Rights and Advocacy for Retarded People

Rights and Advocacy for Retarded People

Stanley S. Herr
Columbia University

LexingtonBooks
D.C. Heath and Company
Lexington, Massachusetts
Toronto

Library of Congress Cataloging in Publication Data

Herr, Stanley S.
Rights and advocacy for retarded people.

Includes index.
1. Mental health laws—United States. 2. Mentally handicapped—Government policy—United States. I. Title.
KF3828.H473 1983 344.73'044 81-47573
ISBN 0-669-04682-5 347.30444

Published simultaneously in Canada

Printed in the United States of America

International Standard Book Number: 0-669-04682-5

Library of Congress Catalog Card Number: 81-47573

To the memory of my parents,
Ruth G. and Louis J. Herr

Contents

Foreword

The second half of the twentieth century will go down in human history as a time of affirmation of individual human rights and dignity. Beginning with the 1948 Universal Declaration of Human Rights, the United Nations and its specialized agencies have issued a series of declarations, recommendations, and resolutions that serve as benchmarks of this development and, significantly, include a Declaration on the Rights of Mentally Retarded Persons, adopted in 1971. That retarded persons now enjoy global support for their rights is a tribute to the worldwide campaign initiated by parents to gain justice for their retarded children. That campaign has done much to remedy long-standing neglect and abuse and to obtain overdue educational, rehabilitational, and other essential services.

In the United States these parents found a champion for their cause in John F. Kennedy, whose President's Panel on Mental Retardation initiated far-reaching programs of federal and state action. What parents had brought into public view, government acknowledged as a public responsibility. But politics and bureaucratic inertia prevented the transformation of that acknowledgment into effective action. A more-forceful sort of advocacy was necessary to bring about requisite policy changes and fiscal adjustments.

Thus, by the time the United Nations adopted the Declaration on the Rights of Mentally Retarded Persons, parents and other advocates were pressing federal courts in the United States to define the rights of disabled children excluded from school and of both children and adults confined, abused, and neglected in institutions for the mentally retarded.

Looking back over those turbulent years and the expansion of judicial activity characterized by such key phrases as *least restrictive alternative, protection from harm,* and *right to treatment,* Stanley Herr presents in this book a comprehensive review that weaves the multitude of legal developments in the various states into a coherent picture. He brings together a variety of perspectives—historical, international, and policy-oriented—that explain and compel the growing awareness that persons with mental retardation have enforceable human and legal rights. The implications of these rights for the courts, for service providers, and for the public are clearly delineated and described. This book focuses on the key role that has been and still must be played by the legal profession in asserting rights and fashioning remedies.

Dr. Herr does not tout litigation as the definitive, all-purpose course of action. To the contrary, he points out that litigation is not an easily applied tool for forging a comprehensive remedy to the complex and enduring problem of neglect in the field of mental retardation. He presents a variety of strategies and provides lucid analyses of all types of advocacy, including the rapidly developing forms of self-advocacy. It is in self-advocacy that Herr sees a new force in the human-services field that will not fade away but will increasingly improve the community's perception of persons with mental retardation in terms of their capabilities and potential.

This is an extremely valuable, sharply etched exposition of the legal and judicial processes that have shaped the field of mental retardation. Because it combines fluid writing with painstaking documentation of governmental, legislative, regulatory, and judicial developments, this book will both appeal to and benefit a wide audience. It provides a powerful counterforce to the retrenchment threatened by pressures on the public fisc. Herr analyzes the causes and bases of legal change and demonstrates the need for continued reform. This book is a chronicle, a resource, and an inspiration.

Gunnar Dybwad
The Heller School
Brandeis University

Acknowledgments

In preparing this book, I have accumulated an abundance of intellectual debts. It is a great pleasure to acknowledge my appreciation to the many individuals and organizations who aided my work.

This book has its origins in a doctoral thesis submitted to the University of Oxford. My supervisor, John Eekelaar, Fellow of Pembroke College, provided strong support and encouragement. Donald R. Harris, director of the Centre for Socio-Legal Studies, and Dr. Joseph Raz, Fellow of Balliol College, welcomed me to membership in those congenial and stimulating circles.

This study has been completely revised and expanded to reflect legal developments through June 1982. Periods as a visiting scholar and a postdoctoral fellow at Harvard Law School and Columbia Law School enabled me to do the further research and writing that led to this book. To the deans, faculties, and library staffs of these two universities I express appreciation for peaceful and productive atmospheres in which to work. Thanks are also due Professor Gary Bellow for the invitation to teach Harvard law students about advocacy for disabled persons, and to my students for having sharpened and tested my ideas in the vivid context of clinical legal practice.

I am especially indebted to Professor Louis Henken and the Center for the Study of Human Rights at Columbia University which he leads. With the collegiality of these associates and the support of the Rockefeller Foundation Fellowship for Human Rights, I gained some rare and splendid time to complete this book.

At the very beginning stages of my career as a researcher, I derived inspiration and financial support from two distinguished sources. Selection as a recipient of the Rosemary F. Dybwad International Award for travel and study, and as a Joseph P. Kennedy, Jr., Fellow in law and ethics opened new possibilities. These permitted me to learn about mentally retarded people and their prospects in ways that no study of precedent and published literature alone could have provided. To Sargent and Eunice Kennedy Shriver and to Gunnar and Rosemary Dybwad, unique pioneers in this field, appreciation is expressed for their encouragement.

By now, it should be clear that this writing has benefited from discussions, interviews, and experiences too numerous to recite in full. Many people from many backgrounds have contributed. In particular, I am grateful to the following for their valuable comments and answers to my queries: Dr. Spencer Eth, Randy Hertz, Sarah McCabe, Steven J. Schwartz, Elizabeth Shafer, and Richard E. Wallace, Jr.

Robert Luzell typed the manuscript with extraordinary skill and meticulous attention.

My tribute to Raquel goes well beyond that due a patient or supportive spouse. As a tireless reader, skillful editor, and loving presence, she has sustained me through these passages.

Part I
The Background

1 Introduction: Hidden Away

Over two million Americans run the risk of being isolated from the rest of society. They are the potential clients of a system of separate housing, separate schooling, and separate medical care. At any given time, more than 250,000 people are in residential facilities for the mentally retarded that all too often make no serious attempt to habilitate their residents.

They have committed no crimes. Nor are they detained to prevent the spread of some infectious disease. Instead, their common fate is to be diagnosed as mentally retarded or developmentally disabled. Typically, they have suffered some added misfortune—poverty, physical handicap, or the loss of family—that has placed them in congregate facilities.

The mentally retarded in America are a hidden minority to most of their fellow citizens. As recently as 1974, the United States Office of Education estimated that 1.75 million handicapped children were entirely excluded from schooling.[1] Nearly half had been classified or misclassified as mentally retarded. Children and adults placed in large, outdated state mental retardation institutions—some 130,000 people—have been rendered practically invisible. Eighty thousand reside in nursing homes where they are no less segregated and where their developmental and habilitative needs cannot be met.[2] Sadly, segregation and dehumanization can occur in institutions with five thousand beds as well as those with as few as ten.

There are 278 public residential facilities for the mentally retarded in the United States. Some are institutions in the most classic sense: state-sponsored and administered facilities that operate on a 24-hour, 365-day residential basis; large central facilities that have "traditionally been separated from the general population."[3] Some have even been described as "human warehouses"[4] and "concentration camps,"[5] their residents faring little better than "prisoners of war."[6]

Regression and deterioration, physical as well as mental, have been repeatedly documented in these deprived environments. Because of insufficient training and activity, many residents develop stereotyped, bizarre, or even menacing behavior. They are thus condemned to a self-fulfilling prophecy of dependency and danger.

In recent years, a new civil rights movement for disabled persons has emerged. One of its major aims is to turn a powerful spotlight on these horrific conditions. Another is to promote a heightened awareness that retarded persons have the same basic rights as other persons.

Among all minorities suffering discrimination, the retarded are the least able to assert their rights. In practice, their rights are often abrogated without due process of law. They exercise little direct political power. Those who are in institutions have no jailhouse lawyers to file court petitions for freedom or correction of barbaric indignities. With training and support in making and expressing choices, many retarded persons can speak up for themselves. For the most part, however, those in congregate care rely on others to be their advocates and to assist them in claiming their rights and equal opportunities.

In less than a decade, the proponents of the civil rights perspective have called into question many patterns of special care and education that sharply segregated the retarded from the rest of society. Although there has yet been no legal equivalent of *Brown* v. *Board of Education*,[7] the thrust of recent statutes, regulations, public policies, and lower court decisions is to invalidate the dual school system that in the past isolated the mentally handicapped. The movement for legal and human rights analyzed in this book has concentrated on three goals: to help retarded people to avoid admission to institutions; to gain protection from physical and psychological harm; and to secure opportunities for community living, including appropriate housing, education, and social services—in short, the elements of normal life.

Families and friends of retarded persons have for many years made appeals for improved services on the basis of compassion and charity. Economists and program planners have bolstered that case with cost-benefit analyses showing that educating and training retarded persons saves society the costs of lifelong dependency, aggravated disability, and unnecessary institutionalization.[8] But only in recent years have consumer groups, lawyers, and lay advocates attempted to establish claims for habilitative services recognized as of right, not as a matter of altruism or sympathy. This *civil rights model* stresses entitlement and choice, whereas the *alms model* it displaces is preoccupied with charitable favor and administrative convenience.

The civil rights imperative has produced more than a wave of litigation. It has led to a heightened professional and public concern for the legal and human rights of persons labeled as mentally retarded. As a result, the typical institution has had to adjust its policies to new realities: stricter regulation, demands to decentralize, and exposure costs for disregard of the rights of the disabled. Yet despite recent progress and a shrinking population, institutions are still prone to an all-too-depressing cycle of scandal, public outcry, symbolic reform, and bureaucratic inertia.

This book examines the legal changes that have resulted at federal and state levels. Willowbrook and other institutional disasters serve as case studies for the role of courts and advocates in reforming residential-care systems. Although New York State alone spends $500 million a year on mental retardation services, the bulk of it goes to maintain dehumanizing institutions now styled as state developmental centers.[9] Despite the fact that less than 10 percent of the retarded live in these public institutions, nearly 85 percent of state funds for mental retardation are spent on institutions. No state institutionalizes a higher proportion of its population, with the result that in 1976 one in eight institutionalized retarded Americans could be found in New York.[10]

Nonetheless, New York is no anomaly. Although it has the largest and one of the oldest institutional systems, its civil rights problems differ more in magnitude than in kind from those of other states. As this study will demonstrate, these problems are of national dimension and require solutions of national scope. From Maine to Florida, from Pennsylvania to the state of Washington, the operations of retardation institutions spark lawsuits and public protests. Litigation has been filed in at least thirty-two states, and investigations have been initiated in most other states. Thus, pressure mounts to devise national strategies to resolve what is clearly a national disgrace.

It is tempting to view the failures of mental-retardation care as predominantly the failures of government. And, in a quite literal sense, government agencies frequently have the greatest difficulty in ridding their own institutions of abuse. The typical institution is the government's own house—located on state land, run with taxpayers' money, and administered by the governor's chosen appointees. It is, therefore, not surprising that the retardation institution is often immune to change even when the powerful and influential demand reform. The late Senator Robert F. Kennedy, whose New York constituency was usually very responsive to him, pleaded in vain for concerted action in the aftermath of the Willowbrook exposés of 1965:

> We hear a great deal, these days, about civil rights, and civil liberties, and equality of opportunity, and justice. But there are no civil rights for young retarded adults—when they are denied the protection of the State education law which commands that all other children must receive an education. There are no civil liberties for those put in the cells of Willowbrook, living amidst brutality, and human excrement, and intestinal disease.[11]

How did the objects of our benevolence become the victims of our gross neglect? This book will examine the legal frameworks that perpetuated the residential segregation of mentally retarded people and thereby consigned them to unnecessarily separate and often inferior educational, social, and medical services. It will also consider the extent to which lawmakers can undo this segregationist legacy, and the legal directions and safeguards that offer promise of a more humane future.

Not that long ago legislatures and the public viewed institutions as the only proper place for the retarded. In countering the legal and attitudinal barriers that have reinforced this view, it is important to consider the uses of legal rights and advocacy services to consolidate the process of social integration. Unless these rights and services are better understood and creatively applied, the resegregation of poor and vulnerable disabled persons in a variety of institutions will accelerate. As military budgets gain at the expense of educational and social services, such people may find less support for community living. Will they then face the unpalatable choice of exposure to neglect in custodial asylums or on city streets?

This book explores some legal rights and policy safeguards that could avert either result. The next two chapters review the legal history of segregated institutions and the public policy that points to a redirection in mental retardation services. Part II includes chapters on the rights of retarded persons to the least restrictive modes of care; to appropriate, individualized habilitation and education; and to community reintegration. Part III discusses the need for an independent advocacy system, and proposes a model for securing trained advocates for mentally disabled persons now living in central facilities as well as in geographically dispersed locations. The concluding chapter addresses the limits of legal reforms and the unfinished agenda for the advocates of genuine community integration of this once-banished minority.

The law's attempts to reform care for the mentally retarded can teach us a great deal about our ability to alter the places reserved for the elderly, the poor, and the dependent young. But there is a larger reason for studying how society tries to protect some of its most vulnerable members. The efforts to define and implement principles of least restrictive care offers an invaluable record of the kind of people we have become, and aspire to be.

Notes

1. 20 U.S.C. § 1400(b)(4). *See* Children's Defense Fund, *Children Out of School* 33 (1974).
2. National Ass'n for Retarded Citizens, "Position Statement on Nursing Homes" (adopted by the Board of Directors on October 8, 1980).
3. American Ass'n on Mental Deficiency, *Manual on Terminology and Classification in Mental Retardation* 5 (H. Grossman ed., rev. 1977).
4. Wyatt v. Stickney, 344 F. Supp. 387, 391 (M.D. Ala. 1972).
5. Nirje, "A Scandinavian Visitor Looks at United States Institutions," in President's Comm. on Mental Retardation, *Changing Patterns in Residential Services for the Mentally Retarded* 53 (R. Kugel & W. Wolfensberger eds., 1969).
6. President's Comm. on Mental Retardation, *Residential Services for the Mentally Retarded: An Action Policy Proposal* at v (1970).

7. 347 U.S. 483 (1954) ("separate but equal" schooling on the basis of race is constitutionally impermissible).

8. *See, e.g.*, R. Conley, *The Economics of Mental Retardation* (1973).

9. *See* G. Jurow, "Financing Long Term Care for the Chronically Mentally Impaired in New York State: An Issue Analysis" at 2, 6 (unpublished paper, June 4, 1979).

10. President's Comm. On Mental Retardation, *Mental Retardation: Trends in State Services* 30 (1976). Of all the states, New York, with over 19,800 people in developmental centers, had by far the largest institutionalized population.

11. Statement of Senator Robert F. Kennedy before the New York Joint Legislative Comm. on Mental Retardation (Sept. 9, 1965), *reprinted in* 111 *Cong. Record* 24,313 (Sept. 17, 1965).

2 The Dismal Legacy

Mentally retarded people have historically been subjected to stigma and oppressive segregation. Centuries of prejudice and enforced isolation have constricted their participation in the most basic social and political processes. Paradoxically, the very laws intended to confer legal protection to retarded people often reinforced their position as degraded and devalued individuals. Under Anglo-American law, special legal status too often was a prelude to subhuman treatment.

The origins of American legal regulation of those who would today be labeled mentally retarded derive from English law. This chapter traces those English roots and the development of American laws and public policies that isolated and stigmatized the mentally handicapped in ways that rivaled even the most oppressive Jim Crow laws. Well into the nineteenth century, New York legal specialists freely acknowledged a jurisprudence of insanity borrowed largely from England.[1] Dr. Isaac Ray, writing in 1838, viewed this reliance on English law with unease. In place of an inconsistent common law, he urged statutes based on scientific learning that would "no longer permit the lives and liberties of our citizens to be suspended on the dicta of men, whose knowledge of insanity was exceedingly imperfect."[2] But the lives and liberties of the mentally retarded were seldom considered.

For historical purposes, this chapter often cites the terminology of the period, even though the labels may be archaic or objectionable by contemporary standards.

The English Roots

Before the nineteenth century, there was little specific legal or medical interest in mentally retarded persons. Despite long-standing distinctions between *idiocy* and *lunacy*, the two conditions were often confused.[3] Under categories such as lunacy, madness, or insanity, people perceived as mentally retarded or mentally ill were often lumped together. Seen as demonically possessed or the products of parental sin, they were often punished or left to perish.[4] Through various devices they could be put away if burdensome to their families or bothersome to their communities.

English law stressed the allocation of the retarded person's property rather than the supervision of his person. By the statute *de Praerogative regis*, the king gained custody of the lands of "natural fools," retaining their profits and acquiring custody over their persons.[5] The law marked a distinction between lunatics and natural fools, for the latter were deemed to have "no understanding from nativity," and to be incapable of recovery, and could therefore be permanently deprived of their property and its profits. Although lunatics and their households were to "live and be maintained competently," the king need only find idiots "their Necessaries," taking the surplus for himself.[6]

Profit, not paternalism, was the real issue. The king's authority over idiots arose only after protracted struggle with his barons, and, unlike his powers over lunatics, it constituted a valuable right.[7] Jurisdiction over the idiot's land and person, originally vested in the Exchequer, was later shifted to the Court of Wards, and then to Chancery along with other profitable rights "belonging to the King as *pater patriae*."[8] Even as late as Blackstone's *Commentaries*, the administration of the affairs of idiots was still described as a branch of the king's revenue.[9]

Determinations of retardation were primitive and subject to manipulation. Idiocy was treated as a question of fact triable by a jury of twelve men. In theory, the chancellor issued a writ *de idiota inquirendo* to a sheriff or commissioner to conduct a trial before a judge and jury. If this disability was proved, the chancellor, on the return of the writ, made a grant or commitment of the party and his estate. Furthermore, the putative idiot could be summoned before the chancellor for inspection.[10] In practice, sheriffs were encouraged to act aggressively to establish the sovereign's rights over persons of property. In the 1628 manual entitled *The Office and Authoritie of Sherifes*, Michael Dalton urged such zeal, instructing that "the King shall have the custody of an Ideots body, and goods, as well as his lands, and that during their lives, providing them things necessary for themselves, their wives and family."[11]

Legal definitions were necessarily loose, such as Fitzherbert's test that a man who knew his own age, his father's and mother's names, and could count twenty pence could not be adjudged an idiot, or Blackstone's that "a man is not an idiot if he hath any glimmering of reason."[12] In finding mental retardation, much depended on the interrogators' motives and approaches. Some examinations seemed calculated to befuddle the hapless subject. Henry Roberts, for example, adjudged incapable of managing his affairs, was "surrounded by Attorneys Clerks, who in his hearing bawled out, 'he won't speak for himself, he cannot answer.' In this deplorable situation he was obliged to sit six Hours, tho' he often complained of being sick."[13] Softer methods might result in a person's discharge from such proceedings, as illustrated by the examination of alleged idiot Katheryne Tothill in 1626, which began by "some gentle entrances by way of discourse, that she might not take any apprehension at our coming thither."[14]

If diagnosis was haphazard, judicial examinations were equally crude. Well into the nineteenth century, judges simply relied on their own cursory observations of the subject's demeanor, looking for such signs as "foolish laughter, a general vacancy of aspect, and . . . other modes which are better understood when seen than by any verbal description."[15]

Parens patriae fictions were developed to justify the guardianship of retarded persons. For those under royal custody, the king was said to acquire a paternal interest in the welfare of his idiots. His purpose, declared Sir George Carew, Master of the Court of Wards in 1612, was to "imitate and approach as neere as may be, the offices and duties of a naturall father."[16] In the Court of Wards and Liveries, however, with wardships bought and sold, protection was secondary to profit making.

In *Beverly's Case*, Sir Edward Coke, the King's Attorney, had spoken of the Crown's benevolent interest in such cases.[17] Unlike other types of persons *non compos mentis*, the idiot was said to suffer a total and irreversible lack of reason. Being under "perpetual infirmity of nature, a nativitate, for he never had any sense or understanding to contract with any man," the so-called fool natural could have his civil acts voided, and his criminal offenses excused. Taking note of the criticism that the civil law assigned no tutor to protect the idiot's interests, Coke argued that the king enjoyed custody over the person and his goods, and because

> every subject is in the King's protection; an idiot who cannot defend or govern himself, nor order his lands and tenements, goods and chattels, the King of right ought to have him, and to order him, his lands, goods, and chattels; and this, it appears was the common law.[18]

To evade the harsh legal consequences of this so-called protection, the distinction between idiot and lunatic was intentionally blurred. According to Blackstone and others, juries were reluctant to render verdicts of mental retardation out of sympathy for the financial hardships imposed, and instead found mental illness by not investigating a party's mental disorder in his or her earlier years.[19]

If the wealthy idiots fared badly, the position of pauper idiots was far worse. They were dealt with like other destitute or vagrant persons through workhouses and houses of correction.[20] Custodial confinement was the limit of early legal measures for the mentally disabled.[21] The law's principal concern was in protecting not the disabled individuals, but the localities they might trouble. Science provided few answers for their treatment, and society spared few resources for their care. As early as 1697, Daniel Defoe criticized the neglect of retarded persons, their exclusion from Bethlem (a public institution for the insane), and called for a public "fool-house." He urged that Parliament erect a separate asylum to maintain them, with funds for such a project levied by a "Tax upon Learning, to be paid by the Authors of Books," that those who have "a Portion of Understanding extraordinary" should support those "as suffer from want of the same Bounty."[22]

For a century and a half, his proposal went unheeded, until the Park House in Highgate, London, for the care and training of idiots was established in 1847. In the first institutions for the insane—Bethlem, founded in 1377; London's St. Luke's in 1751; Manchester's Lunatics Hospital in 1763; York Asylum in 1777—idiots, being regarded as incurable cases, were generally not admitted.[23] Those too disturbed or disturbing to their families might be expelled to workhouses or jails. Eventually, the boarding out of the mentally disabled became a method of discharging local parish responsibilities. Yet many suffered a confinement characteristically more penal than curative.[24] Although a 1763 law required segregation of "persons of insane mind and outrageous behaviour" from other prisoners, it was little enforced.[25] Like so many similar reforms, it was largely intended to benefit sane prisoners, not mentally disordered ones.

Early poor laws distinguished those unable to work by reason of disability from those who refused to do so. By an "Act for the Punishment of Vagabonds and for the Relief of the poore and impotent persons," parish authorities were commanded to "repress idleness and vagabondage" among those deemed "unprofitable members or enemies of the commonwealth," and to provide lodging for afflicted persons unable to work who had resided in the parish for at least three years.[26]

Elizabethan justices of the peace were empowered to assess and tax parish inhabitants to erect and support cottages, "convenient Houses of Dwellinge," for the impotent poor, committing to houses of correction any "who shall not employ themselves to work."[27] Dalton's *The Countrey Justice* offered rough guidance as to various types of poverty, dividing the poor into three categories: those poor by impotency and defect, by accident, or by thriftlessness. Retarded persons were in the first category, along with the infirm aged, unemployable orphans, the chronically sick, and those "naturally disabled, either in Wit or Member, as an Ideot, Lunatick, Blind, Lame, &c." Whereas other poor persons were to be set to hard labor by the overseers, or suffer the house of corrections, Dalton observed that "All those being impotent and not able to work were to be provided for by the Overseers of necessary Relief; and are to have Allowances proportionable, and according to the Continuance and Measure of their Maladies and Needs."[28]

Under the Poor Law of 1601, the parish acquired responsibility for the "Lame, impotent, old, blind, and such other among them, being poor and not able to work."[29] In exceptional cases, a family could petition the local justice of the peace to grant them an allowance for support and maintenance. If a mentally disabled person were dangerous, unmanageable, or without relatives, the justices could order parish officials to assume his safekeeping. The justices could also insist that the person's relatives keep him and if necessary resort to binding, chaining, or hiring special guards.[30]

By 1714, Parliament had singled out pauper lunatics for special regulation and committal. The prospective detainees comprised an amorphous category of persons thought to be mad and dangerous. This statute provided, in an embryonic form, a preventive, civil commitment mechanism:

> whereas there are sometimes in Parishes, Towns, and Places, persons of little or no Estates, who, by Lunacy, or otherwise, are furiously mad, and dangerous to be permitted to go Abroad, and by the Laws in being, the Justices of Peace and Officers who have not Authority to Restrain and Confine them. Be it therefore enacted by the Authority aforesaid That it shall and may be lawful for any Two or more of the Justices of the Peace of any County Town or Place in England Wales or Town of Berwick upon Tweed where such Lunatick or mad Person shall be found by Warrant under their Hands and Seals directed to the Constables Church-wardens and Overseers of the Poor of such Parish Town or Place or some of them to cause such Person to be Apprehended and kept safely locked up in such secure Place . . . as such Justices shall . . . direct and appoint.[31]

This judicial discretion to detain a supposed madman was virtually unlimited. Although the ordinary vagrant had a right of appeal to the next Quarter Session, this act extended no similar rights to the mentally disabled. They received no treatment and could be confined "during such time only as such Lunacy or Madness shall continue." The justices had the power to order these unfortunate persons to their last legal settlements, and charged for the costs of their "keeping and maintaining." Amending legislation in 1744 further broadened the detainable class to include those "so far disordered in their Senses."[32] Vagrancy statutes were, however, to apply only to paupers, not to persons who were of "rank and condition in the world" and whose relatives could apply for lunacy commissions.[33] Thus, the dual track of guardianship for the rich and commitment for the poor began to emerge.

The justices retained supervisory powers over the places in which the mad were confined, principally jails and houses of correction. Under the 1744 act, justices, assembled in General or Quarter Sessions, were authorized to "build, erect, enlarge, . . . buy or hire" new houses of correction. To ensure the act's proper implementation, each session appointed two justices to inspect those houses and report on their conditions of management. Inspecting justices not only appointed and removed house managers, but also issued final orders and regulation for "better governing and regulating" the houses of correction, and for "employing, relieving, and punishing the persons therein." Through fines and removal powers, justices were to hold the custodian accountable for any failure to keep the inmates to hard labor. Managers could be compelled to punish according to the judicial orders by which inmates were "committed to, or detained in their custody." Thus, at the dawn of civil commitment, the judicial authorities were closely involved in the custodial enterprise. But the family still remained the basic unit for care, and the 1744 Vagrancy Act made clear that nothing was to prevent a third party from taking the mad person under his "own care and protection."[34]

Early legal interventions focused on the confinement of the sane and wealthy, and ignored the mad and poor. The controversy, chronicled in pamphlets and lawsuits, eventually led to an Act of Parliament. The "vile Practice," as Defoe described it, consisted of the "better Sort . . . sending their Wives to Mad-Houses at every Whim or Dislike."[35] He also feared that scheming relatives and unscrupulous "mad-doctors" might confine a sane man "under pretence of Madness." By mid-eighteenth century, the King's Bench was granting writs of habeas corpus in the cases of these castoff wives. In *Rex* v. *Turlington*, involving the unhappy Mrs. Deborah D'Vebre consigned by her husband to Turlington's madhouse, the court ordered that Dr. Monroe, as well as her attorney and her nearest relation, be granted visiting rights "at proper times and reasonable hours" in order to "consult with, advise and assist her."[36] By affidavit Dr. Monroe reported that he found the inmate "very sensible, very cool and dispassionate" and had no reason to suspect mental disorder. In court, Mrs. D'Vebre again "appeared to be absolutely free from the least appearance of insanity" and was therefore freed. The following year, Lord Mansfield ordered another of Turlington's inmates released.[37]

The Select Committee of the House of Commons on the State of Private Madhouses investigated such sensational cases and reported that madhouse managers, on the strength of a relative's allegations, would admit anyone into care so long as the charges could be paid. As eminent physicians testified, lax admission practices were also a problem in public madhouses.[38]

In 1774, Parliament passed the first act regulating private asylums, but firmly excluded from its purview the "publick Hospitals within this Kingdom." As a check against arbitrary admissions, commitment authority was lodged with medical persons rather than the patient's relatives. Without a written order signed and sealed by a physician, surgeon, or apothecary that "such Person is proper to be received in such House," the madhouse keeper was forbidden to confine "any Person as a Lunatick."[39] Although the act required annual licensing of houses for the reception of more than one lunatic, licenses could be revoked only if an inspector was denied entry. Outside of London, the act was ineffective, in part because the justices of the peace had a strong aversion to inspecting madhouses.[40]

A dual system of legal regulation had crystallized. For persons of property, Parliament had recognized that "many great and dangerous abuses frequently arise'' in private madhouses, and had attempted to legitimize such commitments. Blackstone, for example, asserted that on the first attack of lunacy, it was ''usual to confine the unhappy objects in private custody,'' the legislature having interposed its authority ''to prevent all abuses incident to such private custody.''[41] But paupers, let alone mentally handicapped paupers, still lacked any special legal protection. Even by the nineteenth century, patients classed as paupers were ignored by licensing statutes: ''The mere fiat of a parish officer [could] send any individual of the whole class of parochial paupers into a madhouse, there to remain unnamed and unseen.''[42]

In sum, English law authorized the stripping away of the rights and legal protection of individuals referred to as idiots. If propertied, their contracts could be voided, lands seized, and judicial remedies for wastage of estates denied. If they were poor, they were destined to be part of a legally invisible mass of deviants. Legal treatises, reflecting social views of the hopelessness of this status, characterized idiocy as a total and ''perpetual infirmity,'' a condition identified by ''an absence of all expression, and a vague and unmeaning look.''[43] Given these bleak images and legal consequences, it is no wonder that juries preferred returning a verdict of lunacy to one of idiocy. These patterns contributed to labeling the simple as mad, and, in turn, to the popular confusion of mental illness with retardation, a confusion that survives to this day.

Excluding and Restraining Mad Persons in Colonial New York

English law shaped the categories and the prejudices that American colonists and jurists inherited in regulating those perceived as mentally deviant. New York not only followed the general patterns set by England, but cast a powerful influence on North American practices. For example, early New York laws tended to blur distinctions between the mentally retarded and the mentally ill. As dependent persons, both were excluded whenever possible and regimented whenever necessary. Under a 1665 amendment to the Duke's Laws, communities were jointly responsible for the care of ''distracted persons'' who were extraordinary threats to public safety.[44] The first poor laws attempted to exclude or remove from the province anyone without a craft, or likely to become a ''burthen or charge'' to a parish. In enforcing these laws, chief magistrates inspected all arriving ships' passengers, and constables denied ''Vagabonds, beggars or others'' entry from one country to another. Should a retarded person somehow obtain settlement or be born in the American colonies, his kin could expect little in the way of public assistance. Citing the English custom of parish and precinct responsibility for the poor, the 1683 poor law simply directed local officials to "make provision for the maintenance support of their poor."[45]

To reduce such expenses, communities often attempted to rid themselves of the indigent and the mentally disordered. Thus, a 1691 act aimed at the "prevention and discouragement of Vagabonds and Idle persons" and a 1701 act declared "people of ill behaviour Discountenanced."[46] Retarded persons without family or fixed settlement could be subject to deportation or penal handling. An "Idle Wandering Vagabond" could be summarily confined to a house of corrections until further order of a Quarter Sessions court. Under a 1721 act, such persons could be punished by removal, whipping, and incarceration.[47] On the finding of two justices, a stranger suspected of "Insufficient abilities" could be ordered transported from constable to constable and removed from the province. If the vagrant returned, each constable was to administer up to thirty-one lashes on the man's bare back or twenty-five lashes for a woman. Even in New York City in 1762, "vagrant and idle Persons" unable to post bail within forty-eight hours of arrest were liable to be corporally punished to any degree short of life and limb and deported out of the city or colony.[48]

The 1773 poor law continued to provide two basic options for dealing with the mentally disabled: to deny them legal settlement, or to fix responsibility for their keeping on relatives. Within forty days of settling, a person who, in the opinion of two justices of the peace, was likely to become chargeable to the parish or town, could be returned to his last place of residence. For those families already settled with "Poor lame or decrepit" members, the justices were to ensure that a financially responsible relative—a parent, grandparent, child, or grandchild—was "to relieve and maintain every such Poor Person . . . in such Manner as the Justices of the Peace . . . at their General or Quarter Session shall order and direct."[49] Notwithstanding these provisions, mentally disordered people in the colonial period were often abandoned or abused, "ordinarily confined to jails, workhouses, poorhouses or in private pens, cages, and strong-rooms."[50]

In New York, as in England, justices of the peace were central participants in local efforts to contain the mad and support the severely afflicted. They appointed overseers for persons "Impotent, old Blind and such others, being Poor and not able to work."[51] In relieving the mentally disabled, the justices, acting as a court of general or special sessions, met annually to supervise any such public expenditures and to fix parish contributions.[52]

In the New York Mayor's Court, churchwardens were directed to relieve individuals described as "non Compos Mentis." For example, in 1720 they paid a sum of four shillings weekly toward the support of Phillipina Schelleux, as an "Object of Charity."[53] If not maintained at home or boarded out, mentally disabled persons were sometimes admitted to the New York almshouse. Between 1736 and 1746, an estimated two hundred persons, perhaps a quarter of whom were described as idiotic, insane, or otherwise disabled, were so housed.[54]

Justices found numerous ways to restrain those seen as mentally deviant. In 1685, citizens in Albany sought orders to remove an "old poor man" from their neighborhood because of their fear of "houses taking fire because of his crazyness." In witchcraft trials, retarded persons were sometimes denounced and even an acquitted suspect could be placed under a sheriff's custody. In 1665, Mary Hall, charged with practicing witchcraft and sorcery, was found innocent, but the court nonetheless ordered that her husband should be bound "body and goods for his wife's appearance at the next session, and so from session to session, as long as they stay within this government, in the meantime to be of ye good Behavior."[55]

New York State's first specific enactment concerning the mentally disabled did little more than authorize confinement for those dangerous to themselves or others. In terms almost identical to the English vagrancy law of 1744, this act of 1788 empowered justices of the peace to detain any persons, "who by lunacy or otherwise are furiously mad, or are so far disordered in their senses that they may be dangerous to be permitted to go abroad."[56] As in England, the justices could commit the madman to a secure and if necessary chained custody. The act reaffirmed two other traditional means of dealing with the mentally disabled: the chancellor's appointment of a guardian or the family's care and protection of its disabled member. Confinement under this statute was a last resort, a means of isolating a person regarded as a threat to the community's well-being.

Governments of this period dealt with the mentally disordered as a problem of containment, not of treatment. New York's first public hospital was not established until 1772, and by 1800 had probably admitted less than one hundred people diagnosed as mentally disordered.[57] The New York Hospital provided basement cells for these inmates, but chronic cases were generally refused. Although the legislature had authorized contracts with the New York Hospital and the Bloomingdale Asylum for the care of pauper lunatics, hospital governors retained a discretion to admit such patients as they chose. It was not until 1827 that New York law prohibited the detention of lunatics in any prison, jail, or house of correction.[58] Thus, those who would today be labeled as mentally retarded were cared for in their own homes, in jails or poorhouses, in boarding arrangements with private families, or else roamed at large. Whatever the merits of family-centered care for those from affluent families, by 1831 a New York legislative committee had concluded that the "whole system as to pauper lunatics and idiots is radically defective."[59]

Retarded Persons in the Age of Asylums

In the first wave of asylum building, special provisions for retarded persons were ignored. In the Jacksonian years, institutions became "the preferred solution" to the problems of poverty, crime, delinquency, and insanity.[60] At first, mental retardation, being viewed as neither curable nor dangerous, remained outside the pale of this attention. Yet by 1838, Edward Seguin had begun the first residential school for the retarded as part of the Bicetre Hospital in Paris, and occasionally retarded children were admitted into the New York Institute for the Deaf and Dumb. Seguin, Jean Itard's pupil and author of *The Moral Treatment, Hygiene, and Education of Idiots and Other Backward Children*, later migrated to New York and became a leading force in the formation of such residential schools in the United States. But at the time of the opening of the State Lunatic Asylum at Utica, New York, the asylum managers had a comparatively free discretion to confine the insane and to exclude the retarded and others thought incurable.[61]

In the 1840s, reformers began to call attention to the neglected condition of retarded persons. Visitors to New York county almshouses and hospitals reported the presence of a few idiots and imbeciles among the old, sick, lame, vicious, unfortunate, and insane.[62] This problem of indiscriminate mixing was scarcely limited to New York. In 1843, Dorothea Dix, an advocate of great force and energy, claimed that "defective legislation" was to be blamed for harsh confinement of "helpless, forgotten, insane and idiotic men and women."[63] She described retarded persons in the Massachusetts prisons as "unjustly committed" and harmless. She also condemned New York's county almshouse for maltreatment of idiots and insane persons, and pleaded for institutions that would provide "vigilant inspection, and faithful care" to this "unfortunate class" of paupers. In her view "the now numerous class of incurables"—idiots and chronic lunatics—had less legal protection than criminals.[64]

In petitioning Congress for federal land grants for asylums, Miss Dix declared that she had seen more than "nine thousand idiots, epileptics and insane . . . destitute of appropriate care and protection . . . bound with galling chains, bowed beneath fetters and heavy iron balls."[65] In New York, she feared that county asylums would "degenerate into mere receptacles," and therefore suggested four to six new state asylums for the "kind care of the incurable." Her goal was nothing less than a comprehensive network of state-funded asylums under strict state supervision and inspection. A year later, Dr. Brigham, superintendent of the State Lunatic Asylum, proposed an idiot asylum. He argued that many of the state's 1,600 idiots could be improved to the point of employment and self-support, and that such an experiment deserved the attention of "the patriot, philanthropist and Christian."[66]

A protracted campaign followed. It began in 1846 with the New York Senate's passage of legislation establishing "an asylum or school for idiots." Although the bill failed in the Assembly, its backers continued to press for public provisions for "imparting instruction to idiots." Dr. Frederick Backus, chairman of the Senate's Medical Societies Committee, obtained supporting letters from prominent asylum superintendents in Massachusetts and England on the feasibility of such a school. The committee report pointed to schools in France, England, Germany, and Switzerland that had taught such persons to govern their "passions and appetites," and promised that similar American schools would release imprisoned minds from such "direful bondage as idiocy imposes." Retarded persons, turned "adrift like the cattle," would instead be taught "to work, to read, to sing."[67] By following the European lead in providing such instruction, New York was urged to set an example for other states.[68]

In 1847, the Senate Committee on Medical Societies reiterated these calls to conscience and patriotism. Idiots, neglected in almshouses, unsafe in insane asylums, and uninstructed at home, needed places where they could be "protected and made useful." The committee now added a new argument for equality of treatment: it was inequitable to make provision for blind or deaf and mute children, or the insane, while those with "the greater affliction of having idiot children" sought relief from public charity or private munificence in vain."[69]

The first institution emerged, however, not in New York but in Massachusetts. In 1848, the Massachusetts legislature approved an experimental school for "pauper idiots," and in 1850 Dr. Samel Gridley Howe appeared with some of these pupils before officials at Albany to demonstrate what could be done and to plead for a similar school in New York. Howe's powerful appeal for equity foreshadowed contemporary claims:

> Massachusetts admits the right of all her citizens to a share in the blessings of education, and she provides it liberally for all her more favored children. If some be blind or deaf, she still continues to furnish them with special instruction at great cost; and will she longer neglect the poor idiot—the most wretched of all who are born to her—those who are usually abandoned by their fellows—who can never, of themselves, step up upon the platform of humanity—will she leave them to their dreadful fate, to a life of brutishness, without an effort in their behalf?[70]

On July 10, 1851, the New York legislature finally voted to launch an experimental school. The New York State Asylum for Idiots was intended for the residential schooling of not more than twenty children.[71] A private home near Albany was rented, and Dr. Hervey Backus Wilbur, a Massachusetts physician who had started the first such private school, was appointed superintendent.[72]

The new asylum operated as an educational, not a custodial institution. It was to be a link in the chain of common schools. Children aged seven to fourteen were admitted for limited periods in order "to impart all the education practicable in each particular case."[73] Pupils were received on a one-month trial basis, and the superintendent, with the advice and consent of the trustee's executive committee, could admit retarded children and others whose deficiency made them incapable of being educated at any regular school. At the outset, Dr. Wilbur stressed the primacy of education over caretaking functions: "It is an establishment for the management and education of young idiots. It is an extension of the blessings of education . . . to a class of persons . . . whose faculties are not susceptible of development under the customary conditions and facilities of a common education."[74]

In comparison to laws concerning the state lunatic asylum, the laws pertaining to the state asylum for idiots were cryptic and vague. The 1851 act establishing the idiot asylum barely filled a page of the statute book and had none of the admission and discharge provisions of the 1842 act organizing the lunatic asylum.[75] The legislature, viewing the experiment a success, granted the idiot asylum permanent status in 1853 and authorized construction of the United States's first specially designed structure for the care and training of retarded persons, a tall building erected on eighteen acres of land donated by citizens of Syracuse. Under the 1862 law reorganizing the asylum, the governor, the superintendent of public instruction, and other leading state officers were appointed to the board of trustees. By statute, the superintendent was required to be "a well-educated physician," and to employ necessary teachers, attendants and assistants; and the trustees were to maintain an "effective inspection" and to visit the asylum at stated intervals.[76]

Although patterned after legislation on lunacy, the 1862 law made no reference to civil commitment or procedural protection. Unlike mental patients, these students could be admitted without the sworn certificate of two physicians, without court order, and without opportunity for judicial appeal and jury trial.[77] Children, let alone mentally retarded children, had no rights. Moreover, the asylum, designated as a place for restorative education, not civil or criminal confinement, received less outside scrutiny than the sometimes bitterly criticized insane asylums.[78]

In its formative period, the New York Asylum for Idiots emphasized education leading to "useful occupation" and the pupil's return to friends and home community. As a small boarding school, its pupils typically entered at age ten and one-half, remained eight years, and were discharged to families or friends.[79] Although the trustees were empowered to discharge state pupils to almshouses or, upon twenty days' notice, to remove any of the paying pupils to their guardians, they were reluctant to do so, fearing that pupils transferred to almshouses would become "depraved and demoralized by association with adult paupers and vagrants of both sexes."[80]

In the face of popular skepticism, Dr. Wilbur, the asylum's superintendent for its first thirty-two years, tried to persuade the legislature that pupils could be trained for occupations. In addition to schoolroom activities and "moral training," he lauded the benefits of practical labor in farm and household work, in the stables, laundry, and grounds of the institution. Education should be available to all pupils, Superintendent Wilbur explained, because "the condition of idiocy did not remove the subject of it beyond the reach of training and instruction, but only made it necessary to modify the method pursued." Except for a handful of children regarded as incurable or unteachable the asylum's pupils were expected to record gains in speech, self-care and other skills. A report to the legislature on the asylum's graduates contrasted their extremely limited activities on entry with their successful training, reciting glowing testimonials from relatives of ex-pupils' community adjustment. Positive results were ascribed not to miracles or cures, but to a system of instruction "developing the intelligence, strengthening the will, and enlarging the resources of the subject."[81]

The Syracuse Board of Trustees therefore urged new public facilities and places for mentally retarded persons of "teachable age and condition." Their plea expressed a developmental view of retarded persons as "human beings, in essence and in possibilities," whose condition "for the time being cramps and hinders their growth and development."[82]

Institutional Expansion and the Perversion of Benevolent Custodialism

These visions dimmed under the pressure of numbers and new ideologies. Seguin had described the early institution as only nominally an asylum, in reality a "training school" for those capable of improvement. To maintain that character, the asylum's bylaws authorized selective admissions, expressly excluding those "epileptic, insane or greatly deformed." But homeless older pupils remained and worked on the institution's farm or laundry, in what Seguin termed "a paternal, not yet legalized, arrangement."[83] Another fateful step occurred when the institution began to develop educational and custodial departments, the latter to render "lower grade cases . . . less troublesome and disgusting" and to make them "comfortable and happy as long as they live."[84] As families refused to take their trained children back, the school departed from its original mission.

For those banished from their families, the county poorhouse offered only a bleak receptacle. Whipped, bound, and confined in "wretched abodes," retarded persons were treated more harshly than criminals or even animals. According to the Poor-Law survey of 1856, the full details of their neglect "would disgrace the state, and shock humanity."[85] Although destitute children were boarded out, by law the child branded "an unteachable idiot" was considered "unfit for family care."[86]

The pioneering superintendents had warned against large institutions. Seguin cautioned that expansion might reduce their schools to "the level of a richly endowed poorhouse."[87] In the same year, Howe strongly condemned the trend toward "permanent life asylums" as unnatural, undesirable, and leading to abuse and the severing of the inmates' ties to kin, friends, and neighborhood.[88] Wilbur had favored building specialized institutions instead of enlarging institutions for omnibus purposes.[89]

Unfortunately, legislatures preferred to expand existing institutions. For example, in 1870, a bill was passed for an extension of the Willard Asylum and the remodeling of adjacent college buildings to be "occupied by insane [persons] or idiots."[90] The New York legislature voted ever-increasing sums for the Asylum for Idiots, and its enrollment swelled.[91] In 1892, the Syracuse institution held 502 pupils, an increase Walter E. Fernald, an influential professional leader, attributed to a more comprehensive admissions policy, and legislatures disposed to enlarge existing institutions rather than fund new ones.[92]

By the end of the nineteenth century, custodial institutions for the retarded had eclipsed educational ones. The first steps in that direction were taken with the New York legislature's appropriation in 1878 of $18,000 for an experimental custodial asylum for the support and maintenance of "adult, idiotic and feeble-minded females."[93] By 1885, New York's Newark Custodial Asylum for Feeble-Minded Women was incorporated for the purpose of segregating mentally retarded females of childbearing age and relieving society from "the burden of supporting illegitimate children." In 1893, the legislature established a new and separate institution for the care and custody of "unteachable idiots." Initially, admission to the Rome State Custodial Asylum required court commitment and testimony as to the subject's idiocy. Such formalities, however, were short-lived: two years later county superintendents of the poor were authorized to commit indigents or almshouse inmates to the Custodial Asylum.[94] By transferring poorhouse inmates to the Custodial Asylum, county expenses were shifted to the state. Given a statute that failed to define *idiot*, let alone *unteachable idiot*, county officials had a free hand to remove social outcasts to the institution.

The Eugenics Peril

The eugenics movement produced new rationales for permanent institutional segregation of retarded people. Popular studies of family degeneracy, such as the Jukes of Ulster County, New York, were misinterpreted to show a close correlation between inherited mental impairment and crime, pauperism, and illness.[95] Although the asylum founders had made many optimistic promises, a skeptical public still viewed idiots as a hopeless and ineducable class. Bowing to that opinion, the professionals of the next generation urged a strict division between the teachable and unteachable, with separate facilities for each.[96] Increasingly, their appeals shifted from the need to protect the retarded from society to the need to protect society from the retarded.

In strident tones, prominent professionals identified the retarded as a social menace and urged their confinement for life. On grounds of "mere economy," Fernald recommended that society assume the permanent care of idiots and imbeciles "before they have carried out a long career of permanent crime."[97] By 1914, the Committee on Provision for the Feeble-Minded had mounted an extensive propaganda campaign for segregationist institutional care, organizing some 1,100 public lectures and lobbying for more institutional facilities in at least 18 states.[98] Leading this frenzy, professionals characterized mental retardation as the source of crime, pauperism, and insanity, an inherited evil to be remedied by "permanent sequestration" and crude preventive detention. Dr. Isaac N. Kerlin, a president and founding member of the American Association on Mental Deficiency, had advocated "an arbitrary but legal isolation of the unfit" as a form of "lifelong moral quarantine."

> How many of your criminals, inebriates, and prostitutes are congenital imbeciles? How many of your insane are really feeble-minded or imbecile persons, wayward and neglected in their early training, and at last conveniently housed in hospitals, after having wrought mischief, entered social relations, reproduced their kind, antagonized experts and lawyers, puzzled philanthropists, and in every possible manner retaliated on their progenitors for their origin, and on the community for their misapprehension?[99]

Indictments of this type provoked demands for stringent civil commitment and eugenics measures. *The Feeble-Minded in New York*, published by the State Charities Aid Association in 1911, described the retarded as a growing danger and social burden. Its solution: total segregation in order to halt their reproduction and "nearly extinguish their race." The report concluded that no consideration of cost, parental affection, or personal liberty should defeat this goal nor outweigh the perceived menace and immorality of the feebleminded. The association pledged to obtain "means of completer segregation": more institutions; a segregation law involving separation of the sexes to prevent "propagation of their kind, and ill-advised contact with the world at large"; and a strict marriage law, granting licenses to only those of "normal mind."[100]

In response, the New York legislature transformed a charities law into a detention law. Informal procedures were replaced by judicial commitments on the basis that detention in an institution was in the best interests of the individual as well as of the state.[101] Magistrates were authorized to commit any child brought before them "appearing to be feeble-minded," simply on confirmation by two doctors.[102] By 1916, the very act of enticing the inmates of such institutions to leave or escape, or promising to "provide a home for or to pay for the service of or to marry such an inmate" had become a misdemeanor.[103] Parole from the Rome State Custodial Asylum was severely restricted, allowed only when "desirable for the best interests of the State," such as to perform domestic, agricultural, or forestry work. By 1918, a permanent state Commission for the Care of the Feeble-Minded was created to register every feebleminded person and obtain more space for them in institutions.[104] Persons were detainable not only for their own welfare, but for the welfare of others or of the community.

The Mental Deficiency Law of 1919 constituted the legal machinery to carry out this sweeping design. Characteristic of the laws of the next decades, custodial civil commitment was its major theme. Court commitment, the primary mode of admission, required a verified petition and the certificate of two qualified examiners.[105] The written report of two physicians or a physician and a psychologist and their "certificate of defect" constituted sufficient proof. Unless the alleged disabled person, his relative or friend demanded a hearing, a judge would immediately issue a commitment order. Although the question of mental deficiency could be tested through a writ of habeas corpus or a jury trial, such challenges were exceedingly rare.[106] Both voluntary admission and the superintendents' discretion to discharge inmates were sharply curtailed.

This legislative scheme, created at a time of extreme prejudice toward the retarded, had a destructive impact. Institutions became places of absolute incarceration. Even at Syracuse State School, voluntary admissions ceased for many years, and were reduced to a trickle between 1929 and 1945 (see table 2-1). On the basis of attorney-general opinions that the Rome State Custodial Asylum had no right to parole inmates, its managers discontinued trial leaves and home visits and temporarily abandoned any attempt to institute a "legal system of parole."[107]

Leading government officials endorsed this legalized segregation as a public-health and a crime-prevention measure. In dedicating the three-thousand-bed Letchworth Village, an institution for "the segregation of the mentally unfit," New York's governor linked mental retardation with venereal disease, moral defectiveness, and homicide.[108] Experts on charities agreed, labeling mental retardation as the "outward sign of degeneracy," a plague to be cut off at its source, even if that meant taking "moron girls" who were "attractive and clever" and putting them under custodial restraint.[109] Across the United States and well into the twentieth century, it had become an apparently settled question of policy that " all mental defectives should be committed to state institutions for life."[110]

Table 2-1
Legal Status on Admission, Syracuse State School

Year	*Court Committed*	*Poor-Law Official Committed*	*Voluntary*	*One-Doctor Certificate*
1929	115	22	—	—
1930	100	57	—	—
1931	62	21	—	—
1932	101	27	3	—
1933	68	33	4	—
1934	75	41	10	1
1935	81	47	—	—
1936	87	54	4	—
1937	86	—	1	7
1938	84	—	3	7
1939	80	—	—	2
1940	77	—	1	1
1941	114	—	2	1
1942	82	—	2	1
1943	82	—	—	—
1944	122	—	2	2
1945	123	—	5	—

Source: New York Department of Mental Hygiene, 78th to 95th Annual Reports of the Board of Visitors of the Syracuse State School (1930-1946).

The Legacy of the Segregationist Movement

When the eugenic alarm subsided, New York State had an entrenched system of laws and public policies promoting segregated, institution-centered care. With disastrous results, officials forgot the founders' plans for small schools and built massive custodial institutions as "areas of detention of undesirable elements for the benefit of society."[111] The Syracuse Board of Visitors even boasted of its long line of innovations in the United States: the first custodial institution for adults and those considered unteachable or intractable; the first special institutions for people with epilepsy and for the "feeble-minded with criminal tendencies"; the first state school in the metropolitan district; and the first institution to establish "proper segregation of the sexes."[112] New York led the nation in another dismal record: by 1934, its seven state schools held 10,800 residents, fully a sixth of the national total.[113]

In time, the branches of the Syracuse School, designed to assume the burden of unteachables, outgrew its parent institution. For several decades, the school maintained a census of over one thousand students and three hundred parolees. The latter were parcelled out to forty-bed "colonies," cottages intended as a "preliminary to re-entry to the home or the world."[114] Not until 1944 was the term *parole*, with its connotations of criminal detention, replaced by the term *convalescent care*, although this "preliminary" status often stretched one to five years or longer.[115] Inmates at the Rome State Custodial Asylum were expected to remain for life. Only a tiny minority whose mental retardation was attributed to faulty diet, nervous exhaustion, or excessive masturbation were thought of as capable of improvement and returning to ordinary family life.[116] For the rest, the Rome Board saw itself as legally bound to uphold a state policy of permanent care.[117] Despite the superintendent's misgivings, babies, young children, crippled children of ordinary intelligence, and "high grade colored children," misclassified through standardized intelligence tests, were all accepted for custodial care.[118] With virtually no outlet, the population inexorably grew from 1,046 residents in 1909 to 3,445 in 1935.

The Newark State Custodial Asylum for Feeble-Minded Women maintained its explicit eugenic purpose for over four decades. Its circulars flatly insisted that women past the childbearing period would not be admitted. Discharges were few; of the 15 released in 1915-1916 out of 875 residents, most were older women past childbearing age and one had secured a writ of habeas corpus.[119] State policies were designed for this isolation, and the inmates' friends were advised not to write anything to dissatisfy residents or raise their hopes of discharge. Education was discouraged because it only increased the inmates' restlessness and desire to leave the institutions.[120]

Segregationist aims were never completely realized. In part, the legal profession was uncomfortable with the notion of lifelong confinement. New York courts had released some asylum inmates, and superintendents devised parole and colony plans as means to stave off more judicially ordered discharges.[121] Fernald also complained of the judiciary's readiness to release as well as to commit retarded persons, and their unwillingness to use existing commitment law without parental consent "except in extreme cases."[122] He referred to "a deep-seated prejudice on the part of lawyers, judges, and legislators toward assuming that every moron will necessarily and certainly misbehave to an extent that he should be deprived of his liberty."[123] But these sporadic legal objections did not slow the rapid growth of institutional rolls: between 1890 and 1916, while the U.S. population increased by 26 percent, the retarded placed under care soared by 753 percent.[124]

Legislative appropriations, however, were never great enough to finance the "life-long segregation of all the feeble-minded." In 1915, the state Commission to Investigate Provision for the Mentally Deficient had recommended vastly expanding New York institutions, then containing 3,000 inmates in order to accommodate 21,000 additional persons. Relying on eugenic arguments, the commission reported that "the mentally defective man or woman at liberty constitutes a serious menace to the State."[125] Despite sustained lobbying pressure, increases in institutional beds, and drastic economies within the institution, the New York program fell short of its expansive goal of segregating the mentally retarded for life, or at least during the reproductive phase.

Yet while asylum managers argued that their care was cheaper than reformatories and hospitals, and that savings of up to 50 percent could be achieved by transfers to their facilities, their reports revealed the inhumanity of that care.

> Because of limited amounts of money available our inmates cannot be properly fed, clothed or bedded. . . . We are running 15 to 25% short in dietary, and we are without proper underclothing, overcoats and other clothing for our inmates and many of the inmates are sleeping on beds without sheets on them and not enough blankets to keep them warm. . . . In addition . . . we have no monies available for nursing services for such inmates in this institution.[126]

Sterilization programs also constituted a dismal failure and a sordid chapter in U.S. law. Though the United States Supreme Court in *Buck* v. *Bell* upheld a state's power to impose compulsory eugenic sterilization on the retarded, this decision was harsh and ill-founded.[127] Earlier New York court decisions had invalidated such sterilization programs on equal protection grounds, and the legislature had declined to reenact that law.[128] The trial judge had reasoned that sterilization of inmates at the Rome Custodial Asylum was unjustified since they were already thoroughly segregated and, as experts testified, involuntary sterilization would only create prejudice against such institutions.[129]

Yet the majority of states had no such qualms. In enacting involuntary sterilization laws in 31 states, over 70,000 Americans in this century fell victim to this degrading procedure.[130] Even in the absence of such laws, retarded persons have been castrated to prevent masturbation or "asexualized" simply as "a protection against ill."[131] Despite these dire methods, institutional segregation and reproductive controls had produced "disappointing results," as their proponents put it, in "eliminating mental deficiency."[132]

This period of panic and repression left its imprint on New York's statute books. The Consolidated Laws of 1930 bore an almost penal nomenclature: state institutions for mental defectives; inmates and colonies; paroles and parole agents.[133] Parole agents, referring to their clients as "damaged goods," regarded even "normal interest in the opposite sex" as grounds for recommittal.[134]

Though the Syracuse institution never completely lost its educational role, and some education and training was provided elsewhere, the dichotomy hardened between so-called custodial and educable cases.[135] Unlike the mentally ill who were promised treatment, the mentally retarded were still targeted by law for segregated custodial care.[136] Despite the fact that the once popular solutions of euthanasia and sterilization were tarnished, the eugenics program would be redirected by those who advocated increased provision of institutional care.[137] This segregation also had a racial dimension. In complaining that "feebleminded colored children" were at large and contributed to the "general social burden," Virginia officials created a separate institution for them. Without such a facility, officials feared that their compulsory sterilization act would remain "comparatively ineffective" for the younger black population for lack of a *locus operandi*.[138]

Other states also replicated these laws and practices. As the postwar period loomed, the American Association on Mental Deficiency could renew its official call for more institutional construction and permanent segregation of the mentally retarded in custodial institutions.[139]

The retarded in the United States had been treated as an outcast class. Retarded persons, as the Syracuse State School Board conceded, had been destined, "unless in a family of wealth," to become public charges and to lead brief, "neglected and unhappy" lives.[140] Special institutions had started as schools but had been trapped into a different mission: rescuing victims of abusing homes and neglecting poorhouses, and lifting the burden of care from families. The progressive schools had all too soon been turned into prisons. Given repressive laws and static populations, they had become places of despair and detention. Even though some of those institutions could recall their origins as small boarding schools for the education and training of the retarded, they had forgotten the advice of their founders, who had stressed the importance of returning students to the community. As Samuel Gridley Howe explained, "Even idiots have rights which should be carefully considered."[141] For long decades, that admonition went unheeded.

Summary

From the Middle Ages to this century, laws have marked the mentally retarded with badges of inferiority and scorn. Although the nomenclature changed, statutory references to idiots, fools, imbeciles, and mental defectives have generally signaled guardianship, institutional isolation, and other crushing restraints. To these impositions, Americans in the late nineteenth and early twentieth centuries added some disgraceful refinements: compulsory eugenic sterilization laws, wholesale exclusion from public schooling, and a total restriction of rights amounting to a virtual civil death. As a banished and brutalized class, the mentally retarded were isolated and stigmatized in ways that matched and sometimes exceeded the most vicious regimes of racial separation.

Persons labeled as mentally retarded pose a classic example of a "discrete and insular minority," a minority for whom the conventional political processes have failed.[142] Scandalous conditions in the public institutions reserved for them is, sadly, a very old story. But the special tragedy of contemporary horrors is not only that they have persisted so long, but how reminiscent they are of earlier exposés and of the reports officials feared would disgrace and shock. This record of suffering and the absence of rights is bound up with other inheritances of the past: massive institutions, outmoded concepts of care, and a legal framework that too often codified the wrong solutions to the wrong problems.

There is also a human side to this legacy. It includes several generations whose members spent childhoods without education and adult lives without hope of release. Though some are still within the law's power to compensate, others are not. Miss Martha Nelson, for example, died in 1975 at the age of 103, after almost a century of confinement.[143] No one even knew why she had been committed as a four-year-old, or why she had been held so long.

Notes

1. Ordronaux, "The Proper Status of the Insane and Feeble Minded" (Feb. 25, 1875), reprinted in *Papers Read before the Medico-Legal Society of New York* (No. 3, rev. ed. 1886); *see also* J. Kent, II *Commentaries on American Law* 450, 452 (6th ed. 1848); J. Story, II *Commentaries on Equity Jurisprudence as Administered in England and America* 564-69, 591-95 (2d ed. 1836).

2. I. Ray, *A Treatise on the Medical Jurisprudence of Insanity* 55 (1838).

3. The term *lunatic* was sometimes applied as including the idiot and at other times as a distinct category. L. Shelford, *A Practical Treatise of the Law Concerning Lunatics, Idiots and Persons of Unsound Mind* 6, 12 (2d ed. 1847); *see also* G. Zilboorg, *A History of Medical Psychology* 420-21 (1941).

4. L. Kanner, *A History of the Care and Study of the Mentally Retarded* 7-9 (1964); Dunn, "A Historical Review of Treatment of the Retarded," *Mental Retardation* 14 (J. Rothstein ed. 1961).

5. This so-called statute may be dated between 1255 and 1290. W. Holdsworth, I *A History of English Law* 473 (7th ed. 1956).

6. W. Blackstone, I *Commentaries on the Laws of England* 292, 294 (1765); *see In re* Fitzgerald, 2 Sch. & Lefr. 432, 437 (Ir. Ch. 1805).

7. F. Pollock & F. Maitland, I *The History of English Law* 481 (2d ed. 1968).

8. W. Jones, *The Elizabethan Court of Chancery* 383-84 (1967).

9. W. Blackstone, I *Commentaries, supra* note 6, at 292. The subject was committed, with "suitable allowance for his maintenance," to some friend, called a committee, but next heirs were not appointed "to prevent sinister practices."

10. A Fitzherbert, *New Natura Brevium* 232-33 (1652 ed.).

11. M. Dalton, *The Office and Authoritie of Sherifes* 36 (1628).

12. Fitzherbert, *supra* note 10, at 583; Blackstone, *supra* note 6, at 294.

13. Anonymous, The Case of Henry Roberts, Esq.; a gentleman, who, by unparalleled cruelty was deprived of his estate, under the pretense of idiocy (London, 1747), in R. Hunter & I. Macalpine, *Three Hundred Years of Psychiatry* 374 (1963).

14. H. Bell, *An Introduction to the History and Records of the Court of Wards and Liveries* 132 (1953).

15. Harrod v. Harrod, 1 Kay & J. 4, 9, 69 Eng. Rep. 344, 346 (Ch. 1854).

16. H. Bell, *supra* note 14, at 112.

17. 4 Co. Rep. 123b, 76 Eng. Rep. 1118 (K.B. 1604).

18. *Id.* at 125b, 76 Eng. Rep. 1124.

19. W. Blackstone, I *Commentaries, supra* note 6, at 293; H. Theobald, *The Law Relating to Lunacy* 3 (1924); T. Powell, *The Attourney's Academy* 216-17 (1623).

20. *See* M. Hale, *A Discourse Touching Provision for the Poor* 11 (1683).

21. *See* N. Walker, I *Crime and Insanity in England* 43-44 (1968).

22. Defoe, "An Essay Upon Projects" 179-181 (1697), *reprinted in* R. Hunter & I. Macalpine, *supra* note 13, at 265-66: "We use [natural fools] in England with the last Contempt, which I think is a strange Error, since tho' they are useless to the Commonwealth, they are only so by God's direct Providence, and no previous Fault."

23. Private madhouse owners also excluded retarded persons: not until 1805 did one suggest that future efforts might "even go so far also to endeavour to relieve idiots." Bakewell, "The Domestic Guide in Cases of Insanity" (1805), *id.* at 705.

24. G. Rosen, *Madness in Society* 274 (1968); K. Jones, *Lunacy, Law, and Conscience 1744-1845* 2 (1955): "whether he was rich or poor, he was almost certain to be confined, neglected, and intimidated, if not treated with open cruelty."

25. 3 Geo. III, c. 27 (1763).

26. Edw. 6, c. 3, § 9 (1547).

27. An Act for the Relief of the Poor, 43 Eliz. 1, c. 2, §§ 2, 4 (1601).

28. M. Dalton, *The Countrey Justice: containing the Practise, Duty and Power of the Justices of the Peace* 176-77 (1762 ed., with indications to 1618 ed. text).

29. 43 Eliz. 1, c. 2 at § 1 (1601).

30. Fessler, "The Management of Lunacy in Seventeenth Century England," 49 *Proced. of the Royal Society of Medicine* 901, 904 (1956), noted in Dershowitz, "The Origins of Preventive Confinement in Anglo-American Law," 43 *U. Cin. L. Rev.* 1, 36 (1974).

31. 12 Anne, c. 26, § 22 (1714).

32. An Act to amend and make more effectual the Laws relating to Rogues, Vagabonds and other idle and disorderly Persons, and to Houses of Correction, 17 Geo. 2, c. 5 (1744).

33. Case No. 49, Lunatick Petitions, 2 Atk. 52, 26 Eng. Rep. 429 (Ch. 1740).

34. 17 Geo. 2, c. 5, §§ 21, 30-31 (1744).

35. Defoe, "Augusta triumphans, or, the way to make London the most flourishing city in the universe" 30-34 (1728), in R. Hunter & I. Macalpine, *supra* note 13, at 266.

36. 2 Burr. 1115, 97 Eng. Rep. 741 (K.B. 1761).

37. Mrs. Hawley's case and confinement are described in 15 *Parliamentary History of England* 1284-85 (1763). She had complained of being taken to a madhouse where she was "shut up night and day in a chamber, locked and barricaded; refused the use of pen and paper; no notice permitted to be carried to any relative or friend; and treated with severity; and she added, that during the whole time she was never visited by her mother, nor ever desired to take any medicines whatever."

38. *Id.* at 1288-89.

39. 14 Geo. 3, c. 49 § 21 (1774).

40. W. Parry-Jones, *The Trade in Lunacy: A Study of Private Madhouses in England in the 18th and 19th Centuries* 265-66 (1972).

41. W. Blackstone, I *Commentaries on the Laws of England* 305 (8th ed. 1788).

42. "Lunatic Asylums," 28 *Edinburgh Rev.* 466 (1817), quoted in Parry-Jones, *supra* note 40, at 242.

43. P. Phillips, *The Law Concerning Lunatics, Idiots & Persons of Unsound Mind* 1, 5 (1858).

44. I *Colonial Laws of New York* 79 (1896). As early as 1677, the New York City Mayor's Court ordered a strong-house built for Peter Paull, "a lunatick." A. Deutsch, *The Mentally Ill in America* 42 (2d ed. 1949).

45. An Act for the Defraying of the publique & necessary Charge . . . & for maintaining the poore & preventing vagabonds, 1683 Laws, ch. 9, in *Colonial Laws, supra* note 44, at 132-33.

46. 1691 Laws, ch. 6, *id.* at 238; 1701 Laws, ch. 96, *id.* at 456.

47. An Act to prevent Vagrant and Idle Persons from being a Charge and Expense to any of the Counties, Cities, Towns, or Precincts within this Province, 1721 Laws, ch. 410, in II *Colonial Laws of New York* 56-58 (1894).

48. An Act for the Speedy punishing and releasing . . . Persons from Imprisonment . . . ," in appendix to *Laws, Statutes, Ordinances & Constitutions of the City of New York* 75 (1763).

49. An Act for the settlement and relief of the Poor, 1773 Laws, ch. 1600, V *Colonial Laws of New York* 513, 520 (1894).

50. A. Deutsch, *supra* note 44, at 420. For the view that the insane fared no worse than other dependent groups in colonial America, see G. Grob, *Mental Institutions in America: Social Policy to 1875* 12 (1973).

51. An Act to Enable the City of New York to Relieve the Poor . . . , 1695 Laws, ch. 47, in I *Colonial Laws of New York* 348.

52. 1701 Laws, ch. 96, *id.* at 456-57; Ms. Kings Co., Ct. & Rd. Recs. 1692-1825, in J. Goebel & T. Naughton, *Law Enforcement in Colonial New York* 28 (1944).

53. Minutes of Mayor's Court, 1718-1720 (May 10, 1720), in *Select Cases of the Mayor's Court of New York City* 68 (R. Morris ed. 1935).

54. D. Rothman, *The Discovery of the Asylum* 38-39 (1971).

55. A. Chester, I *Legal and Judicial History of New York* 277 (1911); A. Deutsch, *supra* note 44, at 43.

56. 1788 N.Y. Laws, ch. 31.

57. 1772 Laws, ch. 1550, V *Colonial Laws of New York* 367 (1894). *See* G. Grob, *supra* note 50, at 31.

58. 1827 N.Y. Laws, ch. 294.

59. New York Assembly Document No. 263, 29 (March 10, 1831).

60. D. Rothman, *supra* note 54, at xiii (1971). On the lack of provisions for idiots, see D. Schneider, *The History of Public Welfare in New York State* 238 (1938).

61. 1836 N.Y. Laws, ch. 82. *See* L. Brockett, *Idiots and the Efforts for their Improvement* 7 (1856).

62. D. Dix, Memorial to the Legislature of the State of New York, *Assembly Doc. No. 21* at 5 (Jan. 12, 1844). Concern focused not on retarded persons, but on the mentally ill and the "large accumulation of incurables" in county poorhouses. Report and Memorial of the County Superintendents of this State on Lunacy and its relation to Pauperism, and for Relief of Insane Poor, *N.Y. Sen. No. 17* at 15 (Jan. 23, 1856).

63. Memorial to the Legislature of Massachusetts, at 5 (Jan. 1843), *reprinted in* D. Dix, *On Behalf of the Insane Poor* (1971).

64. *Id.* at 1, 9, 55. Miss Dix declared:

> The basest criminal . . . is still protected by the laws which he has outraged, and his prison opens to admit the minister of religion bearing the holy word of life, the humane instructor and frequent visitor, whose counsels may inspire repentance towards God, and purposes of amended practice; but the poor wretch whom broken capacities and darkened understanding disqualify for self-care and moral accountability—who, as a young feeble infant, is helpless and unconscious—he is unprotected, unprovided for, forsaken of friends, forsaken of all!

65. D. Dix, Memorial to the United States Congress 7, 30th Cong. 1st Sess., Sen. Misc. No. 150 (1848).

66. A. Brigham, *Third Annual Report of the New York State Lunatic Asylum* 59 (1845).

67. New York Senate, Report No. 23, at 11 (Jan. 23, 1846).

68. On the rise and fall of Abendberg, an early Swiss institution, and its influence on American visitors in the 1840s, see L. Kanner, *supra* note 4, at 24-27.

69. New York Senate, Report No. 44, at 12 (Feb. 16, 1847).

70. S.G. Howe, *Report Made to the Legislature of Massachusetts Upon Idiocy* 53 (1848).

71. 1851 N.Y. Laws, ch. 502, §§ 1-2.

72. First Annual Report of the Trustees of the New York State Asylum for Idiots to the Legislature of the State (Feb. 9, 1852).

73. By-Laws of the New York State Idiot Asylum, art. IX, in Appendix A to Syracuse State School, Twenty-Eighth Annual Report, New York Senate Report No. 6, at 34 (1888).

74. H.B. Wilbur, First Report of the Superintendent, to the Trustees of the New York Asylum for Idiots, at 12 (Jan. 23, 1852).

75. *Cf.* 1851 N.Y. Laws, ch. 502 §§ 1-6 *with* 1842 N.Y. Laws, ch. 135, §§ 1-51.

76. 1862 N.Y. Laws, ch. 220, §§ 9, 12-13.

77. *See* 1842 N.Y. Laws, ch. 135, §§ 9, 21-23.

78. On the agitation for stricter legal safeguards in committing the insane, see Ordronaux, *supra* note 1, at 69-71; E. Packard, II *Modern Persecution or Insane Asylums Unveiled* 332 (1875); *In re* Baker, 29 How. Pr. 485 (N.Y. Sup. Ct. 1865); J. Bucknill, *Notes on Asylums for the Insane in America* 65-69 (1876).

79. New York Asylum for Idiots, *Fifteenth Annual Report* 29 (1866).

80. W. Fernald, "The History of the Treatment of the Feeble-minded," *Proceedings of the Twentieth National Conference of Charities and Corrections* 210 (1893).

81. *Fifteenth Annual Report, supra* note 79, at 13, 63.

82. *Id.* at 64.

83. E. Seguin, *New Facts and Remarks Concerning Idiocy* 12 (1870) (lecture before the New York Medical Journal Association, Oct. 15, 1869).

84. W. Fernald, *supra* note 80, at 217-18.

85. New York State Senate Select Comm. to Visit the Charitable and Penal Institutions of the State, "Report," in Senate I *Documents* No. 8, 79th Sess. (1856), quoted in D. Schneider, *supra* note 60, at 250.

86. 1875 N.Y. Laws, ch. 173, § 1.

87. E. Seguin, *Idiocy and its Treatment by the Physiological Method* 291 (1866, republished by Columbia Univ. Teachers College, 1907).

88. S. Howe, *Ceremonies on Laying the Corner-Stone of the New York State Institution for the Blind* 39-43 (1866).

89. H. Wilbur, "Status of the Work," *Proceedings of the Association of Medical Officers of American Institutions for Idiotic and Feeble-Minded Persons* 96 (1879).

90. 1870 N.Y. Laws, ch. 492, § 2 at 1113.

91. *E.g.*, 1879 N.Y. Laws, ch. 148, § 1 at 218 ($45,000 appropriated); 1883 N.Y. Laws, ch . 243, § 1 at 255 ($53,500); 1884 N.Y. Laws, ch. 240, § 1 at 417 ($63,000).

92. W. Fernald, *supra* note 80, 214-15.

93. 1878 N.Y. Laws, ch. 252, § 1.

94. *Cf.* 1893 N.Y. Laws, ch. 348, § 6 *with* 1895 N.Y. Laws, ch. 59, § 6.

95. R. Dugdale, "Hereditary pauperism, as illustrated by the 'Juke' family," *Proceedings of the Conference of Charities* 81 (1877), *reprinted in* M. Rosen, G. Clark, & M. Kivitz (eds.), I *The History of Mental Retardation: Collected Papers* 270-282 (1975).

96. *See* 1893 N.Y. Laws, ch. 348; Goldberg, "Social Aspects of the Treatment of the Insane," 97 *Studies in History, Economics and Public Law* 32 (Columbia U. 1921).

97. W. Fernald, *supra* note 80, at 211.

98. S. Davies, *Social Control of the Mentally Deficient* 128-29 (1930). For an example of the tone of the committee's writings, see A. Johnson & M. Lane, *The Menace of the Mentally Defective* 18-19 (American Unitarian Ass'n, Bulletin No. 37, 1910): "Whatever the method, whether segregation or sterilization, it is the imperative duty of the state to see to it . . . that the baby who is defective by inheritance shall not be given a chance to come into the world."

99. I. Kerlin, Provision for Idiotic and Feeble-minded Children, in *11th Conference of Charities and Corrections* 246, 258 (1884).

100. A. Moore, *The Feeble-Minded in New York* 3, 89-92 (1911).

101. 1914 N.Y. Laws ch. 405, § 1, amending 1909 N.Y. Consol. Laws, ch. 55, § 460.

102. 1915 N.Y. Laws, ch. 480, § 1.

103. 1916 N.Y. Laws, ch. 320, § 1.

104. 1918 N.Y. Laws, ch. 197, § 1.

105. 1919 N.Y. Laws, ch. 633, § 24.

106. *Id.* §§ 34, 35. *See In re* Larner, 68 App. Div. 320, 74 N.Y.S. 70 (1902) (attorney's fees and expenses of habeas corpus proceedings are charged to inmate's estate).

107. Rome State Custodial Asylum, *Sixteenth Annual Report of the Board of Managers* 11-12 (1911).

108. Address by Gov. Charles S. Whitman, published in Letchworth Village Board, *Seventh Annual Report* 50-51 (Sen. No. 5, 1916).

109. A. Warner, *American Charities* 333-34 (M. Coolidge, rev. 3d ed. 1919).

110. Kuhlmann, "One Hundred Years of Special Care and Training," 45 *Am. J. of Mental Deficiency* 8, 14 (1940).

111. L. Kanner, *supra* note 4, at 86. The creation of Letchworth Village, for example, was rationalized on grounds of social defense: ". . . the law is being flagrantly violated through failure on the part of the state to make adequate provision for these classes of [mental] defectives. . . . This it can do only by making provision for all dependent feeble minded and epileptic in the state of both sexes and all ages, taking them at the earliest possible age, training them to the highest efficiency of which they are capable, and then providing them with permanent custodial care." Letchworth Village Bd. of Managers, *Second Annual Report* 19-20 (Sen. No. 8, 1911).

112. Syracuse State School, *Seventy-Seventh Annual Report of the Board of Visitors* 10-11 (1928).

113. J. Grimes, *Institutional Care of Mental Patients in the United States* 126 (1934).

114. *Seventy-Seventh Annual Report, supra* note 112, at 16.

115. Syracuse State School, *Ninety-Fourth Annual Report* 15 (1944).

116. Rome State Custodial Asylum, *Sixteenth Annual Report* 11 (1911).

117. Rome State Custodial Asylum, *Seventeenth Annual Report* 10-12 (Assembly Doc. No. 18, 1912).

118. Rome State Custodial Asylum, *Twenty-Fourth Annual Report* 16-18 (Leg. Doc. No. 99, 1919).

119. State Custodial Asylum for Feeble-Minded Women, *Thirty-Second Annual Report* 22, 36 (Sen. Doc. No. 24, 1917). Inmates past child-bearing age were removed by county poor law officials, and not until 1932 were men admitted.

120. *Id.* at 37; *Report of the Royal Comm'n on the Care and Control of the Feeble-Minded* 297-98, 300 (Cmd. 4202, 1908).

121. *See* Syracuse State School, *Seventy-Eighth Annual Report* 6 (1929).

122. Fernald, "What is Practical in the Way of Prevention of Mental Defect?" *Proceedings of the National Conference of Charities and Corrections* 96 (1915), quoted in Wolfensberger, "The Origin and Nature of Our Institutional Models," in President's Comm. on Mental Retardation, *Changing Patterns in Residential Services for the Mentally Retarded* 68 (1976).

123. Fernald, "State Programs for the Care of the Mentally Defective," 24 *J. Psycho-Asthenics* 119-20 (1919).

124. Baker, "History of the Care of the Feeble-Minded," in 14 *Bulletin of the Mass. Dep't of Mental Diseases* 26 (April 1930).

125. *Report of the New York State Comm'n to Investigate Provision for the Mentally Deficient* 253 (1915).

126. Rome State Custodial Asylum, *Twenty-Second Annual Report* 8 (1917).

127. 274 U.S. 200 (1927). *See* Cynkar, "*Buck* v. *Bell*: 'Felt Necessities' v. Fundamental Values?" 81 *Col. L. Rev.* 1418 (1981).

128. Osborn v. Thomson, 103 Misc. 23, 169 N.Y.S. 638 (Sup. Ct. Albany Co.), *aff'd* 185 App. Div. 902, 171 N.Y.S. 1094 (1918) (statute applying only to inmates of public institutions unconstitutional since inapplicable to persons not in institutions).

129. 169 N.Y.S. *supra* at 640-42.

130. *See* N. Kittrie, *The Right to be Different: Deviance and Enforced Therapy* 325 (1971).

131. Barr, "Results of Asexualization," 9 *J. of Psycho-Asthenics* 129 (1905); Kansas Bd. of Trustees of the State Charitable Institutions, *Ninth Biennial Report* 86 (1894), *reprinted in* II *Children and Youth in America: A Documentary History* 855-57 (R. Bremner, ed. 1971).

132. *See, e.g.*, S. Davies, *Social Control of the Mentally Deficient* 125-26 (1930); A. Tredgold, *Mental Deficiency* 502 (5th ed. 1929).

133. N.Y. Mental Hygiene Law §§ 120, 121, 138 (Cahill's Consol. 2d ed. 1930).

134. Potter & McCollaster, "A Résumé of Parole Work at Letchworth Village," 31 *J. of Psycho-Asthenics* 165 (1926), *reprinted in* M. Rosen, II, *supra* note 95, at 141.

135. J. Grimes, *supra* note 113, at 48 (1934) (educable children distinguished from "lower grade, ineducable children, who need custodial care until gentle death removes that need"). *But see* 1917 N.Y. Laws, ch. 553.

136. *Cf.* 1927 N.Y. Laws, ch. 426, § 120 ("state institutions for the care, training and custody of mental defectives") *with id.* § 60 ("state hospitals . . . for the care and treatment of the poor and indigent insane").

137. *See* W. Trattnor, *Homer Folks: Pioneer in Social Welfare* 129 (1968); R. Kelson, *The Science of Public Welfare* 329 (1928): "the principal function of such institutions must be the segregation of hereditary defectives to prevent procreation."

138. Memorandum to Governor Peery, 1936, "Some Public Welfare Needs" *reprinted in* A. James, *The State Becomes A Social Worker: An Administrative Interpretation* 337, 340 (1942).

139. 49 *Am. J. of Mental Deficiency* 1 (1944).

140. Syracuse State School Board of Visitors, *Seventy-Seventh Annual Report* 10, 12 (1928).

141. S. Howe, *Twenty-Seventh Report of the Superintendent of the Massachusetts School for Idiotic and Feeble-Minded Youth* 24 (1874).

142. United States v. Carolene Products Co., 304 U.S. 144, 152 n.4 (1933).

143. *See, e.g.*, "Miss Nelson, 103, Dies; Confined for a Century," *New York Times*, Feb. 1, 1975, at 30, col. 2.

3 From Custodial to Habilitative Policies

On August 28, 1981, delegates to the Second South Pacific Conference on Mental Retardation proclaimed a Code of Rights. Recognizing that "everybody living in institutions has the right to community living," their code demanded "the closing of all institutions for intellectually disadvantaged persons."[1] Others have called for a shift from custodialism to community care, but this appeal was different: the code's authors were sixty intellectually handicapped delegates. "We are humans first and disadvantaged second," they explained in asserting their right to choose where to live and work, the right to lead their own lives.

Increasingly, the voices of people with disabilities are being heard in a movement that is international in scope. As part of the 450 million disabled people around the world, those with mental disabilities will not remain a silent minority for much longer. They have now begun to stand up for their own rights. This chapter describes three of the major themes in their quest for change: human rights, habilitation, and community integration.

Human Rights and Retarded People

For too long, mentally retarded people have been treated as if they were less than human. Their dehumanization has taken many guises: systematic exclusion from education, forced sterilization, and the stripping away of all rights through coercive commitment and plenary guardianship. Even their very lives could be sacrificed. Under the so-called euthanasia program of Nazi Germany, an estimated 300,000 "mentally and physically deficient" persons were exterminated.[2] This systematic killing occurred with the full knowledge of institutional superintendents.[3] Ordinary Germans knew it, too, fearing that when "the feeble-minded have been finished off, the next useless eaters whose turn will come [would be] the old people."[4]

Even today, the survival of handicapped infants and children can hinge on arbitrary and arrogant judgments concerning their quality of life.[5] Yet in the developed as well as the developing world, discrimination against retarded people has added man-made disabilities to congenital impairments. It was not just Third World children left to starve in the bush; the minds of socially invisible children were left to waste in the United States. Writing in 1971, federal circuit judge Skelly Wright was shocked to discover the systematic exclusion of school-age disabled children from any schooling, "a human tragedy, unbelievable as it is in the capital of the richest country on earth."[6]

In the 1950s and 1960s, references to mental retardation as a legal and human rights problem began to appear. Reports of the World Health Organization condemned legislative overprotection that led to early institutionalization, discrimination, and isolation of the mentally retarded person from family and community.[7] Through symposiums on guardianship and legislative aspects of mental retardation, the International League of Societies for the Mentally Handicapped explored ways in which retarded people could exercise "the right to choose a place to live" and obtain "complete integration in society."[8] At its Jerusalem Congress of 1968, the International League sought sweeping reforms by proclaiming the Declaration of General and Special Rights of the Mentally Retarded. From its very first article, the declaration struck an unblushing egalitarian position: "The mentally retarded person has the same basic rights as other citizens of the same country and the same age."[9]

This, in fact, was the underlying principle expressed in Denmark's pioneering law[10] and in the United States' awakening interest under President Kennedy in "a network of authorized checks and balances" to safeguard such rights.[11] Step by step, nations began to build a legal framework consistent with the idea of retarded persons living in a manner as close to normal as possible.

The United Nations Declaration on the Rights of Mentally Retarded Persons, adopted on December 20, 1971, forcefully expressed this principle of normalization. By a General Assembly vote of 110 to 0, member states pledged to promote the integration of mentally retarded persons "as far as possible in normal life" and their participation in community life.[12] Article 4 stressed home-based care, and placed priority on retarded persons living with their natural or foster families and giving those families practical assistance. Linking normalization to habilitation, this provision recognized that the individual should be served in "surroundings and other circumstances as close as possible to those of normal life."[13] This historic declaration also called for "proper legal safeguards" against every form of abusive or unwarranted restriction of rights,[14] and "a right to protection from exploitation, abuse and degrading treatment."[15] But who would enforce these rights and determine the limits of the possible? Would nations take these rights seriously and honor this call for national and international action?

The International League has kept these questions from being forgotten. Though its name has changed (it is now the International League of Societies for Persons with Mental Handicap), its purposes have not. Through international surveys it has confirmed that no country, not even the most industrialized, has realized fully in law or practice the rights set out in the United Nations and League declarations.[16] As a nongovernmental organization with consultative status to the United Nations and its agencies, the League continues to prod the international community to take action to implement these human rights. At its behest, the World Health Organization emphasized that the retarded person is "part of the human family, and as such should enjoy the same rights, dignity and compassion accorded to his more fortunate peers."[17] The League's Committee on Rights and Legal Planning labored toward that end: organizing international seminars, preparing legal briefs, and publishing guidelines to assess and stimulate progress in achieving national compliance with human rights standards.[18] Working through organizations of parents, professionals, and disabled persons in sixty-six member countries, the International League has nurtured a global human rights movement of and for mentally retarded people.

In many countries, that movement is expressed in efforts to change discriminatory attitudes, laws, and public policies. The international community, through the Advisory Committee of the International Year of Disabled Persons and the UN Economic and Social Council, has repeatedly urged governments to pass legislation to achieve fuller integration of disabled persons in the community.[19] Yet outdated and inappropriate laws continue to inhibit new approaches to mental care. Inertia, tradition, and vested interests stand in the way of legal protection for the individual rights, welfare, property, and dignity of mentally retarded persons and their families.[20] To counter these obstacles, voluntary associations in the Netherlands, New Zealand, and elsewhere have lobbied for advocacy and limited-guardianship laws.[21] English activists have succeeded in amending the medically oriented Mental Health Act of 1959,[22] an example which may inspire others in India, Pakistan, and Bangladesh to shed similar coercive measures.

New human rights expectations for intellectually disabled persons and their families have influenced the course of legal reform. Examples abound. In Norway, Sweden, and Denmark, involuntary civil commitment on the basis of mental retardation has recently been abolished.[23] England and Scotland have implemented laws prohibiting the exclusion of mentally handicapped children from the educational system.[24] Many jurisdictions have amended, or are in the process of amending, antidiscrimination laws to cover mentally retarded persons.[25]

Nowhere have these initiatives been more dramatic than in the United States. In less than a decade, a coalition of consumers, advocates, and professionals has reshaped the law relating to mental retardation. Retarded persons, when confined in institutions or otherwise shut out from society, had enjoyed neither equality before the law nor protection of basic rights. In theory, they had all the rights normally held by other citizens but their rights were liable to suffer from "unauthorized or unsanctioned curtailment."[26]

In the 1970s, federal court cases forcefully reminded society of the gap between its benevolent promises and its neglectful treatment of retarded people. The first of these cases focused on the misclassification and exclusion of school-age disabled children from public education. The callous disregard of these children's rights was more than a local aberration: by the time national legislation was adopted, lawsuits in over thirty states revealed that vast numbers of mentally and physically handicapped children were barred from school.[27]

Legal activists signaled a second major initiative by placing institutions on trial. *Wyatt* v. *Stickney,* the first class action on the right to treatment, questioned the very legitimacy of institutions in future programming. Dr. Gunnar Dybwad and Dr. Philip Roos, as principle expert witnesses, stressed the destructive effects of custodial institutionalization. "In the long run, I see no need for Partlow [State School and Hospital]," Dr. Dybwad testified, "but if Partlow will exist over the next years, it will be to take itself out of business."[28] Ten years later, Partlow still remains in business. But as with the other fifty public institutions under litigative attack, it is a declining enterprise. Like so many similar facilities, Partlow is now subject to constitutional standards and continuing federal jurisdiction. Yet even after years of judicial supervision, only one court has so far found an institution in compliance, although judicial oversight continues with regard to the community-care portions of that consent judgment.[29]

Court suits also sparked a wave of legislative and regulatory reform. Most importantly, they have vitalized coalitions of consumers, advocates, and professionals determined to defend, and if possible extend, hard-won human rights. One group, for example, has demanded "a real bill of rights," federal legislation which ties funding to guarantees of effective services in the community.[30]

In the 1980s, the attention of advocates will increasingly shift from a federal to a state focus. Though the states have long had the primary responsibility for caring for retarded persons, the policies pursued by President Reagan's administration seek to reduce federal categorical assistance and federal regulatory roles. Coupled with state-administered block grants and state taxpayer revolts, this has set in motion a scramble at the state level for shares of a shrinking social-services budget. In this political climate, vigorous advocacy is more vital than ever. But as exemplified by the Reagan administration's threat to eliminate the Legal Services Corporation, the very survival of advocacy organizations may be at stake.

The attack on human rights advocates is a thinly veiled attack on community integration. As this book's case study demonstrates, state governments remain resistant to redirecting their own funds away from institutions and into quality community-based care. In trying to capture as many federal dollars as possible, the states devoted $2.72 billion to the institutional sector and only $520 million on the community-services sector.[31] The advocates dramatize the inconsistencies between these facts and the official rhetoric that promised disabled citizens the "independence that is their right."[32] Thus, while four out of five dollars for state retardation purposes were going to institutional services, Governor Hugh Carey of New York publicly announced that "Our primary goal must be to provide people with alternatives to confinement in institutions, to expand the special network of housing, employment opportunities and medical care that ends forever the shameful segregation of the disabled."[33]

Ending this segregation will not be easy. As chapter 6 explains, moving retarded persons into community homes raises complex political, economic, and legal problems. For example, implementation of the Willowbrook Consent Decree began in 1975, but the conclusion of this case is still not in sight. Under the latest court order, the state of New York has until 1985 to resettle the remnant of a population that once numbered 5,209.[34] If Willowbrook once had the dubious distinction of being the world's largest residential institution for the retarded, it is now another midsized institution, midway to oblivion. But the issues raised by this case go far beyond the well-being of the 1,215 people who remain there in 1982.

Spurred by the *Willowbrook* decree and intense advocacy pressure, New York has placed approximately three thousand persons with profound and severe developmental disabilities in community residential settings.[35] On a statewide basis, it has halved institutional censuses, from over 25,000 to 12,830 residents within a decade. Indeed, a recent state study confirms that not only are small community-based residences "safe, attractive, comfortable and homelike environments" for this population, but they offer better, more personalized, and less expensive care than the state developmental centers.[36] The state Commission on the Quality of Care has also concluded that the state-operated community residences are costlier and inferior to those run by voluntary agencies.[37] Similar findings have been issued before, but here an arm of state government has questioned why the state is providing more restrictive and less therapeutic forms of care when it can purchase and monitor superior services for fewer dollars. In this context, it is no wonder that Willowbrook, like Partlow or Pennhurst,[38] has become an international symbol of shameful custodialism and the role of law in stimulating social change.

The Triumph of Habilitation

The right to habilitation challenged the destructive, self-fulfilling prophecies of mental retardation as a hopeless condition. Article 2 of the International League declaration enunciated the retarded person's right to "such education, training, habilitation and guidance as will enable him to develop his ability and potential to the fullest possible extent, no matter how severe his degree of disability."[39] With only minor technical changes in language, the United Nations proclaimed this right.[40] A federal court, in citing this United Nations declaration and applicable U.S. law, recognized legal claims to habilitation as the analog to treatment for the mentally ill or rehabilitation for the physically disabled.[41] On the basis of expert testimony, courts in the United States concluded that all mentally retarded persons can benefit from a program of education and training.[42] Since every retarded person is capable of development and growth if given suitable habilitation,[43] custodial institutions were left without a rationale. Congress, in accepting this developmental model of retardation, stressed that "the assumption that certain individuals are essentially incapable of development . . . must be rejected."[44]

Habilitation served as both a broad organizing concept and a process. As a concept, it recognized that mentally retarded persons, like all other persons, undergo behavioral changes that are influenced by learning and living environments. The term *habilitation,* being broader than *rehabilitation,* referred to a total environment and set of activities by which individuals gained new skills, rather than compensated for lost ones. As defined by courts and accreditation councils, habilitation includes, but is not limited to, programs of formal, structured education and training.[45] It is the entire process by which individuals are assisted to acquire and maintain the life skills to "cope more effectively with the demands of their own persons and of their environments, and to raise the levels of their physical, mental and social functioning."[46]

Overwhelming evidence demonstrates that such improvements are possible. Even the most profoundly retarded individuals "can and do profit from habilitation efforts."[47] But to be effective, programs of habilitation require individually tailored goals, a sequential plan of implementation, and a multidisciplinary staff. Furthermore, nationally accepted standards exist by which to judge the adequacy and suitability of habilitation programming.[48]

Confining retarded persons in large, total institutions contravene these standards. The architects of custodial policies offered to protect society from retarded persons, and retarded persons from themselves and their exploiters. But habilitation professionals disproved the stereotype that the retarded represent any significant danger to society, and condemned the injustice of punishing the retarded victim for the victimizer's wrongs.[49] Ill-informed physicians had urged parents to sever their ties to their retarded children and to institutionalize them at an early age to preserve family harmony and emotional health.[50] Habilitation professionals rejected this sacrifice of the child's interests and helped identify ways in which children with handicaps could grow and be supported within their own families.[51] Despite this knowledge, custodial centers still exist. They are characterized by regimented group activities and the subordination of the individual resident's needs to the facility's convenience.

Reacting against the bleak conditions on crowded wards, reformers articulated principles of individualization and normalization. Although persons with mental retardation have varying degrees of capability, they share the right to live as normal a life in as normal an environment as possible. The older presumptions of incompetence had led to overprotection and a destruction of human potential. This could occur not only in gross ways, such as putting retarded people away for life, but in more subtle ways, by denying them access to everyday experiences, opportunities to make mistakes, and to fail like any other member of society.

Habilitation has now become the reigning ideology of the mental retardation field. Along with other organizations of professionals, the American Association on Mental Deficiency (AAMD) endorses the "right to a publicly supported and administered comprehensive and integrated set of habilitative programs designed to minimize handicap or handicaps."[52] Normalization and the least restrictive setting are explicit corollaries of this right. Thus, the AAMD recognizes the right to live in the "least restrictive individually appropriate environment."[53] Given lifelong institutional care costs that can exceed $2 million per retarded person,[54] this position was both just and prudent.

Still, there is a great difference between adopting statements of philosophy and carrying them out. The AAMD reminded its members of their obligation to implement the basic rights of retarded persons, and to remedy any violations. Toward this end, professionals were urged to use legislative, judicial, or job action or "whatever public and private means are available, moral, ethical, and legal."[55] The association, as plaintiff and *amicus curiae* in pathbreaking cases,[56] set an example of leadership. But the association was no monolith, and its proinstitutional forces were distinctly uncomfortable at the specter of supporting suits against some of its own members. By the late 1970s, the AAMD had gone to the sidelines. Moreover, the expert consensus expressed in the *Wyatt* trial in 1972 had frayed by the *Wyatt* implementation hearings of 1978.

That consensus has, however, been reconstituted around Phillip Becker's case and the issues of detriment it poses. In August 1982, the AAMD, joined by the National and California Associations for Retarded Citizens, and California's protection and advocacy program, filed a brief as *amici curiae* marshaling the empirical data and the law supporting rights to medical care and habilitation. On the basis of the "voluminous scientific literature," they concluded that institutionalization can be detrimental to a retarded child's mental, emotional, educational, and linguistic growth. For adults as well, "prolonged exposure to an institutional environment and the lack of continuity of care and stimulating interventions can cause regression and deterioration in skills previously acquired."[57]

Strong evidence also exists that habilitation programs cannot be effective unless the client's surroundings reinforce communication and social skills and encourage the client to increase his or her capacities.[58] A segregated institution cannot provide full habilitation because it lacks this critical social dimension.[59] And, as an integral part of this habilitation process, retarded people need training in recognizing, exercising, and asserting their human rights. Indeed, to a far greater extent than previously assumed, retarded persons can participate in making choices and giving or withholding consent to the habilitative interventions in their lives.[60] This partnership will require greater sensitivity to the feelings of clients, such as avoiding blanket labels such as "the retarded," "the retardate," or "the developmentally disabled"; minimizing intrusions on privacy; and explaining processes and proposed treatments in language that the client is most likely to understand. In one bizarre protest, a resident of a state school actually buried his personal file in an attempt to defend his privacy and to keep people, as he put it, from talking behind his back.

There is a sharp distinction between client-oriented and institution-oriented practices. Unfortunately, policy planners neglect to ask clients what services make them feel better or more satisfied with their lives. Yet when deinstitutionalized persons have been asked or given the option to stay in the community or return to the institution, the overwhelming majority prefer community living.[61]

Community Integration and Public Policy

Despite policy goals of community integration, the government has maintained perverse disincentives to deinstitutionalization. For two decades, United States presidents have reiterated a national policy of community placement as a means of opening "better lives for the mentally retarded."[62] President Reagan, too, has spoken in favor of funding alternatives to institutionalizing retarded persons, expressing astonishment that Medicaid regulations are biased toward institutionalization rather than care in a "home atmosphere." Referring to a case of a brain-damaged, three-year-old girl whose care cost $12,000 a month in a hospital (with federal Medicaid payments) but less than $2,500 a month at home (which her parents could not afford and Medicaid would not pay), he criticized "hidebound regulations" resulting in "a tremendous expense to the taxpayers and doing no good to the patient."[63] But Mr. Reagan and his administration are no longer the outsiders campaigning against Washington. They must now redirect a Medicaid program truly out of control—Intermediate Care Facilities for the Mentally Retarded (ICF-MR). Under that program the federal government has poured billions of dollars into inadequate and segregated institutional care, while community programs are poor competitors for ICF-MR funds or alternative social-services grants.[64] As in the case of individual parents, economic rationality also encourages the states to capture federal funding for institutional approaches rather than using a higher percentage of their own monies for community ones. Recent federal waivers and changes in the deeming rules, as described in chapters 4 and 6, represent only minor tinkerings with this system.

Clearly these funding patterns are a serious obstacle to realizing the principle of the least restrictive alternative. That principle offers a way of accommodating the requirements of law, social policy, and habilitation. But it is a formula for frustration if the bulk of federal and state dollars goes to the most restrictive of care options. It should be recalled that after the Supreme Court's *Pennhurst* decision,[65] Congress reaffirmed the right of developmentally disabled persons to "habilitative services in a setting which is least restrictive of their personal liberty."[66] Once again, Congress pledged to ensure that federal funds are expended on habilitation programs "designed to maximize the developmental potential of a person."[67] Despite this mandate, states continue to invest 83 percent of all capital spending for retardation facilities on institutional renovation or construction, and to use ICF-MR funds primarily to improve existing institutions rather than to create community-based residences.[68] Even in states which use Medicaid monies for smaller community facilities, ICF-MR requirements impose medical-model features that are often contrary to normalization goals.

In its constitutional context, the doctrine of the least restrictive alternative serves the purpose of limiting government's intrusion on personal liberty. Of course, it must first be established that government has a legitimate interest in intervening in a particular person's life. The doctrine thus offers a way of reconciling potentially competing human rights and habilitation goals. For example, a state might have a legitimate interest in training and caring for a retarded individual incapable of surviving safely. But that alone does not warrant confining that individual in a custodial program. Nor does it justify denying the resident opportunities to gain skills for a greater degree of independence, and eventual release or transfer to community surroundings. Furthermore, retarded persons require immediate relief from "warehouse-type facilities."[69]

Scandals in congregate care are far from over. And because habilitation professionals can harm as well as help, scrutiny should be greatest where their interventions are most intrusive and long-lasting. Given these criteria, and the appalling historical record, institutionalization is a logical focus for searching professional and citizen review. Client abuse, both physical and psychological, remains an endemic feature of institutional life.[70] Scientific studies and judicial findings reveal that certain institutional conditions are not only dangerous, but result in the deterioration of a resident's physical, emotional, and intellectual functioning (see chapter 5).[71]

In terms of the resources invested, fiscal and human, efforts at institutional reform yielded disappointing results. Even after years of improving staff-to-resident ratios and upgrading physical facilities, the changes at Partlow or Willowbrook were largely cosmetic. Gradually, a wide variety of courts and experts have come to the conclusion that such institutions are obsolete and beyond repair. Thus, the federal court in the *Willowbrook* case found that the "goals of normalization and development of the mentally retarded cannot be met until every effort is made to physically and socially integrate the class members into the community."[72] Even the American Psychiatric Association acknowledged that those institutionalized as mentally disordered, "rendered invisible by removal to large and remote state institutions," are at risk of "mere custody in an environment that does not allow a minimum level of human care."[73]

Community integration also had its critics. Some cautioned against eliminating institutions, arguing that this would reduce the spectrum of services and hence limit professional discretion and the choices of clients, or their surrogates. A few skeptics believed that the most capable residents had already been creamed-off (released or transferred to community care), leaving only the so-called unplaceables behind. But many groups, including the World Health Organization, disagreed, urging active habilitation programs in order to prepare more people for community living.[74] While deinstitutionalization has not gone far enough, some researchers raised warning flags, pointing to custodial practices creeping into programs labeled as community care, or questioning the wisdom of prescribing small family-style care for everyone.[75] Yet according to an AAMD publication, "certain means of service delivery or settings can be so restrictive of liberty and so damaging to individuals that their continued existence is not justified."[76] The reformer's dilemma was how to mobilize support to close those institutions and at the same time create a stable system of long-term care.

Experience in depopulating mental hospitals colored the public's acceptance of a policy of returning retarded people to their home communities. Between 1955 and 1978, the census of residents of public institutions for the mentally ill plunged from 559,000 to 149,000.[77] In contrast, the peak came later and the decline was more gradual in the census of public mental retardation institutions: from 195,000 residents in 1967 to 139,432 in 1978.[78] Compared to the mental hospitals' policies, fewer retarded people placed in community facilities returned to institutions, and aftercare arrangements were generally better. Members of the general public, with visions of ex-mental patients dumped in their neighborhoods, were not likely to make distinctions between mental retardation and mental illness.[79] The mental health clients had arrived first: more than 200,000 deinstitutionalized people left mental hospitals even before the first decline in retardation institutions. And state and local government had done little to inspire confidence that the needs of former state wards would be well-served. It was therefore not surprising that community residential facilities for the retarded were often perceived as another threat to local security, life-styles, and property values. Community-education approaches, rather than calming those fears, may have even stimulated local opposition.[80]

Clinicians drew different cautionary lessons from the hasty discharge of chronically mentally ill patients. Some observers warned that many ex-patients had simply been "trans-institutionalized" to nursing homes and prisons, and that the scarcity of decent community care reflected the public's "enduring unwillingness to pay for high-quality care for the mentally ill."[81] Respected authorities such as Dr. John A. Talbott believed that with steps such as community-support services, case-management systems, and full civil rights for patients, the disasters of the past could be avoided.[82] In learning from this social engineering, advocates for retarded people vowed to construct remedies that were the very antithesis of dumping.

Instead of releasing retarded persons without supervision or supportive services, the reformers sought assurances of integrated, individually tailored habilitation in community-based programs. Advocates had essential roles in making such community integration work. In many states, they joined in creating, virtually from scratch, a coordinated, carefully monitored, and professionally staffed network of community-living arrangements and daytime services. On a national level, advocacy groups fought for laws and appropriations that would give disabled persons access to community education, health, rehabilitation, and long-term care services. That battle has both defensive and affirmative aspects; preserving human rights measures, such as the Education for All Handicapped Children Act and its regulations, and redirecting Medicaid funds from costly institutional renovations to small, normalized community-living settings.[83] Meanwhile, statewide advocacy organizations pursued a parallel agenda: monitoring local programs, influencing policies, and campaigning for state laws and regulations consistent with community integration.[84]

To secure such integration, advocates must struggle against restrictive zoning practices, denials of client entitlements, and cutbacks in community programming. This requires a high degree of grass-roots activity, and close contact with the people whose choices one hopes to expand. It means speaking up for retarded persons without family support, and training those who can to speak up for themselves.[85] Most critically, the advocate's participation can improve the quality of least-restrictive-alternative determinations so as to fit the chosen alternative to the individual client's needs and desires.

In those places where advocacy is vigorous and human rights respected, people with mental retardation thrive. In Sweden and Denmark, where the goals of integration and habilitation are embedded in public policy and programs are carefully planned and monitored, residents of community facilities enjoy enviable opportunities for normal living.[86] In England, the Wessex Project shows that a completely locally-based pattern of care can serve even the most profoundly retarded individuals.[87]

Increasingly, programs in the United States report similar findings. Michigan's Macomb-Oakland Regional Center is helping to avoid institutionalization by creating family-care training homes, group homes, supervised apartment living, and respite care.[88] Through Nebraska's pioneering legislation in 1969, the Eastern Nebraska Community Office of Retardation (ENCOR) offers a comprehensive network of local services to prevent institutional admissions in a five-county area.[89]

Transfers from large institutions to family-style living arrangements can encourage community contact. As a result, individuals experience increased personal freedom and improvements in the quality of their lives and their adaptive abilities.[90] But even for those in independent living placements, service providers should offer continuing training and assistance. With proper support services, the community-based habilitation of deinstitutionalized people can succeed, even for those with profound impairments.[91] Perhaps the most poignant evidence of this comes from retarded people and their families. One mother testified that her son has learned more in three years in the community than in his thirty-eight years at an institution; in contrast to those earlier years, he now is able to talk, walk, and hold a job.[92] Another former resident, contrasting the chaos and violence at Pennhurst State School, summed up his new life in a group home in these words: "I am a different kind of man now."[93]

Summary

Because of the powerful juncture of habilitation, community integration, and human rights imperatives, the law relating to mental disability had to be transformed. With the shift from custody to habilitation, that law identified a new objective: to ensure that the retarded person has "a right to be a part of society—not apart from society."[94] But despite broad agreement on principles, implementation of such a right met considerable resistance. Turning to the legal process, advocates sought effective tools for bringing discordant practices in line with humane ideals.

Notes

1. The Australian Voice of Intellectually Disadvantaged Citizens, "Code of Rights" (Resolutions of the Second South Pacific Conference on

Mental Retardation, Melbourne, Australia, presented by members of the Fifth Strand to Senator Fred Chaney, Federal Social Security Minister, August 28, 1981).

2. F. Wertham, *A Sign for Cain: An Exploration of Human Violence* 170 (1966); Wolfensberger, "The Extermination of Handicapped People in World War II Germany," 19 *Mental Retardation* 1, 3 (Feb. 1981).

3. Letter from L. Schlaich, Chief of the Institution for Feeble-Minded in Stetten, to Dr. Frank, Reich Minister for Justice (Sept. 6, 1940) (requesting that euthanasia be carried out only after legal basis was created), United States v. Brandt, Trials of War Criminals Before the Nuremberg Military Tribunal Under Control Council Law No. 10, vol. 1, at 854.

4. Letter from Dr. Hilfrich, Bishop of Limburg, to the Reich Minister of Justice (Aug. 13, 1941) , *id.* at 845-46.

5. Compare *In re* Phillip B., 92 Cal. App. 3d 796, 156 Cal. Rptr. 48 (1979), *cert. denied sub nom.* Bothman v. Warren B., 445 U.S. 949 (1980) *with* Guardianship of Becker, No. 101981 (Cal. Super. Ct., Santa Clara Co. Aug. 7, 1981), *aff'd,* No. 53419 (Cal. Ct. App., 1st Dist. Jan. 25, 1983) (guardianship transferred from biological parents who refuse to consent to medical treatment to psychological parents who provide child with a substitute home).

6. Hobson v. Hansen, No. 82-66, Ruling on Motion to Intervene at 3 (D.D.C. July 23, 1971).

7. World Health Organization (WHO), Technical Report Series, No. 75, *The Mentally Subnormal Child* 39 (1954). *See* World Health Organization, Technical Report Series, No. 392, *Organization of Services for the Mentally Retarded* (1968) (Fifteenth Report of the WHO Expert Committee on Mental Health).

8. International League of Societies for the Mentally Handicapped (ILSMH), *Symposium on Legislative Aspects of Mental Retardation* 7, 15 (Stockholm, June 17, 1967); ILSMH, *Symposium on Guardianship of the Mentally Retarded* (San Sebastian, Spain, May 31, 1969).

9. International League of Societies for the Mentally Handicapped, Declaration of General and Special Rights of the Mentally Retarded, art. 1 (adopted in Jerusalem Oct. 24, 1968).

10. Act No. 192 of June 5, 1959, concerning the Care of the Mentally Retarded and other Exceptionally Retarded Persons, *as amended by* Act No. 228 of May 27, 1970, concerning Service Administration.

11. President's Panel on Mental Retardation, *Report of the Task Force on Law* 19 (1963). *See* President's Panel on Mental Retardation, *A Proposed Program for National Action to Combat Mental Retardation* (1962) (statement of President John F. Kennedy regarding the need for a national plan in mental retardation, Oct. 11, 1961: "We must provide for the retarded the same opportunity for full social development that is the birthright of every American.").

12. Declaration on the Rights of Mentally Retarded Persons, G.A. Res. 2856, 26 U.N. GAOR, Supp. (No. 29) 93-94, U.N. Doc. A/8429 (1971), preamble and art. 4. Only nine states abstained, consisting of the Soviet Union, its nearest allies, and the Republic of Tanzania. *U.N. Yearbook* 368 (1971).

13. G.A. Res. 2856, art. 4.

14. *Id.*, art. 7.

15. *Id.*, art. 6.

16. Herr, "Rights Into Action: Protecting Human Rights of the Mentally Handicapped," 26 *Cath. U.L. Rev.* 203 (1977); R. Sterner, *Social and Economic Conditions of the Mentally Retarded in Selected Countries* (1976).

17. Joint Comm'n on International Aspects of Mental Retardation, *Mental Retardation: Prevention, Amelioration and Service Delivery* 95 (Jan. 1980, commissioned by the World Health Organization).

18. ILSMH, *Step by Step,* in *2 Proceedings of the Seventh World Congress of ILSMH on Mental Handicap* 428-89 (1978) (printed in English, Spanish, French, and German).

19. U.N. Economic and Social Council Res. 1921 (LVIII), May 6, 1975 (Prevention of Disability and Rehabilitation of Disabled Persons), 58 U.N. ESCOR, Supp. (No.1) 30, U.N. Doc. E/5683 (1975); U.N. Dep't of Information, "First Session of Advisory Committee for 1981 Year for Disabled Persons, Recommends Draft International Programme for Year," Doc. No. SOC/4014 at 2 (March 26, 1979).

20. *See* Harding & Curran, "Promoting Mental Health through the Law," 32 *WHO Chronicle* 109 (1978) (of 43 countries surveyed, only 6 had separate legislation covering the needs and rights of retarded people, while 12 were operating informally with no specific legislation covering treatment for mental disorders).

21. The New Zealand Institute of Mental Retardation, *Guardianship for Mentally Retarded Adults: Submissions to the Minister of Justice* (Sept. 1982); Meiresonne, "Information About the Dutch System of Guardianship for Mentally Handicapped People and about Some Recent Proposals to Fill Gaps in this System" (Dutch National Ass'n for the Care of the Mentally Retarded, Feb. 23, 1977); D. Beattie, Advocacy and Attainment of the Rights of the Intellectually Handicapped 27-34 (paper presented at the annual conference of the New Zealand Society for the Intellectually Handicapped, April 1976). *See generally* International Information Service on Mental Retardation, Report on Guardianship of the Mentally Retarded Throughout the World (1974).

22. Mental Health Act, 1959, 7 & 8 Eliz. 2, c. 72; Mental Health (Amendment) Act 1982, c. 51.

23. Dybwad & Herr, "Unnecessary Coercion: An End to Involuntary Civil Commitment of Retarded Persons," 31 *Stan. L. Rev.* 753, 761 (1979);

Bank-Mikkelsen, "Abolition of Involuntary Civil Commitment of Retarded Persons" (paper presented at the Eighth World Congress of the ILSPMH, Nairobi, Kenya, Nov. 22, 1982).

24. Education (Handicapped Children) Act, 1970, c. 52; Education (Mentally Handicapped Children) Act, 1974, c. 27 (Scotland).

25. *E.g.,* The Canadian Charter of Rights and Freedoms, § 15 (1), being Part I of the Constitution Act, 1982; Quebec Charter of Human Rights and Freedoms, Que. Stat. 1975, c. 6, as amended by an Act to Secure the Handicapped in the Exercise of their Rights, Que. Stat. 1978, c. 7, §§112-113; Ontario Human Rights Code, Ont. Stat. 1981, c. 53, §§ 1-6, 9(b)(ii).

26. *Report of the Task Force on Law, supra* note 11, at 13, 20.

27. *See* Children's Defense Fund, *Children Out of School in America* 280-85 (1974).

28. Trial Record at 26, Wyatt v. Stickney, 344 F. Supp. 387 (M.D. Ala. 1972, *aff'd sub nom.* Wyatt v. Aderholt, 503 F.2d 1305 (5th Cir. 1974), discussed in chapter 5, *infra.*

29. Wuori v. Concannon, Civil No. 75-80 P, Order of Discharge (D. Maine Sept. 18, 1981) (upon parties' concurrence, Pineland Center discharged from the court's jurisdiction, but community care aspects of case remain under judicial supervision).

30. Letter to author from "Operation Real Rights: Ad Hoc Committee to Make Real the Rights of All Persons with Disabilities" (Sept. 17, 1981).

31. C. Wieck & R. Bruininks, The Cost of Public and Community Care for Mentally Retarded People in the United States (Developmental Disabilities Project on Residential Services and Community Adjustment, University of Minnesota, 1980).

32. New York Governor Hugh L. Carey, Annual Message to the Legislature at 19 (Jan. 7, 1981).

33. *Id. Accord,* W. Jones, *Communitization: An Alternative Approach to Social and Service Reform* 3, 10 (1979).

34. New York State Ass'n for Retarded Children, Inc. v. Carey, No. 72 Civ. 356/357 (E.D.N.Y. April 28, 1982). The "Willowbrook Case," as it is popularly known, is discussed in chapters 5 and 6, *infra.*

35. New York State Comm'n on Quality of Care for the Mentally Disabled, Willowbrook: From Institution to the Community, A Fiscal and Programmatic Review of Selected Community Residences in New York City, at 1 (Aug. 1982).

36. *Id.* at 75. Although the annual costs of developmental centers in New York City ranged from $40,201 to $106,356 per resident, community residential facilities had average costs per resident of $28,639.

37. In comparing the median per-year cost per client, the cost for state-operated residences was $43,093, while the cost for voluntary agencies was $27,876. *Id.* at 76.

38. On the implementation histories of the federal cases on Pennhurst and Partlow State Schools and Hospitals, see chapters 5 and 6, *infra.*

39. ILSMH Declaration, *supra* note 9, art. 2.

40. U.N. Declaration, *supra* note 12, art. 2. For example, they substituted the term *rehabilitation* for *habilitation.*

41. *E.g.*, Wyatt v. Stickney, 344 F. Supp. 387, 390 n.6, *aff'd sub nom.* Wyatt v. Aderholt, 503 F.2d 1305 (5th Cir. 1974). Chief Judge Johnson cited article 2, which reads: "The mentally retarded person has a right to proper medical care and physical therapy and to such education, training, rehabilitation and guidance as will enable him to develop his ability and maximum potential."

42. Pennsylvania Ass'n for Retarded Children v. Pennsylvania, 343 F. Supp. 279, 296 (E.D. Pa. 1972). *See* Halderman v. Pennhurst State School and Hospital,446 F. Supp. 1295, 1298 (E.D. Pa. 1978): " 'Habilitation' is the term of art used to refer to that education, training and care required by retarded individuals to reach their maximum development."

43. Welsch v. Likins, 373 F. Supp. 487, 495 (D. Minn. 1974).

44. Senate Rep. No. 160, 94th Cong., 1st Sess. at 28 (1973).

45. Wyatt v. Stickney, 344 F. Supp. 387, 395 (M.D. Ala. 1972), *aff'd sub nom.* Wyatt v. Aderholt, 503 F.2d 1305 (5th Cir. 1974); Accreditation Council for Services for Mentally Retarded and Other Developmentally Disabled Persons, *Standards for Services for Developmentally Disabled Persons* 21-22 (1980). [Hereinafter referred to as ACMRDD Standards].

46. ACMRDD Standards, *supra* note 45, at 21.

47. Welsch v. Likins, Civ. No. 4-72-C 451 (D. Minn. Oct. 1, 1974) (memorandum findings of fact and conclusions of law).

48. *E.g.,* Wyatt v. Stickney, 344 F. Supp. 387, 395-407 (M.D. Ala. 1972); ACMRDD Standards, *supra* note 45.

49. Kivowitz, "Mental Retardation and the Law," in *Modern Legal Medicine, Psychiatry and Forensic Medicine* 862 (W. Curran, A. McGarry, & C. Petty eds. 1980); W. Jones, *supra* note 33, at 3.

50. *See* American Medical Ass'n, *Mental Retardation: A Handbook for the Primary Physician* 63 (1965); Quindlen, "About New York: A Child Comes Home from Willowbrook," *New York Times*, Oct. 7, 1981, at B3 (parents express guilt at following doctor's advice that the best thing was to send one-year-old infant to Willowbrook).

51. F. Menolascino, *Challenges in Mental Retardation: Progressive Ideology and Services* 37 (1977).

52. American Ass'n on Mental Deficiency (AAMD), "Rights of Mentally Retarded Persons: An Official Statement," 11 *Mental Retardation* 56 (Oct. 1973).

53. *Id.* at 58.

54. *See* Haywood, "Reducing Social Vulnerability is the Challenge of the Eighties, 1981 AAMD Presidential Address," 19 *Mental Retardation* 190, 194 (Aug. 1981).

55. AAMD, *supra* note 52, at 56.

56. *E.g.,* Wyatt v. Stickney, *supra* note 45; Morales v. Turman, 364 F. Supp. 166 (E.D. Tex. 1973); Souder v. Brennan, 378 F. Supp. 808 (D.D.C. 1973); Townsend v. Treadway, Civil No. 6500, slip op. at 10-11, 15 (M.D. Tenn. Sept. 21, 1973) (Thirteenth Amendment applies with full force to persons in mental institutions; practice of using seclusion rooms as a means of enforcing work assignments eliminated).

57. Brief of Amici Curiae, the Ass'n for Retarded Citizens of the United States, American Ass'n on Mental Deficiency, Ass'n for Retarded Citizens—California, Protection and Advocacy, Inc. for the State of California at 29, Guardianship of Becker, No. 53419 (Cal. Ct. App. Aug. 19, 1982).

58. *See* Deno, Gutmann, & Fullmer, "Educational Programs for Retarded Individuals," in *Behavior Modification of the Mentally Retarded* 235 (2d ed. T. Thompson & J. Grabowski 1977); T. Thompson, A. Carey, & J. Grabowski, "A Structured Approach to Residential Normalization: Behavioral Intervention in Institutional and Group Home Settings" (1978) (after living in a community-based group home for two years, previously institutionalized severely and profoundly retarded women dramatically improved language and social skills and increased their IQ levels by 10 to 30 points).

59. *See* A. Stone, *Mental Health and Law: A System in Transition* 123 (1975) and the literature collected in Brief of Amici Curiae, *supra* note 57, and Post-Hearing Brief of Plaintiffs and Amicus Curiae United States at 120, Wyatt v. Hardin, No. 3195-N (M.D. Ala. Feb. 18, 1979). *See also,* Affidavit of William E. Jones, Ricci v. Mills, No. 72-469-T (D. Mass. July 12, 1982).

60. *See* AAMD, *Consent Handbook* 52-54 (1977); ILSMH, *Step by Step, supra* note 18, at 449. *See generally* D. Howie, J. Cuming, & N. Raynes, "The Retarded Resident as Respondent: An Empirical Exploratory Study" (1981); Edgerton & Bercovici, "The Cloak of Competence—Years Later," 80 *Am. J. of Mental Deficiency* 485 (1976).

61. B. Baker, G. Seltzer, & M. Seltzer, *As Close as Possible: Community Residences for Retarded Adults* 222 (1977) (75 percent of residents preferred community residence to previous living arrangement); Antosh, "Long Journey into the Community," 32 *Temple U. Alumni Review* 8 (Spring 1981); J. Conroy, "Survey of Families of Clients Deinstitutionalized from the Date of the Court Order to April 30, 1980: Pennhurst Study Brief Report No. 10," (Temple U. Developmental Disabilities Center, prepared

under U.S. Dep't of Health and Human Services Contract No. 130-81-0022, July 31, 1981) (families of relocated clients also perceive clients to be happier, and families are more satisfied and involved with community living arrangements than the institution).

62. President Nixon's statement following his meeting with the President's Comm. on Mental Retardation, 7 *Weekly Compilation of Presidential Documents* 1530 (Nov. 16, 1981); President Ford's statement following his meeting with the President's Comm. on Mental Retardation, 10 *Weekly Compilation of Presidential Documents* 1270-71 (Oct. 11, 1974).

63. President Reagan's News Conference in Washington, D.C. (Nov. 10, 1981), *New York Times*, Nov. 11, 1981 at A24.

64. *See* Center for Human Policy, *Title XIX and Deinstitutionalization: The Issue for the 80s* (Syracuse U. 1981) (ICF-MR funds totaled $1,337,846,369 in 1978).

65. Pennhurst State School and Hospital v. Halderman, 451 U.S. 1 (1981).

66. H.R. Rep. No. 97-208, 97th Cong., 1st Sess. 800 (1981).

67. *See id.* and 42 U.S.C. § 6010(2) (1977).

68. Braddock, "Deinstitutionalization of the Retarded: Trends in Public Policy," 32 *Hospital and Community Psychiatry* 607, 611 (1981); Landesman-Dwyer, "Living in the Community," 86 *Am. J. of Mental Deficiency* 223, 229 (1981).

69. President's Comm. on Mental Retardation, *Mental Retardation: Century of Decision* 60 (1976).

70. B. Blatt, *Exodus from Pandemonium* (1970); *see* R. Scheerenberger & S. Jones, Administrative Problems: Resident Abuse, Salaries, Turnover, Overtime, and Union Activity 2-8 (National Ass'n of Superintendents of Public Residential Facilities for the Mentally Retarded, 1980). Besides the difficulty of disciplining abusive employees, other "reported deficits in state abuse program protections included lack of sufficient, appropriately trained staff, poor staff attitudes about reporting above and, consequently presumed failure to either report abuse or to report it in a timely fashion." *Id.* at 7.

71. *E.g.,* Pennhurst State School v. Halderman, 451 U.S. 1, 7 (1981), citing undisputed findings of fact, 446 F. Supp. 1295, 1308-10 (E.D. Pa. 1977); Spitz, "Hospitalism: An Inquiry Into the Genesis of Psychiatric Conditions in Early Childhood," in 1 *The Psychoanalytic Study of the Child* 53 (1945); Sternlicht & Siegel, "Institutional Residence and Intellectual Functioning," 12 *J. Mental Def. Research* 119 (1968) (average decrease of 10 IQ points over four-year period for institutionalized children, and trend toward depression for adolescents and adults). As one review of the scientific literature concluded, "most institutional environments which have been studied do have adverse effects on the development of retarded children." D. Pilling, *The Handicapped Children: Research Review* 80 (1973). *Accord, Integration of Developmentally Disabled Individuals into the Community* 21-34 (A. Novak & L. Heal eds. 1980).

72. New York State Ass'n for Retarded Children v. Carey, No. 72-C-356/357, Memorandum Decision and Order, slip op. at 11 (E.D.N.Y. June 10, 1977).

73. "Position Statement on the Right to Adequate Care and Treatment for the Mentally Ill and Mentally Retarded," 134 *Am. J. of Psychiatry* 354 (1977).

74. Joint Comm'n on International Aspects of Mental Retardation, *supra* note 17, at 79.

75. S. Bercovici, *Barriers to Normalization: Restrictive Management of Retarded Persons* (1982); Landesman-Dwyer, *supra* note 68, at 231.

76. R. Turnbull et al., *The Least Restrictive Alternative: Principles and Practices* 32 (1981).

77. Braddock, *supra* note 68, at 608.

78. *Id.* at 607.

79. *See generally* H. Cobb & P. Mittler, Significant Differences between Retardation and Mental Illness: A Position Paper of the International League of Societies for Persons with Mental Handicap (Sept. 1980).

80. *See* Sigelman, Spanhel, & Lorenzen, "Community Reactions to Deinstitutionalization," 45 *J. Rehabilitation* 52 (Jan. 1979).

81. Borus, "Deinstitutionalization of the Chronically Mentally Ill," 305 *New Eng. J. Med.* 339, 342 (1981).

82. Talbott, "Deinstitutionalization: Avoiding the Disasters of the Past," 30 *Hospital and Community Psychiatry* 621, 624 (1979).

83. *See* Herr, "The New Clients: Legal Services for Mentally Retarded Persons," 31 *Stan. L. Rev.* 553, 607-08 (1979); Center for Human Policy, *Title XIX and Deinstitutionalization, supra* note 64.

84. *See* U.S. Comptroller General, *How Federal Developmental Disabilities Programs Are Working* 61 (Report to the Subcomm. on the Handicapped, U.S. Senate Comm. on Labor and Human Resources, Feb. 20, 1980).

85. *See* Hammond, Sternlicht, & Deutsch, "Parental Interest in Institutionalized Children: A Survey," 20 *Hospital and Community Psychiatry* 338 (1969); Massachusetts Dep't of Mental Health, Regulations for the Operation of Programs for Mentally Retarded Persons, 104 CMR § 20.14 (b)(ii)-(iii) (1978) (program clients should have training and opportunities to exercise their rights to "the fullest extent of their capacities and interests").

86. Herr, "Rights Into Action: Protecting Human Rights of the Mentally Handicapped," 26 *Cath. U. L. Rev.* 203, 216-44, 287-99 (1977); Wahlström, "Where to Live and How to Live," 1 *Proceedings of Seventh World Congress of the ILSMH on Mental Handicap* 224 (1978); Bank-Mikkelsen, "Denmark," President's Comm. on Mental Retardation, *Changing Patterns in Residential Services for the Mentally Retarded* 241 (R. Kugel & A. Shearer eds. 1976).

87. Kushlick, "The Need for Residential Care," in *The Handicapped Person in the Community* 307, 311 (D. Boswell & J. Wingrove eds. 1974); Kushlick, "Wessex England," in President's Comm. on Mental Retardation, *supra* note 86, at 297, 307: "The Wessex experiment indicates that even the most severely multiply-handicapped child can be cared for in a domestic setting near his own home, at least as well as in an existing traditional institutional ward—that indeed these children are the very ones who seem to make the best progress under such a regime."

88. From 1976 to 1980, Macomb-Oakland, with a catchment area of nearly 1.8 million people, had only two admissions and six or seven readmissions to institutions for the retarded. *See generally* President's Comm. on Mental Retardation, *MR 78 Report to the President, MR: The Leading Edge—Service Programs That Work* 39-41 (1979).

89. D. Braddock, *Opening Closed Doors: The Deinstitutionalization of Disabled Persons* 18 (1977); Lamont, "A Community System: Eastern Nebraska Community Office of Retardation," in National Ass'n for Retarded Citizens, *National Forum on Residential Services* 125 (1976).

90. Hemming, Lavender, & Pill, "Quality of Life of Mentally Retarded Adults Transferred from Large Institutions to New Small Units," 86 *Am. J. of Mental Deficiency* 157 (1981); Wahlström, *supra* note 86, at 226.

91. C. Feinstein & J. Conroy, "Update on the Status of the Pennhurst Deinstitutionalization: Pennhurst Study Brief Report No. 12" at 6 (Temple U. Developmental Disabilities Center, August 31, 1981) (success of 141 ex-Pennhurst clients placed in community living arrangements predictive of successful adaptation of remaining 662 Pennhurst residents); H. Cobb & P. Mittler, *supra* note 79, at 4; K. Wehbring & C. Ogren, *Community Residences for Mentally Retarded Persons* (NARC Research and Demonstration Institute Monograph No. 3, 1976).

92. Testimony of Mrs. Grace Auerbach, Joint Appendix at A 612-16, Pennhurst State School v. Halderman, 451 U.S. 1 (1981).

93. Testimony of Robert Troester, *id.* at A 594.

94. President's Comm. on Mental Retardation, *People Live in Houses: Profiles of Community Residences for Retarded Children and Adults* 56 (1975).

Part II
The Law

4 Admissions and the Right to Least Restrictive Care

Myths of Benevolence

Because the decision to admit a person to long-term residential care raises such emotional discomfort, powerful myths of justification develop. Mentally retarded persons, falsely perceived as permanent children or as a social menace, were once assumed to be better off if put away for life in segregated facilities. Although such decisions are rationalized as in the client's best interests, other family members, law enforcers, or social agencies may be the primary beneficiaries of out-of-home placement. The institution itself is characterized as an asylum from a hostile world, and a center for sophisticated behavioral intervention. Benevolent intentions are accepted at face value.

As long as those traditional assumptions prevailed, the law paid little attention to the rights and needs of persons committed or admitted to mental retardation institutions. Courts and legislators basically kept their hands off, lulled by beneficent promises of treatment and heedless of responsible warnings. Yet even a generation ago, physicians made no secret of the inadequacies of these large residential institutions, "designed primarily to segregate . . . and only rarely fulfilling the objectives implied in their title of 'Training Schools.' "[1] By 1968, the World Health Organization (WHO) joined those urging a sharp reversal in direction. According to WHO, retarded persons should be served in their own communities whenever possible, since "segregation, whether well-meaning or not, breeds prejudice and discrimination."[2] Despite such findings, the legal rules did little to inhibit such segregation and its cruel consequences.

Until recently, institutions for the mentally retarded had virtually a one-way door. Those who entered were committed to spend "the rest of their dreary lives within."[3] Most admissions were highly informal and unreviewed, if not unreviewable by independent authorities. Institution directors had vast discretion, and unnecessary and inappropriate admissions were common. The rare court opinions questioning the commitment of retarded persons found such statutes "obscure" and devoid of anything that "savor[ed] of due process of law."[4] With little or no choice in care options, families basically confronted an all-or-nothing proposition: commit their relative to a large state institution, or shoulder the financial and social burdens of care alone. Given a shortage of community-based group homes and other residential alternatives, desperate compromises were sometimes struck. Parents even subjected their children to nontherapeutic experimental research or to custodial conditions in order to obtain an institutional place.[5] One parent described his son's admission to a five-thousand-bed institution as follows:

> I received a letter from the present director at Willowbrook advising me that, although there was no room for Barry at Willowbrook, if I signed a release agreeing to allow Barry to enter a "research program" the long waiting list could be by-passed and he would be immediately admitted. The letter stated that the research program involved injecting the child with a hepatitis virus.[6]

Do advocates and courts have any role in regulating entry into care? On a de jure if not a de facto basis, institutional admissions are already governed by laws, regulations, and state-approved procedures. Ideally, this legal regulation should reflect the liberty interests of the retarded individual, the therapeutic interests of avoiding inappropriate admissions and family guilt, and the public interest of doing social justice and spending wisely on residential care. But these interests were frequently distorted by laissez-faire admission policies, political pressures, and the tendency of adult professionals to be more loyal to other adults than to children in their care. The question of who speaks for the retarded child, or for the retarded adult unable to speak for himself or herself, was all too often glossed over in the institutionalization context. The rights of the family were protected without consideration of the child's right to live within his family or a substitute family. Under modern statutes, advocates and tribunals can aid in the search for less drastic alternatives.

In many states, actual practices bear little resemblance to the legal and professional norms. Public institutions continue to admit and serve a relatively high percentage of moderately, mildly, and borderline retarded persons. Of all new first admissions in 1979, over 39 percent involved persons with these milder forms of retardation, primarily children and young persons aged six to twenty-one.[7] Thus, institutions still provide a highly restrictive form of care to many handicapped individuals, despite a strong professional consensus in support of integration into the community. The literature abundantly documents patterns of unnecessary, inappropriate, and prolonged institutionalization.[8] It also hints at some reasons for this: racial bias, parental inadequacy, social deprivation, careless screening, lack of resources in the community, and "the enormous pressures administrators receive to institutionalize a student for incarcerative rather than service reasons."[9]

Even by conservative assessments, surveys of institutionalized populations in the 1960s revealed that one out of every three residents should never have been admitted.[10] Today, controversy rages over whether anyone should be required to enter large facilities. Yet the statistics and the polemics do not convey the personal pains of those swept up in an omnibus institution. A wide variety of upsetting individuals—abandoned babies, neglected children, sexually promiscuous females, alleged law offenders, and physically handicapped people—were cast into state schools for the retarded.[11] In some cases, they were literally dumped on institutional doorways.[12] But the more common problem was the state's failure to secure substitute homes for retarded children and adults.[13] Even week-old infants could be consigned to institutions.[14]

The Supreme Court and Deference to Doctors

The United States Supreme Court has failed to resolve the difficult policy and constitutional issues of commitment of persons with mental retardation. Even after years of litigation in the federal courts, and three hearings before the Supreme Court, we still have no definitive ruling on the constitutionally required procedures for admitting and retaining a child in a mental institution. Resolving that controversy could have wide consequences, especially in the field of mental retardation: over two-thirds of all first admissions to public institutions for the retarded are persons below the age of fifteen.[15] Although the Supreme Court has heard several right-to-treatment cases, it has not squarely faced questions of the procedural and substantive due process safeguards that should apply in mental-retardation admissions.

In 1979, the Supreme Court ignored its own admonition to "stop, look and listen" when it carelessly swept mentally ill and mentally retarded children under the same legal rule. Two lower federal courts had ruled that the so-called voluntary commitment of minors under eighteen to inpatient mental facilities without preadmission hearings violated the Due Process Clause of the Fourteenth Amendment. In *J.L.* v. *Parham*, a trial court held Georgia law constitutionally deficient because of its failure to provide young persons with an opportunity to contest their placement in state mental hospitals.[16]

In *Bartley* v. *Kremens*, a three-judge district court struck down as unconstitutional Pennsylvania statutes that permitted a parent, guardian, or individual standing in loco parentis to admit a minor to a mental facility with the concurrence of the facility's director.[17] In a sensitive analysis balancing the interests of the child, the parents, and the state, the *Bartley* court found that this compromised the child's due process rights and provided insufficient protection against erroneous, unnecessary, and detrimental confinement in mental institutions.

This was the issue the Supreme Court ducked in 1977 by its controversial use of the mootness doctrine.[18] In remanding the *Bartley* case, the Court urged that the lower court, in formulating the class definition, pay careful attention to the "differences between mentally ill and mentally retarded, and between the young and the very young."[19] Yet when the Supreme Court ultimately consolidated and passed judgment on the Georgia and Pennsylvania cases, those distinctions and subtleties were conspicuously lacking.

On remand, the district court in the Pennsylvania case, starkly captioned *Institutionalized Juveniles* v. *Secretary of Public Welfare*, had recognized major differences in the nature of mental retardation and mental illness. Yet for members of either subclass, institutionalization threatened constitutionally protected liberties including the protection of "good name, reputation, honor [and] integrity."[20] Certain hazards were also common: risks of stigma, error in diagnosis and identification, and conflicts between parents and the best interests of the child. But the shared handicaps of retarded juveniles of all ages—the inability to read, write, or understand abstract concepts—added to their vulnerability. Thus, the district court rejected procedures that rely on the child to understand his rights, object to his institutionalization, and bear the burden of triggering remedial safeguards. For some, these burdens would be insurmountable. Therefore, the court concluded that

> especially in the case of retarded children, who may lack the ability to understand the notice given to them, due process rights are violated in the absence of an automatic post-commitment hearing, to be scheduled within a reasonable time, and the presence of counsel to speak solely for the child's interests.[21]

Remarkably, the Supreme Court's decision neither addressed that problem nor settled this controversy. Instead, the majority in the *Institutionalized Juveniles* case deferred ruling on postadmission procedures, endorsed the constitutional sufficiency of preadmission procedures for retarded children in a cursory paragraph, and, once again, sent the case back to the lower court for further proceedings.[22] The Court agreed that the placement of juveniles in public or private mental institutions constituted state action implicating constitutionally protected liberty interests and requiring due process procedures. It was also common ground among the justices that preadmission psychiatric interviews could constitutionally suffice for the entry decision initiated by parents and approved by hospital authorities.

Beyond that the Court was sharply divided. The majority's analysis dodged the problems of the mentally retarded child by unreflectively applying the holding and reasoning of a mental health case to a far different factual and professional context. But, unlike the long-term and even permanent institutionalization of the retarded, the *Parham* v. *J.R.* holding is derived from a record in which children placed in psychiatric facilities had average stays as relatively brief as seventy-one and ninety-two days. Against that background, the Court concluded that

> the risk of error inherent in the parental decision to have a child institutionalized for mental health care is sufficiently great that some kind of inquiry should be made by a "neutral factfinder" to determine whether the statutory requirements for admission are satisfied. . . . That inquiry must carefully probe the child's background using all available sources, including, but not limited to, parents, schools and other social agencies. Of course, the review must include an interview with the child. It is necessary that the decisionmaker have the authority to refuse to admit any child who does not satisfy the medical standards for admission. Finally, it is necessary that the child's continuing need for commitment be reviewed periodically by a similarly independent procedure.[23]

On the record before it, the Supreme Court could not and did not give focused attention to the distinct processes affecting retarded children. *Parham* was purely a mental health case and even within that sphere the record is sparse on critical points. Thus, the district judges visited only mental hospitals, but their opinion tells us little of their observations, the physical facilities, or the patients' daily routines.[24] In both the *Parham* and *Institutionalized Juveniles* cases, evidentiary gaps loomed large, on the actual process for each child's admission, specific instances of dumping or other unfair practices, the quality or duration of the preadmission psychiatric interviews, and the neutrality of such decision making. For example, the sole witness testifying about Pennsylvania's decision-making process was a state-hospital director offering a highly generalized description of how adolescents become psychiatric inpatients. All this sheds no light on admissions of retarded persons. Moreover, oversimplified accounts of highly variable processes permit the Supreme Court to extoll the virtues of "trained" admitting psychiatrists exercising their "independent medical judgment."[25]

Indeed, the Burger Court's recurrent motif is deference to physicians. This is singularly jarring when medical expertise plays only a small role as in the commitment process. Thus, the majority in *Institutionalized Juveniles* sweeps far too broadly in asserting that "no child is admitted without one and often more psychiatric examinations by an independent team of mental health professionals whose sole concern . . . is whether the child needs and can benefit from institutional care."[26] By transposing its confidence in "traditional medical investigative techniques," "well-established medical procedures," and "the traditional tools of medical science" to the nonmedical realm of retardation institutions, the Court has further obscured reality.[27] Although recent Supreme Court opinions acknowledge the fallibility of psychiatric diagnosis, they show a disposition to limit review of opinions of experts by judicial or administrative authorities.[28] But do talismanic phrases such as "independent medical judgment" and "individual medical decision" really describe what happens when the hospital administrator is the so-called neutral and detached finder of fact, and the decisions are as much social and educational as they are medical?

The Supreme Court is also unduly deferential to social workers or others acting in loco parentis. The result in *Parham* is to deny their wards a more stringent preadmission review. By treating identically the rights of children committed by their parents and the rights of children committed by the state's social workers, the Court makes a troubling equation. Are those state officials as reliable protectors of a child's best interests as natural parents? Do guardians really have the same emotional stake in the child they institutionalize as would a psychological parent? Justice Brennan, in dissent, offered the better view that juveniles confined upon the recommendation of their social workers should not have their rights waived by those workers and are therefore entitled to a preadmission commitment hearing.[29] In addition, such hearings could prod the search for parental substitutes and help avoid the use of institutions as homes.

Even when parents initiate commitments, family autonomy is compatible with processes requiring full exploration of noninstitutional alternatives. In the field of mental retardation, the duration and character of institutionalization in no way compares to a parent's decision to seek "a tonsillectomy, appendectomy or other medical procedure" for a child.[30] The better analogy is not, as the Supreme Court asserts, to physical medicine, but to parental petitions for the state's assistance under the "persons in need of supervision" (PINS) jurisdiction. By asking for a long-term or semi-permanent placement outside their home, often at state expense or subsidy, parents invite the state to intervene in the lives of children beyond their coping abilities. That decision may seriously disadvantage the child, and may create a burden of guilt for the family that time does not relieve.[31] Careful screening and review procedures can do more than prevent erroneous commitment decisions arising out of family disruption, parent-child disputes, or neglect. Unnecessary confinements also result from well-intentioned but ill-informed assessments by family members and their medical advisers of the benefits of institutional care.[32] Here again, the Supreme Court's dissenting justices had a clearer grasp of the pitfalls of commitment:

> It ignores reality to assume blindly that parents act in their children's best interests when making commitment decisions and when waiving their children's due process rights.
>
> Children incarcerated in public mental institutions are constitutionally entitled to a fair opportunity to contest the legitimacy of their confinement. They are entitled to some champion who can speak on their behalf and who stands ready to oppose a wrongful commitment.[33]

Existing safeguards, such as medical inquiry, peer review, and the writ of habeas corpus, are not reliable methods for protecting retarded people who may be lost in the shuffle. Although the *Parham* majority acknowledges this risk for a child without natural parents, it offers no persuasive remedy.[34] The

Court describes habeas corpus as an "important means of obtaining individual relief,"[35] but as this chapter will point out, in practice such petitions are almost never filed by residents of retardation institutions.[35] Professional peer review has also been notably ineffective. Instead, the literature reveals patterns of overinstitutionalization for retarded persons for whom other alternatives would be more beneficial.[36] In this context, a staff physician is poorly positioned to reverse these patterns or to press for a less harmful disposition.

Yet the states remain free to establish stringent preadmission and post commitment standards that recognize these realities. As the *Parham* opinion notes, states may provide adversary hearings or other judicial or administrative process, although such preadmission process is not constitutionally compelled.[37] Because of the constitutional questions not reached by the Court, and the fact-sensitive nature of policy-making in this field, we can anticipate further revision of admission standards and procedures. Scholarly commentary and model laws already urge reforms to keep childrens' due process rights and interests from being lost through "inadvertence, inaction, or incapacity."[38] Beacon lights in federal and state law also point to exploration of less drastic alternatives and development of habilitation plans that truly benefit the retarded individual.[39] Even the Supreme Court's own precedents seem at odds with its pronouncements in *Parham*.

Consider the process due if you are eighteen years old or older and your mother tries to commit you because of your mental difficulties. In deciding just that case, a unanimous Supreme Court held that the trial court must employ the standard of "clear and convincing" evidence in an involuntary civil commitment hearing.[40] *Addington* v. *Texas* thus joins a long line of decisions recognizing that civil commitment "for any purpose" imposes a significant deprivation of liberty and inflicts a "stigma" or other "adverse social consequences" that warrant due process protection.[41] Although criminal-justice standards of proof are not constitutionally compelled, the Court's opinion emphasizes the value society places on individual liberty and the freedom of states to adopt stricter barriers against inappropriate commitment. Noting the "expanding concern of society" with rights of the mentally disabled and the uncertainties of diagnosis, the High Court concluded that "the individual's interest in the outcome of a civil commitment proceeding is of such weight and gravity that due process requires the state to justify confinement by proof more substantial than a mere preponderance of the evidence."[42]

Chronological age is an arbitrary standard by which to ration due process rights when both children and adults in retardation institutions suffer disadvantages. Earlier Supreme Court opinions drew no such lines. In 1972, Theon Jackson, "a mentally defective deaf mute with a mental level of a pre-school child," petitioned the Court for release from Indiana's Muscatatuck Institution.[43] At age twenty-seven, he had been found incompetent to stand trial by reason of his scant communication skills. Three and one-half years later, he still remained in limbo at Muscatatuck—untreated, untried, and unlikely to improve. With a state lacking the facilities to help him and a counsel preparing to barter his client's freedom for special institutionalization, Jackson faced a lifelong confinement in barren custody.

In *Jackson* v. *Indiana*, the Supreme Court rejected the constitutionality of such a fate. Justice Blackmun, writing for a unanimous Court, ruled that a person committed on the basis of incapacity to stand trial cannot be held more than the reasonable period of time necessary to determine if there is a substantial probability of attaining that capacity in the foreseeable future. Otherwise, the state must institute civil commitment proceedings or release the defendant. Taking note of modern trends favoring community-based care, the Court acknowledged that imposing even civil commitment on Jackson on the basis of his mental deficiency would be "problematical."[44]

The risk of being condemned to permanent institutionalization—constitutionally proscribed in *Jackson*—is no less substantial for persons committed to public retardation facilities through civil channels. Where state institutions predicate release on attaining the skills for an independent life, while denying the retarded person even minimal programs for acquiring those skills, they become places of no return. In *Jackson*, the Court not only cites studies that cast doubt on the treatment capabilities of "most of our mental institutions," but finds "remarkable" the lack of litigation probing the constitutional limits of civil commitment.[45] Thus, the Court enunciated a rule establishing a minimum test of the legality of these commitments: "due process requires that the nature and duration of commitment bear some reasonable relation to the purpose for which the individual is committed."[46]

The *Jackson* rule of substantive due process is frequently invoked in mental disability cases, but the civil commitment of retarded persons is seldom tested in the courts.[47] Given the low visibility of such proceedings and the limited capacities of subjects to resist institutional impositions, this is hardly surprising. The case of Kenneth Donaldson is a devastating example of the legal obstacles mentally disabled (or allegedly disabled) persons face and the insensitivities of routine medical and judicial review. Donaldson, kept in custodial confinement for fifteen years, spent much of that time seeking legal assistance and preparing the nineteen appeals and the four attempts at Supreme Court review that culminated in his release from unconstitutional confinement in a state mental institution.[48] If such exertions were required of an intelligent and articulate person like Donaldson, virtually insurmountable barriers confront retarded persons with limited understanding and minimal verbal skills.

The civil commitment power has historically been justified on the basis either of the subject's risk of harm to himself or others, or of his inability to care for himself and his presumed need for care and treatment. Civil hospitalization statutes of the former type are generally justified under the state's police power; the latter under the state's *parens patriae* power. Courts have traditionally assumed that the state's *parens patriae* power to act as guardian of persons under legal disabilities can justify the institutional commitment of mentally retarded persons for care and treatment or protection from harm.[49]

Parens patriae reasoning, however, can be a fiction masking less benign purposes.[50] Courts have thus insisted that benevolent state intentions will not insulate *parens patriae* commitments from judicial scrutiny, or constitutional requirements of substantive due process.[51] Substantive due process analysis requires that state action must promote a proper public purpose by means reasonably necessary to effectuate that purpose. Moreover, a compelling state interest must be identified to warrant the infringements on fundamental interests entailed in compulsory institutionalization.[52] Incarceration of harmless retarded persons in segregated facilities will not meet this test.

The logic of *O'Connor* v. *Donaldson* offers powerful, indeed compelling, support for that conclusion. Although Donaldson's commitment was initiated by his father and approved under a state law described as "less than clear," the legality of his original commitment was not at issue.[53] Even though brought as a "right to treatment" case, the Supreme Court avoided that issue and instead decided Donaldson on the basis of the constitutional right to liberty.[54] Focusing on Donaldson's involuntary custodial confinement and his doctor's refusal to release him, the Court observed that neither state law authorizing confinement of the harmless mentally ill nor a constitutionally permissible original commitment provide a constitutional justification for unnecessary continuing confinement. Thus, the Court held that "a State cannot constitutionally confine without more a nondangerous individual who is capable of surviving safely in freedom by himself or with the help of willing and responsible family members or friends."[55]

This formulation leaves a variety of questions open. The ambiguous phrase "without more" is an invitation to fine distinctions. Can a state confine a person who is not dangerous, if it provides him with treatment? Can a state confine without treatment a person it adjudges dangerous? Furthermore, this opinion offers no guidance as to the criteria or degree of risk to consider in sorting the dangerous from the nondangerous person. Yet at minimum, *Donaldson* puts the helping professions on notice that "simple custodial confinement" is unlawful.

Writing for the unanimous Court, Justice Stewart marked some impermissible constitutional grounds for enforced custodial confinement. For instance, the state may not involuntarily confine a person solely on the basis of mental illness, or to spare the community from unease or exposure to harmless mental deviants.[56] The Court also rejected the paternalistic rationale that the mentally disabled can be confined to ensure them higher living standards, that the "mere presence of mental illness does not disqualify a person from preferring his home to the comforts of an institution."[57]

Similarly, mental retardation alone is no basis for confining persons against their will. Nor is the imposition of the discomforts of an institution a logical or necessary condition for saving retarded persons from harm to themselves, or harm from others. Moreover, the *Donaldson* opinion casts serious doubt on the constitutional adequacy of commitment standards based on the need for care and treatment, absent a finding of the individual's incapacity for community living. Thus, the Supreme Court expressly approves the doctrine of the least restrictive alternative in the civil commitment context, and encourages stricter safeguards where the state claims to act in the individual's best interests. This leaves to future cases the looming question of the state assistance owed to inmates who lack the help of willing and responsible relatives and friends, but who are capable of benefiting from less onerous alternatives to custodial care.[58] Properly understood, *Donaldson* should provoke a reassessment of admission and retention standards, and the state's obligation to equip residents of retardation institutions with the skills for survival and social adaptation in independent or sheltered community-living situations.[59] Indeed, a lower federal court, in construing the Supreme Court's opinion, has declared that the state cannot confine a mentally retarded or physically handicapped child for "simple custodial purposes."[60]

Supreme Court cases dealing with broken promises of treatment for children suggest other limits of paternal and state benevolence. *In re Gault* reminds us that the child's loss of liberty mandates substantial due process rights, notwithstanding the state's promises of individualized care and regenerative treatment.[61] Like the developmental center or the state school for the retarded, "however euphemistic the title, a 'receiving home' or an 'industrial school' for juveniles is an institution of confinement in which the child is incarcerated for a greater or lesser period of time."[62] *Planned Parenthood of Missouri* v. *Danforth* teaches that parental authority is not an absolute barrier to a child's exercise of constitutional rights.[63] If a minor's right to an abortion can override family opposition, surely a child's removal from her home and right to freedom from inappropriate, long-term institutionalization merits a truly independent review. The facts behind *Stump* v. *Sparkman*—a case holding a judge immune from damages for wrongfully approving the sterilization of a fifteen-year-old, "somewhat retarded" girl—reveal the hazard of *ex parte* proceedings conducted without an advocate for the child.[64] Even though Indiana law prohibits a parent from having a minor sterilized,[65] the girl's mother petitioned for such an operation, doctors agreed to perform it, and the state judge endorsed the petition. Linda Sparkman was not informed of all this; she was told her appendix was being removed. Tragically, she only learned the truth after her marriage and her futile attempts to become pregnant. To be labeled "somewhat retarded" is apparently a magic formula jeopardizing the most fundamental human rights.

Federal Legislation and Least Restrictive Living

For nearly two decades, the federal government has tried to curb loose admission practices and abusive institutionalization. In 1963, President Kennedy had personally asked state governors to aid retarded persons "locked-up in institutions, shunned and neglected in their communities."[66] The President's Panel on Mental Retardation had urged that programs for retarded people should be community-centered, and called for a thorough reappraisal of the laws relating to their care. The panel had proposed automatic judicial review at two-year intervals for persons admitted to institutions, and a protective service agency to monitor the treatment of residents.[67] Its Task Force on Law, chaired by Chief Judge Bazelon, recommended admission procedures that ensured the retarded person's easy access to a partisan advocate and to the courts. Their report foresaw statutes that would lead rather than follow public opinion, since the law relating to mental retardation "must combat many years of general ignorance, prejudice and superstition."[68]

Federal laws on funding have had a more decisive impact than federal exhortations to change. Reforms were gallingly slow in coming, as Senator Robert Kennedy demonstrated in his much-publicized visits to the Willowbrook and Rome State Schools. He described residents as "slipping into blankness and lifelong dependence," and children condemned "to live without hope," more terribly confined than "animals in a zoo."[69] Legislative committees substantiated these criticisms, planning commissions pondered, bureaucrats blamed budgets or reacted defensively,[70] but the human warehouses went unchanged. Even six years after Senator Kennedy's exposé and eight years after President Kennedy's appeal, the President's Committee on Mental Retardation was still deploring "the institutionalized dehumanization and neglect to which we have so long relegated many of our mentally retarded under the guise of care and concern."[71] But with the growth of federal financial assistance to state mental-retardation programs, officials gained a powerful lever for upgrading and redirecting care.

State programs are eager to capture that assistance, even if its receipt imposes stricter standards, requirements, and policies. Most of those federal funds are derived from Medicaid Title XIX reimbursements, with other funds drawn from education, vocational rehabilitation, and developmental disabilities programs. Title XIX of the Social Security Act is the principal means of federal reimbursement for institutional care and services.[72] Under this scheme, those facilities for the mentally retarded classified as "intermediate care facilities," (ICFs) are subject to outside reviews and minimum standards.[73] As checks against unnecessary care and services, facilities receiving Medicaid reimbursement must participate in utilization and independent professional reviews. Under Section 42 U.S.C. 1396(a), such reviews must include a ". . . medical evaluation of each patient's need for intermediate care and a written plan of service prior to admission or authorization of benefits in an intermediate care facility as determined under regulations of the Secretary."[74]

Regulations specifically designed for mental retardation facilities, called ICF-MR regulations, attempt to curb inappropriate admissions and to "insure the civil rights of all residents."[75] Under those regulations, a facility may not admit an individual unless his needs can be met by the facility. An "interdisciplinary professional team" must determine that admission is the best available plan for that individual.[76] The ICF-MR must provide residents with an extensive array of habilitative services based on their needs.[77] There is, however, a large loophole. The facility's inability to meet those needs does not preclude admission, since ICF-MR regulations permit, without any limitation of time, institutional stays of recognized unsuitability. As part of the preadmission procedure, the professional team must evaluate the individual and define his need for service "without regard to the availability of those services." They must then review "all available and applicable" care, treatment, and training programs, and record their findings. If admission is not the best plan, but the individual must be admitted, the facility must clearly acknowledge that the admission is inappropriate, and initiate "plans to actively explore alternatives."[78]

If faithfully enforced, Medicaid regulations constitute important safeguards of human dignity and rights. For example, a facility must not admit more residents than its rated capacity and its ability to provide adequate care.[79]

In the past, Medicaid regulations only required facilities to summarize laws, regulations, and procedures concerning admission and release, and to have a "written statement of policies and procedures concerning the rights of residents."[80] Current regulations, however, impose affirmative obligations to inform residents of their rights.[81] Thus, each resident must be "fully informed, before or at the time of admission, of his rights and responsibilities" and must acknowledge "in writing" receipt of information on residents' rights.[82] These regulations only make sense if residents are literate, are trained to recognize their rights, or have the assistance of attentive family members, friends, or advocates. Despite the siren calls of deregulation,[83] residents' rights save the government from costly, inappropriate institutionalization. They should be strengthened, not eliminated.

The new Medicaid waiver to provide home- and community-based services is a step in the right direction. States may now avoid unnecessary institutionalization for certain individuals whose costs of care in a Medicaid facility would likely exceed the medical assistance costs of their community-based care.[84] Although this Medicaid waiver does not include room and board, the written plan of care can go well beyond conventional medical services. Thus, the Secretary of Health and Human Services may approve state requests for respite care, adult-day health services, homemaker services, personal-care services, case management, habilitation services, and other services.[85]

Congress clearly intended more than short-term cost savings. It sought to encourage community care by funding options for those who believe there is no place like home. Legislative history left little doubt that Medicaid waivers should subsidize a service package of comprehensive community-based habilitation, including "health and social services needed to insure optimal functioning of the mentally retarded and the developmentally disabled."[86] Whether states' requests for waivers would be narrowly or generously framed, whether the congressional intent to preserve the integrity of patient choice will be honored, and whether the coverage in terms of populations and services will be liberally interpreted are all difficult to predict. Once again, vigorous advocacy will be required in resolving such issues and benefiting eligible individuals.

The Developmentally Disabled Assistance and Bill of Rights Act funds advocates and takes aim at reducing or eliminating the need for institutional care. Congress declared that persons with developmental disabilities have "a right to appropriate treatment, services, and habilitation" for such disabilities.[87] Under this mandate, such treatment, services, and habilitation should be provided in "the setting that is least restrictive of the person's personal liberty."[88] Congress further specified that habilitation programs should be "designed to maximize the developmental potential" of the disabled individual. But the central controversy sparked by the act goes to the very existence of substandard facilities: the federal government's and the states' obligations to assure that "public funds are not provided to any institutional or other residential program" for the developmentally disabled that "does not provide treatment, services, and habilitation which is appropriate to the needs of such persons."[89] Implementing these obligations could profoundly change admission and retention practices. Defaults, however, on the part of the federal executive branch and the states have forced disabled persons to struggle through the courts.[90]

Out of that struggle, the policy of the United States, as expressed by Congress and affirmed by the courts, is to speed the integration of retarded citizens into the community. The Education for All Handicapped Children Act mandates the least restrictive individually appropriate educational environments, thus enabling parents to participate in educational decisions and obtain a range of community-based services for a child who might otherwise be institutionalized.[91] Section 504 of the Vocational Rehabilitation Act bars discrimination against "qualified handicapped persons" across the entire spectrum of federally assisted programs.[92] Under the recent Social Services Block Grant Act, each state is encouraged to furnish services aimed at "preventing or reducing inappropriate institutional care by providing for community-based care, home-based care, or other forms of less intensive care."[93] Thus, federal law outlines the rights and services which, properly applied and funded, can divert retarded people from institutions and provide them with quality habilitation, education, and support in their home communities.

Despite this policy, government agencies often regard laws conferring rights on retarded persons as mere aspirational statements or unenforceable declarations of principle. Because of the political costs, they are reluctant to stop funding even substandard custodial programs. With its relatively modest appropriation, administrators of the developmental disabilities program have little leverage to exert. In contrast, Medicaid is a giant program, albeit a muscle-bound giant. The administering state agencies, hampered by lack of staff to inspect facilities and monitor reports, have had enormous difficulties in upgrading care conditions.[94] Particularly in the case of a state institution, it is politically difficult for a sister state agency, such as a health department, to impose exacting standards or to compel diversion of resources to more beneficial programs. In such contexts, termination of funds to the noncomplying institution is simply not regarded as a realistic or viable enforcement tool. Federal officials prefer negotiating correction plans to withholding federal funds to retardation institutions for noncompliance, since this draconian measure may harm the residents. The resulting minuet may yield greater compliance with ICF-MR standards, but the institutional subculture still breeds a cynical disregard for residents' rights. To counter this disregard, dynamic elements are needed to educate and keep the disability system honest.

Federal Courts and Institutional Gatekeepers

Two of the most effective—and controversial—responses to institutional problems are the federal courts and legal services for retarded persons. They are effective as outsiders who can alter the rules, perceptions, and resource distributions that determine whether rights are real or token. They are controversial for the very same reason: because of their direct and indirect impact on the status quo of jobs, relationships, and power.

Judges were not eager for this extra work.[95] In fact, federal courts acted only after persistent abdications by executive and legislative branches of their responsibilities to protect residents from gross harm.[96] As reformers, lawyers were also comparatively recent arrivals on the mental-retardation scene. They were the products of a public-interest and legal-services movement that in the 1960s was preoccupied with more assertive clients. But to veteran social critics such as Professor Gunnar Dybwad, the litigation begun in the 1970s was an act of last resort, an expression of profound frustration and failure.

> Intervention through the Federal courts came only after all other avenues for assistance and remediation inherent to our system of government had failed as much as had the informal system of checks and balances represented, for instance, through the functioning of our professional organizations, special interest groups, consumer organizations, citizen sponsored better government groups, or mass media, and last but not least, the forum of public opinion. Resort had been taken to all of them, over and over again . . . but no effective action resulted.[97]

The doctrine of the least restrictive alternative (LRA) offered a strategy for combating intolerable conditions and reducing government intrusion in the lives of retarded people. Developed by the courts in constitutional adjudication and now widely accepted by treatment professionals, the LRA principle recognizes that when the state restricts fundamental rights, it has the duty to do so in the least drastic manner consonant with the purpose of the restriction.[98]

Thus, when rights such as personal liberty or associational freedoms are at stake, the court may require an inquiry into alternatives to the challenged regulation or practice that would permit legislative interests to be fulfilled with the least abridgement of the individual's constitutional rights. But the principle of the least restrictive or least drastic alternative, as it is interchangeably known, has developed meanings beyond its judicial origin. It is more than a tool for resolving compelling, but often competing, constitutionally and legislatively protected interests. It is also a concept for testing service provisions against libertarian principles, normalization philosophies, and individual needs in contexts as diverse as residential care, school systems, counseling, guardianship, employment, and medical assistance.[99]

In recent years, this doctrine has gained a firm foothold as a limitation on civil commitment powers. Congress and state legislatures have employed the principle as a broad check on inappropriate institutionalization of mentally retarded persons, whether the commitment be described as involuntary, voluntary, or nonconsensual. Federal courts have applied this principle to placement and retention decisions affecting residents of mental-retardation institutions,[100] mental hospitals,[101] juvenile institutions[102] and facilities serving both mentally ill and retarded persons.[103] State courts have also invoked the doctrine to impose limits on state powers to admit and detain mentally disordered persons.[104] While citing this doctrine with approval in *O'Connor* v. *Donaldson*, the Supreme Court has not yet definitely ruled on its scope or application.[105] In view of the wide judicial and professional support for the LRA concept and the enhanced sensitivity in the last decade to due process safeguards for the mentally disabled,[106] the Supreme Court should uphold the principle as an integral part of retardation care.

Without a system of advocacy, the announcement of a new legal rule tends to have little effect on the lives of its retarded beneficiaries. For example, in *Heryford* v. *Parker*, the United States Court of Appeals for the Tenth Circuit upheld the due process right to legal counsel for persons subject to mental retardation commitment.[107] At age nine, Parker was committed by his mother to the Wyoming State Training School under a statute requiring certificates by two doctors and a judicial order. Seventeen years later, he was released to her care, but at age twenty-eight he was returned to the Training School against the wishes of his parents. Under the rule enunciated in *Heryford*, a retarded person must have the opportunity for "the guiding hand of legal counsel at every step" of the commitment proceeding. Following *Gault*,[108] the court of appeals reasoned that the state's benevolent objectives could not serve as a basis for denying basic rights:

> It matters not whether the proceedings be labelled "civil" or "criminal" or whether the subject matter be mental instability or juvenile delinquency. It is the likelihood of involuntary incarceration—whether for punishment as an adult for a crime, rehabilitation as a juvenile for delinquency, or treatment and training as a feeble-minded or mental incompetent—which commands observence of the constitutional safeguards of due process.[109]

Although this important, early precedent exposed a system that resulted in "indefinite and oblivious confinement" as well as "shameful injustice,"[110] it failed to attract wide attention. Yet the right to counsel rule could have revolutionized pre- and post-commitment proceedings. In extending this rule retroactively, the court of appeals recognized this possibility, brushing aside the state's argument that retroactivity would result in an opening of the "floodgates" and a "wholesale release of inmates in the Wyoming institutions and like institutions all over the country."[115]

This prediction has proved dramatically inaccurate. That many retarded people might benefit from the *Heryford* rule was viewed by the court as a strong reason for "the desirability, if not necessity" of its retroactive application. However, the chance of an institutional resident filing a writ of habeas corpus or other commitment challenge is miniscule. Even though the right to counsel in civil commitment proceedings is now well established, the promise of *Heryford* remains unfulfilled in the field of its origin. As with other new declarations of law intended to benefit retarded or allegedly retarded persons, rights are unknowingly waived and vigilant advocates are distressingly few.

Federal class actions have applied least restrictive standards with more effective results. They have identified state interests and state-federal resources that support integration of retarded people with other people. Although the states have a valid interest in meeting the special habilitative needs of mentally retarded children and adults, they can employ less drastic means than confinement in segregated, remote institutions. Thus, a line of cases, contested as well as by consent, require community living for retarded people, help in gaining release from institutions, and protection from harm and warehouse-like conditions.[112] These decisions establish a strong presumption in favor of care and habilitation in community-based settings.

From the outset, the federal courts sought to discourage the use of institutions. *Wyatt* v. *Stickney*, in articulating constitutional standards for habilitation, barred admissions if community services could afford adequate habilitation. Any new admission would require a prior determination that residence in the institution constituted the least restrictive habilitation setting for the particular individual.[113] The *Wyatt* standards, setting a direction followed by other courts and policymakers, declared that

> Residents shall have the right to the least restrictive conditions necessary to achieve the purposes of habilitation. To this end, the institution shall make every attempt to move residents from (1) more to less structured living; (2) larger to smaller facilities; (3) larger to smaller living units; (4) group to individual residence; (5) segregated from the community to integrated into the community living; (6) dependent to independent living.[114]

With mounting emphasis and specificity, class actions focused on remedies to secure this right. *Welsch* v. *Likins* held that retarded persons are constitutionally entitled to the benefit of the least restrictive environment consistent with their needs and conditions, and required state officials to make good-faith efforts to encourage the placement of residents or prospective residents in such settings.[115] The Court of Appeals for the Eighth Circuit upheld those rights as positive, constitutional requirements enforceable by the district court.[116] As discussed in chapter 6, *New York State Association for Retarded Children* v. *Carey* produced plans to dismantle the Willowbrook Developmental Center, and *Halderman* v. *Pennhurst State School and Hospital* sought a basis for holding institutions for the mentally retarded illegal.[117] In cases of this type the legal issues have now centered on the state's duty to provide potential or present residents with the least stringent practicable alternatives.

The dust of court battles has still not settled on the underlying question of whether a state can be compelled to create alternatives to institutional care.

In the 1982 Supreme Court term, once again, the *Pennhurst* case is under review. Meanwhile, the district and circuit courts have permitted remedial orders to proceed that promise "safe and beneficial community living arrangements" for retarded residents.[118] Other legal battles have been waged, sometimes unsuccessfully, to block construction of expensive new institutions.[119] And as cases proliferate, federal and state courts may disagree on the scope of the right to treatment for mentally disabled persons in the least restrictive environment.[120]

Sensitive issues of federalism hang in the balance. It is generally conceded that the state has no direct federal constitutional obligation to provide care and habilitation to mentally retarded persons.[121] However, by statute, most states have undertaken a substantial program of residential care and treatment, and many already recognize the right to the least restrictive alternative. In theory, a class-action demand for less restrictive services involves a legal bluff. If the state undertakes to provide residential services for the retarded, courts can require that the operation of those facilities conform to constitutional standards. As a hypothetical matter, some courts have assumed that a state could evade that obligation by leaving this field entirely; however, as a practical, moral, and political matter, a state legislature could ill afford to exercise that unpalatable option.

To avoid constitutional confrontation, state and private litigants can bargain in good faith for services and plans compatible with the least restrictive alternative. The firm urging of a federal district court is often essential in this type of negotiating process. For example, through judicial prodding and a structural planning process, a detailed settlement in *Brewster* v. *Dukakis* entitles six thousand handicapped persons, potential or current residents of Northampton State Hospital (Massachusetts), to treatment alternatives less restrictive than the state institution.[122]

Some facilities are so clearly dangerous and antitherapeutic that courts may be forced to halt new admissions. Since 1971, further admissions to Willowbrook have ceased, and this moratorium has continued indefinitely under the *Willowbrook* decree.[123] Following a trial documenting the neglect and deterioration of residents, the court issued a decree embodying least restrictive principles and timetables for transfer of the plaintiff class to more suitable alternatives. According to Judge Judd's opinion, residents confined in closed wards without a meaningful waiver of their freedom are entitled to due process and other constitutional protection from harm.[124] As a result, the *Willowbrook* case, consistent with *Wyatt* and other federal decisions, extended the reach of least restrictive principles to persons admitted under voluntary as well as involuntary admission procedures. These cases question whether any consensual relation is truly possible in so destructive and coercive a context, and whether the illusion of voluntary status should permit prolonged and avoidable institutionalization.

Cases like *Willowbrook* recognize that family pressures at the time of admission can result in a "fundamental conflict of interest between a parent who is ready to avoid the responsibility of caring for an abnormal child and the best interests of the child." The plaintiffs' approach to this problem in the *Pennhurst* case would have withdrawn the destructive option. Therefore, the court's original order had enjoined state officials from admitting any retarded person to "residence and/or habilitation" at this facility, and prohibited county and state officials from "recommending or in any way counselling that any individual be committed to Pennhurst."[125] At Michigan's Plymouth Center for Human Development, new admissions have been halted under an order and stipulation that acknowledges that "[a]ll mentally retarded individuals can and should live in the more normalized environment of the community and do not require institutionalization."[126] Other class-action suits in Ohio, Massachusetts, and Washington, D.C. have also stemmed the flow of new admissions to anachronistic settings.[127]

Where commitment statutes give short shrift to liberty interests or fail to provide stringent admission-screening procedures, federal courts can test their constitutionality. In *Dixon* v. *Attorney General*, mentally ill and mentally retarded civil detainees were granted substantial procedural protection, including prior notice, hearing, assistance of counsel, an appointed independent mental examination if indigent, as well as opportunities to present evidence, subpoena witnesses, and confront and cross-examine all witnesses.[128] As a result of the landmark case of *Lessard* v. *Schmidt*, a three-judge district court enjoined the enforcement of the Wisconsin involuntary-commitment statute as a violation of the Fourteenth Amendment Due Process Clause.[129] In a comprehensive opinion, the federal court required a full panoply of procedural safeguards. Such cases reflect the general rule that in the absence of a voluntary, knowing, and intelligent waiver, adults facing commitment to mental institutions are entitled to "a full and fair adversarial hearing" before a neutral tribunal, including the rights to be present with counsel, to be heard, to cross-examine, and to offer evidence.[130] While some have feared that strict procedures will frustrate compelling state objectives, traumatize patients, or dull judicial sensitivity through routine invocation,[131] unwanted or unwarranted confinement in a mental institution may be even more traumatic. Only a thorough testing of expert opinion and underlying fact can pierce the veils of the *parens patriae* rationale and the therapeutic mystique.

Experience demonstrates that workable processes can explore less drastic alternatives and devise habilitation plans that truly benefit persons with disabilities. In *Saville* v. *Treadway*, a three-judge federal court struck down a Tennessee statute that permitted the admission of mentally retarded persons by their parents, guardians, or custodians, or by any health, welfare, or school official.[132] Like many other states, the law authorized institutional admission simply on third-party consent and a licensed physician's certification that the individual was retarded and in need of institutional care and treatment. In reviewing the potentially lifelong duration of such institutionalization and the absence of effective review of these proxy consents and medical opinions, the court held that

> The procedures required by due process vary with the nature of the case, and the more serious the deprivation the more extensive the procedural safeguards which precede its imposition. . . . [w]here individual liberty is at stake to the extent it is in the instant case, it is absolutely essential that such confinement be preceded by adequate procedural safeguards. Given the possible conflicts of interests between a mentally retarded child and even a parent, it seems obvious that the "voluntary" commitment procedures of T.C.A. § 33-501 fall far short of those required by due process.[133]

Unlike *Parham* v. *J.R.*,[134] a plan for preadmission review of proposed admissions of children and adults was developed by Tennessee's treatment professionals and approved by the court. That plan provides for a two-stage process for any long-term admission. On the basis of their own intake, testing, information-gathering, interdisciplinary assessment and counseling procedures, state officials must warrant that the admission decision is made in "the best interest of the client, even if it conflicts with the family's desires."[135] Moreover, this decision must reflect evidence of the type of treatment appropriate to the proposed resident and any feasible alternatives to institutionalization. To ensure the exploration of less drastic means, each proposed resident must automatically be represented by an independent advocate, or private retained counsel.

Whether by statute, case law, or consensus, the legal process should recognize that the decision to institutionalize a retarded person is not simply a medical decision. It is much more—a moral, social, and educational decision carrying lifetime consequences for a child or adult. Therefore, the proposed resident should have an independent right to be heard, and a partisan advocate who can insist on a thorough professional search for and review of residential alternatives. Through informal but orderly review, a hearing process can prevent unnecessary admissions and uncover other placement possibilities. As a result of careful screening and active advocacy, participants in this process can avoid the rubber-stamp rituals of the past.

Rights and Remedies in the State Arena

The Reagan administration has advanced the dubious proposition that federal regulatory and judicial roles can safely recede because states already provide adequate legal protection for their needy citizens. That argument, to put it kindly, is especially unpersuasive in relation to mentally retarded citizens. National surveys of state laws on institutionalization, including those conducted in 1967, 1977, and 1981,[136] consistently reveal grave due process defects. And despite the obvious merit of achieving minimum and uniform standards in this field of care, state laws vary enormously and generally lag behind federal laws in their attention to least restrictive principles, periodic reviews, and preadmission safeguards.[137] Even some of the largest and richest states limp along with badly obsolescent statutes that perpetuate false assumptions and misleading images. New York is a clear case in point.

In theory the New York Mental Hygiene Law offers a detailed, comprehensive, and uniform legal framework for the admission and retention of persons in schools for the mentally retarded. The law specifies that mentally retarded persons can only be admitted into a school through one of three statutory modes: voluntary, nonobjecting, or involuntary.[138] However, the term *school* is misleading, since these procedures apply not only to the twenty large state institutions (formerly known as state schools, now renamed developmental centers), but to any other departmental residential facility or private facility licensed by the Commissioner of the Office of Mental Retardation and Developmental Disabilities (OMRDD). Despite the large number of persons affected, these legal provisions have not previously been the subject of critical, scholarly analysis.

The Mental Hygiene Law has become a relic, largely irrelevant to the problems encountered in day-to-day practice. It focuses on involuntary commitment at a time when those procedures have fallen into disuse and disrepute.[139] It fails to define admission criteria for entry into developmental centers, or into community-based residences. By statute, mental retardation is broadly defined as "sub-average intellectual functioning which originates during the developmental period and is associated with impairment in adaptive behavior."[140] Other statutory definitions are circular: a person "in need of care and treatment" is defined as a retarded person who would benefit from care and treatment as a school resident.[141] All this provides little guidance to professionals or the public, leaving each institution largely free to determine its own practices. To search for the actual criteria applied, one must go outside the statute and regulations to the shifting area of administrative policy and staff philosophies.[142] The ingredients are all here for improper admissions: broad statutory eligibility, diagnostic disagreements, and the temptation to misuse diagnostic labels as a basis for justifying a particular administrative action.[143]

Role of the Mental Health Information Service

On paper, the New York Mental Health Information Service (MHIS) assured the propriety of all admissions and cleaned up the commitment system. To retarded residents, it is described as "a Court agency independent of the school and established to protect your rights."[144] Its basic duty is to "study and review the admission and retention of all patients," retarded as well as mentally ill, and to inform those persons, their relatives, and friends of review procedures and their rights to a judicial hearing, representation by legal counsel, and an independent medical opinion.[145] According to the courts, MHIS thus constituted the linchpin to the constitutionality of the Mental Hygiene Law.[146] To its architects, MHIS was conceived as a legal-protective service, a watchdog to relieve the plight of the forgotten man.[147] If abuse occurred, MHIS would investigate it. If residents failed to understand legal notices, one need not fear, MHIS would make those notices intelligible or act on its own initiative. If unsuitable or unwilling persons were detained as "voluntary residents," MHIS would liberate them.[148] The agency was billed as all things to all men; as neutral information service, advocate, guardian, ombudsman, and friend of the court.

In fact, the retarded person's access to legal services depended on where he or she happened to live. Instead of a uniform statewide agency, MHIS functioned as four autonomous regional offices, each with its own philosophy and staffing pattern.[149] For instance, the MHIS in the Fourth Department had no lawyers on staff.[150] The availability and appearance of partisan advocacy was also undermined by the service's statutory responsibility to "assemble and provide the court with all relevant information as to the patient's case, his hospitalization, his right to discharge if any."[151] Thus MHIS is cast in the double-agent role of screening cases for the court, making *ex parte* recommendations, and at the same time maintaining the client's confidences and providing the client with the zealous representation required under the Code of Professional Responsibility. Representing clients in court and advising the same court as to how to dispose of their cases produced an ethical tightrope, and certainly the appearance of an ethical conflict.

In fairness, the line staff faced enormous difficulties: a vast number of persons entitled to MHIS assistance, lack of public familiarity with the program, and a traditional focus on civil commitment of the mentally ill. The residents of retardation institutions (belatedly added in 1972 to the MHIS case load) were, and are to this day, the Cinderellas of the service. While individual staff members expressed their concern, the agency was conspicuously absent from the *Willowbrook* case. As a former MHIS staff attorney explained,

> I never heard of any mental retardation cases being brought by the Mental Health Information Service. It always was a low priority. I wanted to bring judicial actions, reviews of retentions, that sort of thing, but the MHIS Director didn't want it. He saw it as just a placement and social science matter. He didn't want us to burden the courts with it. I wrote

> him a memorandum describing the types of cases that should be raised, particularly the need for care, the least restrictive alternative, and similar issues. But I was told to forget it; that all this was basically a social work issue. I went to the Willowbrook MHIS office, but nothing was being done there. Mental retardation work is still not a priority.[152]

Voluntary Admission

The low priority of this work may have been rationalized on the basis that, compared with mental patients, few retarded residents are under involuntary confinement. At least in theory, voluntary admission implies consent and avoids the evils of involuntary institutionalization. Indeed, New York law encourages the admission of residents on a voluntary basis. A facility director can admit any person he deems "suitable for care and treatment, who voluntarily makes written application therefore."[153] But for a person under the age of eighteen, a parent, legal guardian, or next of kin must make application for a "minor voluntary" admission, a status that requires no expression of the minor's willingness to enter into care.[154]

A person eighteen years or older can be admitted and retained as a voluntary resident upon a written application and a demonstration of willingness and suitability for voluntary care and treatment. For this purpose, a resident need not possess the legal capacity to contract.[155] He must, however, not only understand that he is requesting and applying for admission to a school for the mentally retarded, but also understand the "nature of the voluntary status and the provisions governing release or conversion to involuntary status."[156] Satisfying this three-part test constitutes no small mental feat: few people admitted on a voluntary basis are likely to grasp that if the facility director denies their written request to leave they can be forced to stay as an involuntary resident. Since mental-retardation institutions are intended to care for severely disabled persons, keeping a person in a development center who is capable of giving truly informed and free consent is contrary to public policy.

In such contexts, there are numerous questions as to the integrity of voluntary admissions. It may be difficult to prove that a retarded person actually sought "to be admitted to [a] school for the mentally retarded of [his or her] own free will."[157] Legalistic declarations bearing the resident's signature or mark provide no assurances that such a consent has, in fact, been tendered.[158] The resident's application states that "I have read or had read to me, and understand the contents" of the notice of status and rights.[159] There is no requirement, however, that this statement be witnessed or countersigned. The Mental Health Information Service must conduct its own annual review of the resident's suitability and willingness to remain in such a status.[160] But its representatives need not be present when the resident first offers his written consent or annually renews it. The resident can be retained only upon his written consent to stay and only after receiving notice as to his status and rights as a voluntary resident, including the right to leave and the right to receive MHIS assistance.[161] But residents are not advised as a matter of course to request MHIS assistance,[162] and such procedures do not offer a reliable guarantee of actual and informed consent.

Courts have long questioned the hollow rituals whereby mental patients convert to voluntary status, thus forgoing vital rights through inaction or inadvertence. Over a decade ago, New York's highest judges warned that, without the prior assistance of the MHIS, patients being converted from involuntary to voluntary status might acquiesce to pressures from hospital officials and make unknowing, confused decisions of doubtful integrity.[163] In a concurring opinion, Judge Keating emphasized due process infirmities of this classification process and the hazards of leaving "the correction of errors to family or mental institutions from whence may come the abuse."[164] In an analysis equally apposite to retarded persons, he concluded:

> A state may not, consistent with "due process," place any mentally ill person in the custody of any person or institution unless it makes some provision for periodic review of the propriety and suitability of the confinement before some impartial forum in which the incompetent is represented by a person or agency wholly committed to that person's interests.[165]

Despite this admonition, procedures for minor voluntary admission make no pretense of securing the young person's consent or providing such a forum and advocate. By law, if the minor is under eighteen and "suitable for care and treatment," the decision to "volunteer" him for long-term institutional care is wholly left to a relative (or guardian) and a school director. Although the minor may request release, there are no provisions requiring periodic notification of his rights and status or written consent to a continued stay.[166]

The decision requires no inquiry into the minor's competence or willingness to be admitted. Thus, to classify the minor's admission as a voluntary admission is conceptually illogical and confusing.[167] Given the emphasis attached to voluntary admission, the legislature should take greater pains to specify the criteria for such admission, to strengthen safeguards of informed consent, and to restructure the consent-giving to maximize the possibilities of real choice by the prospective resident. For residents incapable of such choice, New York law provides a separate procedure for nonobjecting admission that thereby avoids the problems of pseudo-voluntary admission and suggests a more candid approach.

Nonobjecting Admission

By providing for the admission of certain nonobjecting residents, section 15.25 of the New York Mental Hygiene Law permits the institutionalization of persons incapable of taking affirmative action on their own behalf. Unlike voluntary admission, such admission is explicitly limited to a retarded person with a severe degree of impairment, namely, "any person in need of care and treatment who does not object thereto and who is so profoundly or severely mentally retarded that he does not have sufficient understanding to make him suitable for admission as a voluntary resident."[168]

Procedures under this section provide more stringent safeguards than those for voluntary admission. They closely resemble involuntary admission procedures, except that only one certificate of a physician or psychologist is required, and the applicant must make a declaration on pain of perjury that the prospective resident does not object to being admitted to the institution. As a further safeguard, a staff physician at the receiving school, other than the certifying physician, must approve the admission.

Here again, admission status is largely a matter of administrative convenience. A resident admitted or converted to nonobjecting status who requests release may be detained if the facility director has reasonable grounds to believe that involuntary care and treatment are required. The resident, a friend, or the MHIS acting on his or her behalf may then request a hearing in a court of record.[169] Under procedures similar to those for judicial authorization of involuntary retention, the court can order involuntary care and treatment in the school for a period not exceeding sixty days. Further applications for retention can be made for one- and then two-year periods.

This form of admission gives legal recognition to a large group of residents whose admission is neither truly voluntary nor involuntary. The statute wisely provides checks against inappropriate admission or misclassification, and requires information and safeguards closely patterned after involuntary procedures. Thus, the MHIS must conduct reviews immediately after a nonobjecting admission and at least once in every twelve months of retention.[170] Such an admission requires at least two separate examinations, each agreeing on the diagnosis of severe or profound retardation and the anticipated benefit of admission. By limiting its purview to the most severely handicapped, this section at least narrows the scope of residential commitment.

Involuntary Admission

Involuntary admission refers to the civil confinement of a resident in a state-operated or state-certified residential facility for the "residential care, treatment, training, or education" of the retarded.[171] The commitment standard requires a dual finding: mental retardation coupled with a "need of involuntary care and treatment," and is defined in *parens patriae* terms: "that a person is in need of in-patient care and treatment as a resident in a school, that such care and treatment is essential to his welfare, and that his judgment is so impaired that he is unable to understand the need for such care and treatment."[172]

Although members of the public and even some legislators mistakenly believe that such admission is based on court certification,[173] the Mental Hygiene Law authorizes involuntary admission on medical certificate alone. In fact, the statute creates a hybrid administrative-judicial procedure for admitting and retaining residents against their will. The doctors provide the necessary certification and the court's function is essentially ministerial, that is, it has no independent power to commit the individual to the Mental Hygiene Department for involuntary admission.[174] The school director and staff physician, not the court, are responsible for making the initial admission. To avoid unnecessary confinement, the Mental Hygiene Law requires periodic reviews, including MHIS review, and judicial authorization for continued retention. Accordingly, the legislature repealed the judicial power to make a "final order" authorizing a retarded person to "thereafter remain in such institution."[175] The question now framed for judicial consideration is the resident's need for retention, not his or her need for admission.

Application. An involuntary admission begins with the filing of a written application, supported by medical certification. A wide variety of persons can make an application: the alleged mentally retarded person's coresident, nearest available relative, guardian, or welfare officials or officers of any recognized charitable institution, agency, home, or facility in which the subject lives.[176] Although some fourteen persons are listed, some courts have raised the question of adding law guardians, family courts, corporation counsel, or other attorneys to this list.[177] This recommendation seems unwise and inconsistent with trends away from involuntary commitment.

The application must be executed within six months of admission to a school. In contrast, there is a ten-day limitation on applications for involuntary mental hospitalization and a three-month limit on Medicaid institutional admissions.[178] Thus, there is greater risk of dated information serving as the basis of a confinement to a retardation school. Under pain of perjury, the applicant must complete a form showing facts and circumstances causing him to believe that the subject is mentally retarded and would benefit from care and treatment in the school named in the application.

Certification. Each application must be accompanied by the separate certificates of two examining physicians licensed to practice medicine in the state. Alternatively, certificates may be submitted by an examining physician and a state-certified psychologist.[179] One problem is that the Mental Hygiene Law and the admission forms promulgated under its authority are inconsistent in numerous respects. On the forms, the examiner is not asked whether the subject is in need of involuntary care or is suitable for voluntary care. Instead, the physician or psychologist is asked to list the reasons why "[t]his patient needs inpatient care and treatment" in a school for the retarded, and to checkmark a box indicating suitability for admission as either a nonobjecting resident or an involuntary resident.[180] Moreover, the forms entirely overlook two statutory requirements. They do not draw the examiner's attention to the need to consider less restrictive alternatives to commitment, and his duty to consult, insofar as possible, with the professionals furnishing prior treatment.[181] These omissions undermine basic safeguards against precipitous or inappropriate admission.

The application and the certificate fail to pose the right inquiries. The applicant is not asked to form any opinion as to why involuntary care "is essential to the alleged retardate's welfare" but is, instead, asked to reply to a technical, predictive question—to state facts showing that the proposed resident "would benefit from care and treatment in this school."[182] Paradoxically, the experts are not required to address this question of benefit or to determine whether the actual care and treatment facilities available will meet the proposed resident's specific needs. Indeed, under current state policy, the absence of beneficial programming in an admitting facility is not to be construed as the "overriding factor in denying admission."[183]

At present, the examiner's primary function is to certify to the subject's mental retardation. Under this certificate, the examiner attests that he or she has "personally observed and examined" the subject "with care and diligence." But all this stops short of the critical issue: compliance with criteria and procedures for "placement in the least restrictive form of treatment appropriate to meet the patients' needs."[184]

Acceptance by the School. A person certified under Section 15.27 of the Mental Hygiene Law may not be admitted to a school until he has been examined by a staff physician. The physician must find the person mentally retarded and in need of inpatient care and treatment, confirming by a checkmarked box that such care needs to be provided involuntarily.[185] In upholding the constitutionality of analogous provisions for the mentally ill, New York courts have been impressed that three physicians must concur in finding a patient in need of commitment.[186] However, with respect to the commitment of retarded persons, it should be considered that all three professionals may be colleagues in the very same school to which admission is sought, and may be under parental and peer pressures to confirm the opinions of their colleagues.

Notice of Admission. Revision of the Mental Hygiene Law in 1972 eliminated provisions for notice prior to admission and for personal service of notice upon the alleged mentally retarded person. Instead, the school director must give written notice of a person's involuntary admission to the MHIS, to the detainee's nearest known relative (other than the applicant), and to as many as three other persons designated by the resident.[187] Although the statute fails to require notice to the alleged retarded person after the making of the application or at the time of admission, the forms provide for postcommitment Notice of Status and Rights to the resident and to the applicant. That notice advises the resident of his status and his right to a judicial hearing:

> You have been admitted to this school for the mentally retarded as an involuntary resident. You will live, sleep, work and play here unless you are allowed to go somewhere else.
>
> You, your relatives, and your friends should feel free to ask members of the school staff about your condition, your status and rights, and the rules and regulations of the school.
>
> If you, your relatives, or your friends feel that you do not need involuntary care and treatment, you or they may request a court hearing. The request for a court hearing will be forwarded by the school director to the appropriate court and the Mental Health Information Service.[188]

State Judicial Remedies

At first glance, New York statutes seem to offer a wealth of judicial remedies to test the appropriateness of an individual's institutional admission. In fact, those remedies are not available until after the admission process is completed. Yet for a variety of reasons, including the demoralization and the drugs that accompany institutionalization, postcommitment remedies are almost never invoked. Hypothetically, a resident has the right to seek a writ of habeas corpus regarding the cause and legality of the detention, a hearing on the question of need for care and treatment at a school (if requested within sixty days of his admission), a hearing on a court authorization ordering involuntary retention beyond the first sixty days, and a fresh (*de novo*) review and rehearing of any subsequent retention order.[189] None of these hearings, however, are automatic. Unless the resident takes affirmative action within prescribed time periods to make a hearing demand, these rights are effectively waived.[190]

Other proceedings could arise in the family court, in the supreme court (a state trial court) under a cease and desist order, in the supreme court under administrative remedies, or as actions for damages.[191] Yet within the closed world of institutions, residents generally lack the means or capacity to avail themselves of such remedies.

Commitment Hearings. Judicial hearings under the Mental Hygiene Law are poorly described and almost never conducted. If a resident requests release or opposes an application for retention, the court shall "hear testimony and examine the person alleged to be mentally retarded."[192] Hearings may be informal and the examination may be in or out of court. But the statute is silent as to such matters as the burden of proof, the resident's right to be present at the hearing, to cross-examine, or to have access to records and other evidentiary materials.[193] However, the court must fix the date of the hearing no later than five days from receiving the notice-of-hearing request. The court then sends notice of that date to the resident, the school director, the MHIS, any person requesting the hearing, and any other person the court wishes to testify.

After a hearing, the court must either find the resident in need of involuntary care and order retention in the named school, or find him or her not in need of involuntary care and order immediate release. If no request for hearing is made, the court may still order retention solely on the basis of papers, without the presence of the resident, his counsel, or a MHIS representative.

Review of Commitment Orders. Upon the school director's application for a resident's retention beyond the initial sixty-day period, the court may order a continuing retention for a period of no more than one year. Thereafter, the court may order retention for two-year periods. The detainee, or his relative or friend, within thirty days of such order, may petition a trial-court judge (other than the New York Supreme Court justice who issued the original order) to rehear and review the proceedings. In this *de novo* review, a justice or a jury must try the questions of the detainee's mental retardation and need for retention. The right to jury trial must be expressly waived by the resident or party requesting the review on his behalf. A petitioner other than the resident or an immediate family member must first obtain leave of court "upon good cause shown" to seek review.[194]

A weakness of existing law is the limited range of dispositions open to the court. The resident must be discharged upon a finding that he or she is not mentally retarded or is not in need of retention. The only alternative disposition that a court may make between outright release and continued retention is to approve third-party custody. Thus, the court may transfer a resident's care and custody to relatives or a guardian, if they give their written consent and are found "willing and able properly to care" for the detainee at some other place.[195] But the statute fails to prescribe a systematic review of least restrictive alternatives, and sheds little light on how the system actually functions. The *modus operandi*, as one court recently observed, is to "shroud admission into residential facilities with the bureaucratic maze of rules and regulations [and] ultra-technical details."[196]

State Writ of Habeas Corpus. Although habeas corpus petitions have been brought by allegedly mentally ill persons,[197] residents of developmental centers have not filed for the writ. Alternative statutory remedies are only part of the explanation. Unlike federal habeas corpus cases that challenge the place as well as the fact of confinement,[198] the scope of state habeas corpus review has been narrowly construed. In *People ex rel. Anonymous No. 1* v. *LeBurt*, the Court of Appeals found that although a finding of mental illness and the legality of commitment could be attacked under the state writ, the patient's allegations of unconstitutional care and treatment should be remitted to the Mental Hygiene Commissioner for statutory-based administrative remedies for the investigation of treatment inadequacies.[199]

Seven days later, the same court ruled that an indigent mental patient is constitutionally entitled to the assignment of counsel in a habeas corpus proceeding to establish his sanity.[200] But in a dissenting opinion, Judge Bergan argued that the Mental Health Information Service and the possibilities of judicial review were sufficient safeguards, that a right to counsel would offer little benefit to mentally ill patients, and that the judicial review of patients' continued retention represented "a marked improvement over the uneven and haphazard chance of patients making application for writs of habeas corpus."[201] Notwithstanding "the enlargement of litigation" feared by this judge, retarded residents have neither obtained adversarial hearings nor filed habeas corpus applications.

Family-Court Actions. Getting into good residential care can be as great a legal problem as getting out of poor care. Even family-court judges meet with considerable frustration in seeking residential placements for retarded and other handicapped children under their jurisdiction. In *Usen* v. *Sipprell*, a fifteen-year-old girl who had been refused placement in the West Seneca State School brought a class action through her guardian *ad litem* on behalf of indigent mentally and emotionally handicapped children lacking appropriate programs of care, treatment, and education.[202] Representatives of a retarded, emotionally disturbed boy intervened, and both children claimed a right to receive "adequate care, treatment and education" under applicable state social-services, mental-hygiene, education, and family-court laws. The supreme court granted their claims, directing state and county respondents to submit short- and long-term plans for the named children's care and treatment.

New York State courts, hostile to class actions, have relegated claimants to less effective forums. Reversing the trial court on other grounds, the appellate division held that the family court should hold evidentiary hearings to determine the children's particular service needs, the services that respondents would be able to provide, and whether "necessary available services" were arbitrarily or capriciously denied. Despite its concern that family-court action might prove "an exercise in futility," the appellate division refused to permit either the individual or class actions to proceed in the supreme court. Referring to newly granted powers under the Family Court Act, the appellate division reasoned that the family court should schedule prompt hearings and could "solicit and order" appropriate care, education, and treatment for the two children. [203] Under that act, family courts can order any local or state agency or institution to provide "information, assistance and cooperation" concerning a child under "care, treatment, supervision or custody," and to assist the court "in every reasonable way to give the children within its jurisdiction such care, protection and assistance as will best enhance their welfare."[204]

Despite such powers, family courts have had little success in securing residential services for mentally retarded adolescents. For example, the case of *In re Leopoldo Z.* involved a moderately retarded fifteen-year-old juvenile delinquent and his probation officer's fruitless search among a dozen private and public agencies for an appropriate placement.[205] Relying on the earlier-quoted statute, the family court eventually ordered the Brooklyn Developmental Services, a state mental-retardation unit, to explore placement alternatives and report on its efforts. Failure to provide a viable alternative to Leopoldo's incarceration in a juvenile remand center, Judge Rider warned, might lead the court to compel the state to create a suitable placement for this youth. Yet such threats are often idle, and courts in similar situations have not been able to bypass ordinary civil commitment procedures.[206] Like parents who confront the state's lack of proper facilities, they too confront closed doors.

Administrative-Law Actions. Given the lack of decent state institutional placements, some parents have gone to court to seek private residential facilities for their mentally retarded children. While New York education laws authorize state and local contributions for the education of a handicapped child for whom adequate public instructional facilities do not exist,[207] families often face financial hardships when the child reaches adulthood and educational aid ceases.

Court actions can sometimes forestall institutionalization through the funding of a boarding-school placement.[208] In *Seitelman* v. *Lavine*, the appellate division held that the denial of state financial assistance to a mentally retarded young adult living in an out-of-state facility was arbitrary.[209] Until his twenty-first birthday, Seitelman received educational financial aid to attend a private boarding school for the mentally retarded. But the New York Department of Social Services refused to make a contribution toward the cost of his continued care at the out-of-state institution, though such aid for the disabled would have been available for care in a New York institution, on the grounds that the petitioner was not a New York resident because he attended the New Jersey school, and that the school was not approved or licensed by the New York Department of Mental Hygiene (DMH) Commissioner. This determination was upheld by the State Social Services Commissioner after an administrative fair hearing, and the petitioner brought a judicial proceeding.

The appellate division unanimously annulled the commissioner's determination, holding as a matter of law that it was arbitrary to require retarded persons seeking aid to enter an approved institution in New York rather than an out-of-state facility. In affirming this judgment, the court of appeals avoided the state's claim that it had discretion to limit grants to intrastate use, because that ground was not advanced in either the original tribunal or the administrative review.[210] The petitioner's stay at the New Jersey school did not alter his legal residence, except for an intent to change residence demonstrated by more than his presence at the institution. In dictum, the Court of Appeals referred to policy considerations in support of its legal holdings and a statutory framework evidencing "the humanitarian concepts forming the enlightened approaches to the plight and treatment of the mentally retarded."[211] Its decision, the court observed, had avoided a public failure to discharge a legal and humane responsibility to provide the mentally retarded with care in adequate residential facilities.

Judges have sometimes taken extraordinary measures to alleviate such failures. Confronted with the inappropriate hospitalization of two retarded individuals and failures on the part of hospital officials to make applications for more suitable placement, a supreme court ordered their admission to a developmental center upon presentation of the appropriate certification.[212] Referring to the DMH's statutory mandate to provide such persons with high quality care and treatment and to protect their civil rights, the court sharply criticized the MHIS, the hospital, and the state for their passivity and insufficient advocacy in assisting the mentally retarded to enforce their rights under law. The existence of such a mandate, the court observed, "without providing the facilities to assure the proper implementation of programs is meaningless."[213] Clearly, emergency legal actions of this type are no substitute for a system that would offer freedom of choice in the selection of appropriate, publicly supported, and least restrictive care.

Private-Law Actions. Damage actions in the New York courts are not a viable remedy for wrongful or erroneous institutional admission of retarded or allegedly retarded persons. Except for fraud or negligence, no cause of action will lie against the certifying physicians or the receiving authorities.[214] The state will not be liable for errors in medical judgment, even where misdiagnosis is the basis of the committal.[215] Moreover, state employees are not required to look behind an order of commitment that is valid on its face.[216] Even were the order illegal, if it were clothed with the attributes of an authorization to detain, there would be no duty to inquire further. The breadth of diagnostic definitions and the vagueness of commitment criteria also make it difficult to establish medical or other malpractice in the admission process. Indeed, New York cases alleging wrongful commitment to a mental institution have been brought exclusively by persons committed as mentally ill. Except for a case of police misuse of summary arrest powers,[217] such cases alleging wrongful admission have been generally unsuccessful.

With courts reluctant to impose liability for actions during emergencies, damages have usually been reserved for cases of prolonged, grossly unnecessary confinement.[218] Even in federal civil right actions that prove oppressive custodial conditions, state mental-hospital administrators and physicians have a qualified good-faith immunity from tort damages.[219] Although the Supreme Court has found that such state officials may be liable for knowing or malicious violations of patients' constitutional rights, the narrowness of the *Donaldson* holding and its distinctive factual pattern makes a flood of such cases unlikely. The situation remains little changed from Dr. Thomas Szasz's observation of nearly two decades ago, that for those hospitalized as mentally ill "suits for false commitment are almost always ineffective."[220] And for those institutionalized as mentally retarded, such litigation scarcely exists.

Conclusion

The rituals of passage into mental retardation institutions have had more to do with rites than rights. The applicant presented his or her version of reality, and a calculus of benefit that might advantage or disadvantage the handicapped person. The physician, as the sovereign expert, prepared the commitment papers that ratified the admitting institution's acceptance decision. The judge, as a bit player in a hollow ceremony, legitimized that verdict and endorsed the physician's report that imprisoned people in places like Willowbrook, Partlow, and Pennhurst. Legal assistance, if available at all, was essentially pro forma. The person labeled as retarded was rarely seen in these commitment proceedings. Thus its participants could preserve fictions that the prospective resident had no capacity for choice and the institution had no power to harm. Lacking effective preadmission advocacy, the handicapped individual enjoyed neither the forms nor the substance of due process.

In practice, the law still poses few barriers to unnecessary admissions, in part because few, if any, questions are asked and in part because judges, lawyers, and legislators are as likely as any other segment of society to have unrealistically low expectations for handicapped people. Despite the scandals and exposés, the lawmakers have been slow to acknowledge that the benefits to retarded individuals from care and treatment in large congregate-care facilities are often outweighed by their human costs. Thus, state laws still place undue emphasis on institutionalization. By focusing on the decision to commit or not to commit, those statutes tend to ignore points of entry into less restrictive care or the necessity for creating a network of community-based support, residential, and daytime services.

Despite their many defects, involuntary commitment laws for the mentally retarded remain on the books as an ill-examined offshoot of the mental-illness model. Yet there is little analysis of the vague rationales for this coercive power, empirical study of the practice under such laws, or consideration of the feasibility of replacing rather than repairing these commitment statutes.

Distinctions between voluntary and involuntary admissions, seemingly large in legal theory, are drained of meaning if you are a resident of a total institution facing a daily regimen of restriction, a choiceless environment. Notwithstanding informal and unwarranted presumptions of blanket incompetency, retarded persons can make some choices about service provisions. It is therefore ironic, if not misleading, that the majority of institutional residents are considered to be "voluntarily" admitted by relatives without the retarded person's actual consent and that these voluntary residents have fewer rights and safeguards than those who are ostensibly detained. Yet regardless of semantics or procedures, should anyone—minor or adult, willing or unwilling—have to live in the massive segregated retardation institutions that still exist in every state?

Notes

1. Yannet, "The Community Responsibility for the Care of the Mentally Retarded," 50 *J. Pediatrics* 397 (1957).

2. World Health Organization, Technical Report Series, No. 392, *Organization of Services for the Mentally Retarded* 30 (1968).

3. L. Clark, The Martti Wuori Case: Report to the Court: How Maine Cares for its Retarded Citizens 21 (July 20, 1981).

4. *E.g.*, Parker v. Bernstein, 125 Misc. Rep. 92, 210 N.Y.S. 594, 597 (Sup. Ct., Oneida Co. 1925).

5. *See* New York U. Medical Center, *Proceedings of the Symposium on Ethical Issues in Human Experimentation: The Case of Willowbrook State Hospital Research* (Urban Health Affairs Program, May 4, 1972).

6. Affidavit of Melvin F. at para. 3, New York State Ass'n for Retarded Children v. Rockefeller, 357 F. Supp. 752 (E.D.N.Y. 1973).

7. As of Fiscal Year 1978-1979 there were 5,237 new admissions to public residential facilities, with approximately 39 percent comprising mildly and moderately retarded individuals and with some 41 percent of the new

admissions coming from their own homes. Scheerenberger, "Deinstitutionalization: Trends and Difficulties," *Deinstitutionalization and Community Adjustment of Mentally Retarded People* 6 (R. Bruininks et al. eds., 1981).

8. *E.g.*, D. Braddock, *Opening Closed Doors: The Deinstitutionalization of Disabled Individuals* 97 (1977); D. Braginsky & B. Braginsky, *Hansels and Gretels: Studies of Children in Institutions for the Mentally Retarded* 175-76 (1971); New York State Dep't of Mental Hygiene, *Appropriateness of the Continued Institutionalization of the State School Population in New York State* 31 (1969); United States President's Comm. on Mental Retardation, "A Renewed National Commitment," in the President's Comm'n on Mental Health, IV Appendix: *Task Panel Report*, 2022 (1978).

9. Repp, "On the Ethical Responsibilities of Institutions Providing Services for Mentally Retarded People," 16 *Mental Retardation* 153, 154 (1978). *See* P. Morris, *Put Away: A Sociological Study of Institutions for the Mentally Retarded* (1969); Saenger, "Social Factors in the Institutionalization of Retarded Individuals," in *Proceedings of Conference on Scientific Study of Mental Deficiency* 642-49 (1962); Malzberg, "Some Statistical Aspects of First Admissions to the New York State Schools for Mental Defectives," 57 *Am. J. of Ment. Def.* 27 (1952).

10. Jaslow, Kime, & Green, "Criteria for Admission to Institutions for the Mentally Retarded," 4 *Mental Retardation* 2 (1966); New York State Department of Mental Hygiene, *supra*, note 8.

11. *See* G. Rivera, *A Special Kind of Courage: Profiles of Young Americans* 51 (1976); K. Wooden, *Weeping in the Playtime of Others: America's Incarcerated Children* 70-72 (1976).

12. *In re* Stanley P., No. 14934 (Mass. Dorchester Dist. Ct., May 11, 1978) (alleged minor law offender transported to Fernald State School without notice to its staff and detained until civil rights lawyers intervened).

13. *See* W. Wolfensberger, *Normalization* 88-89 (1972); Olshansky & Schonfield, "Institutionalization of Pre-School Retardates," 2 *Mental Retardation* 109, 113 (1969); Project Impact, "Making Impact" (1981) (special needs adoption network established for mentally handicapped and others considered hard to place; such children had been held under Massachusetts state custody for an average of five years).

14. *See, e.g.,* Guardianship of Becker, No. 101981 (Cal. Super. Ct., Santa Clara Co. Aug. 7, 1981) (parents placed six-day-old infant with Down's Syndrome in board-and-care facility, and have opposed foster-home placement); Adamson v. Lackner, No. M243830, Petition for Writ of Habeas Corpus 2-4 (Cal. Super. Ct., Los Angeles Co. Nov. 8, 1977) (parents placed four-year-old in state institution, and resisted subsequent staff attempts to arrange placement in community family care home).

15. U.S. Dep't of Health, Education, and Welfare, *Mental Retardation Source Book* 37 (1972).

16. 412 F. Supp. 112 (M.D. Ga. 1976).

17. Bartley v. Kremens, 402 F. Supp. 1039 (E.D. Pa. 1975), *vacated on other grounds*, 431 U.S. 119 (1977), *reinstated sub. nom.* Institutionalized Juveniles v. Secretary of Public Welfare, 459 F. Supp. 30 (E.D. Pa. 1977).

18. *See* Kremens v. Bartley, 431 U.S. 119, 137 (1977) (Justice Brennan and Justice Marshall, dissenting).

19. 431 U.S. at 135-36.

20. Institutionalized Juveniles v. Secretary of Public Welfare, 459 F. Supp. 30, 43 (E.D. Pa. 1977).

21. *Id.* at 46.

22. Secretary of Public Welfare v. Institutionalized Juveniles, 442 U.S. 640 (1979).

23. Parham v. J.R., 442 U.S. 584, 606-07 (1979) (citations omitted), quoted in Secretary of Public Welfare v. Institutionalized Juveniles, 442 U.S. 640, 646 (1979).

24. Parham v. J.R., 442 U.S. at 597, n.6.

25. *Id.* at 611, 618.

26. 442 U.S. 640, 649-50 (1979).

27. *See* Parham v. J.R., 442 U.S. 584, 607, 609 (1979). *See also*, Pennhurst State School v. Halderman, 451 U.S. 1, 54-55 (White, J., dissenting in part).

28. *Id.* at 609; Addington v. Texas, 441 U.S. 418, 429 (1979); O'Connor v. Donaldson, 442 U.S. 563, 584 (1975) (concurring opinion).

29. *See Parham*, 442 U.S. at 637-38 (Brennan, J., concurring in part and dissenting in part).

30. *Cf. Parham*, 442 U.S. at 603 *with* New York State Ass'n for Retarded Children v. Rockefeller, 357 F. Supp. at 756 (inhumane and hazardous conditions at institution for the mentally retarded endanger the "health, safety and sanity" of its residents).

31. *See* F. Menolascino, *Challenges in Mental Retardation* 250, 320 (1977).

32. People v. Reilford, 65 Ill. App. 3d 177, 382 N.E.2d 72 (1978) (bare assertions from medical experts that treatment is necessary and beneficial are insufficient basis for court to decide to institutionalize a person as mentally retarded); Kelly & Menolascino, "Physicians' Awareness and Attitudes toward the Retarded," 13 *Mental Retardation* 10 (1975); Wilkie, "Mentally Retarded Child: Institutional Care and Life Style," 78 *N.Y. State J. Med.* 1142 (1978) (many physicians who participate in institutionalization decisions are ignorant of the environmental conditions in institutions).

33. *Parham*, 442 U.S. at 632, 638.

34. 442 U.S. at 619.

35. *Id.* at 616, n.22. See notes 197-201, *infra* and accompanying text. *Accord*, Doe v. Gallinot, 657 F.2d 1017, 1023 (9th Cir. 1981) (automatic postcommitment hearings required since mental health commitment deci-

sions found "highly error-prone" and habeas corpus protection found "illusory when a large segment of the protected class cannot realistically be expected to set the proceedings into motion in the first place").

36. *See* National Ass'n for Retarded Citizens, *Residential Services* 6, 23 (Position Statements, Oct. 1976) and the literature cited at note 8, *supra.*

37. Parham v. J.R., 442 U.S. 584, 611 n.18 (1979).

38. Secretary of Public Welfare v. Institutionalized Juveniles, 442 U.S. 640, 652 (1979) (Brennan, J., concurring in part and dissenting in part). *See* Watson, "Children, Families and the Courts: Before the Best Interests of the Child and Parham v. J.R.," 66 *Virginia L. Rev.* 653, 675 (1980); Richards, "The Individual, the Family, and the Constitution," 55 *N.Y.U. L. Rev.* 1 (1980); Ellis, "Model Statute: An Act to Guarantee the Right of Developmentally Disabled Persons to Receive Appropriate Services and to Establish Consent Procedures to Allow the Provision of Those Services," *Disabled Persons and the Law: State Legislative Issues* 425 (B. Sales, D. Powell & R. Van Duizend eds. 1982).

39. For federal laws, *see* notes at 72-93, *infra* and accompanying text. For progressive state laws, see New Mexico Stat. Ann. § 43-1-8 (1979 Pamphlet); California Welfare and Institutions Code §§ 4502-4503 (Supp. 1979); Virginia Code § 37.1-65.1 (Cum. Supp. 1981).

40. Addington v. Texas, 441 U.S. 418 (1979).

41. *Id.* at 426. *See* Jackson v. Indiana, 406 U.S. 715 (1972); Humphrey v. Cady, 405 U.S. 504 (1972); *In re* Gault, 387 U.S. 1 (1967); Specht v. Patterson, 386 U.S. 605 (1967).

42. Addington v. Texas, 441 U.S. 418, 427. *Accord*, Matter of K.M.L., 626 P.2d 574 (Alaska Sup. Ct. 1981) (inadequate proof and procedural safeguards to commit retarded eighteen-year-old son).

43. 406 U.S. 715 (1972).

44. *Id.* at 728-29 n.7, referring to President's Comm. on Mental Retardation, *Changing Patterns of Residential Services for the Mentally Retarded* (1969).

45. *Id.* at 735 n.17, 737 n.23.

46. *Id.* at 738.

47. *See, e.g.*, State v. Kinner, 382 So.2d 75 (Fla. 2d Dist. Ct. App. 1980), *rev'd*, 398 So. 2d 1360 (Fla. Sup. Ct. 1981).

48. *Civil Rights of Institutionalized Persons: Hearings on S. 1393 Before the Subcomm. on the Constitution of the Senate Comm. on the Judiciary*, 95th Congress, 1st Session 8 (1977) (statement of Kenneth Donaldson).

49. *See In re* Wendell, 1 Johnson's Ch. 600, 602 (N.Y. 1815): "The care and custody of idiots and lunatics, being confided to this court, the whole control of the inquisition, and the manner in which that control shall be exercised, would seem to depend entirely on the discretion of the court."

50. *See, e.g.*, Sprecher, "Reaction Comment," *Mentally Retarded Citizen and the Law* 479-80 (M. Kindred et al. eds. 1976); Coleman & Solomon, "Parens Patriae 'Treatment': Legal Punishment in Disguise," 3 *Hastings Const. L.Q.* 345 (1976); DuBose, "Of the Parens Patriae Commitment Power and Drug Treatment of Schizophrenia: Do the Benefits to the Patient Justify Involuntary Treatment?" 60 *Minn. L. Rev.* 1149 (1976).

51. *E.g.*, Wyatt v. Aderholt, 503 F.2d 1305, 1312-13 (5th Cir. 1974); *In re* Gault, 387 U.S. 1, 21, 27-30 (1967); People v. Reilford, 65 Ill. App. 3d 177, 382 N.E.2d 72, 78 (1978): "The due process clauses of both State and Federal Constitutions prevent the involuntary institutionalization of a person by a State solely because he is mentally retarded."

52. *See* Lessard v. Schmidt, 349 F. Supp. 1078, 1103 (E.D. Wis. 1972), *vacated and remanded for specific judgment*, 414 U.S. 473 (1974), 379 F. Supp. 1376 (1974), *vacated and remanded*, 421 U.S. 957 (1975), *judgment reinstated*, 413 F. Supp. 1318 (1976).

53. O'Connor v. Donaldson, 422 U.S. 563, 566-67 (1975); B. Ennis, *Prisoners of Psychiatry* 84-86 (1972) (Donaldson's commitment questionable; cursory examination, hasty judicial hearing, and ineffective assistance of counsel).

54. See 493 F.2d 507 (5th Cir. 1974) and discussion in chapter 5, *infra*.

55. 422 U.S. at 576.

56. *Id.* at 575: "May the State fence in the harmless mentally ill solely to save its citizens from exposure to those whose ways are different? One might as well ask if the State, to avoid public unease, could incarcerate all who are physically unattractive or socially eccentric. Mere public intolerance or animosity cannot constitutionally justify the deprivation of a person's physical liberty."

57. *Id.*

58. *See* Halderman v. Pennhurst State School and Hospital, 446 F. Supp. 1295, 1314 (E.D. Pa. 1977).

59. *Id.* at 1320 (habilitation in the least restrictive setting consistent with *Donaldson* reasoning). *See also* Matter of K.M.L., 626 P. 2d 574, 579 (Alaska Sup. Ct. 1981) (no statutory authority to commit retarded persons, as well as constitutional doubt that an individual can be confined involuntarily "simply because he has a handicap and 'treatment' may be beneficial").

60. Gary W. v. State of Louisiana, 437 F. Supp. 1209, 1222-23 (E.D. La. 1976).

61. 387 U.S. 1 (1967).

62. *Id.* at 27-28.

63. 428 U.S. 52 (1976).

64. 435 U.S. 349 (1978).

65. *See* A.L. v. G.R.H., 163 Ind. App. 636, 325 N.E.2d 501 (1975).

66. Telegram of the President to the Governors, July 24, 1973, and Letter of the President to Dr. Stafford Warren, Sept. 18, 1963, in White House Conference on Mental Retardation, *Proceedings* 7 (1963).

67. President's Panel on Mental Retardation, *A Proposed Program for National Action to Combat Mental Retardation* 153 (1962).

68. President's Panel on Mental Retardation, *Report of the Task Force on Law* 41 (Chief Judge David L. Bazelon, chairman, 1963).

69. "Retarded Children in 'Snake Pits,' Kennedy Says," *New York World Telegram & Sun*, Sept. 9, 1965, at 3.

70. A confidential report of the Joint Legislative Comm. on Mental Retardation substantiated his criticisms. "Kennedy Backed by Secret Report on Mental Homes," *New York Times*, September 11, 1965, at 1. *See, e.g.*, New York State Planning Commission, I *A Plan for a Comprehensive Mental Health and Mental Retardation Program for New York State* 111 (1965); B. Blatt & F. Kaplan, *Christmas in Purgatory: A Photographic Essay in Mental Retardation* (1966).

71. President's Comm. on Mental Retardation, *The Decisive Decade* 1 (1971).

72. This pays part of the costs of "necessary medical services" and rehabilitation and other services to "attain or retain capability for independence or self-care." 42 U.S.C. § 1396 (1974).

73. 42 C.F.R. §§ 442.300-442.516 (1981). An ICF-MR is distinguished from a hospital or skilled nursing facility by the lesser degree of physician direction and medical care provided.

74. 42 U.S.C. § 1396a(a)(31).

75. 42 C.F.R. § 442.403.

76. *Id.* § 442.418(a). The trend is against institutionalization, in part because of the development of alternatives and the administrator's realization that every new admission means achieving two releases in order to reduce institutional censuses, and thus meet statewide ICF-MR plans. *See generally* "Down's Syndrome and Sibling Love," *New York Times*, November 19, 1981, at C1 (since 1974, all Down's Syndrome children born in Nassau County returned to natural family or placed in foster or adoptive homes).

77. 42 C.F.R. § 442.454.

78. *Id.* § 442.418(b)-(c).

79. *Id.* § 442.420.

80. 45 C.F.R. §§ 249.13(a)(2)(ii), (a)(1)(ii) (1974).

81. *See* 42 C.F.R. § 442.311 (1980), captioned "Written Policies and Procedures: Residents' Bill of Rights."

82. *Id.* § 442.311(a)(1)-(3). For a resident adjudicated incompetent under state law or determined by a physician to be incapable of understanding his rights and responsibilities, the resident's guardian, next of kin or sponsoring agency is expected to act as the resident's delegate. *Id.* § 442.312.

83. *See* "Nursing Homes Services Facing Federal Repeal," *New York Times*, Jan. 8, 1982, at A14.

84. 42 U.S.C. § 1396n(c) (Pamphlet No. 4, Dec. 1981).

85. 42 U.S.C. § 1396n(c)(4)(B).

86. H.R. No. 97-208, 97th Congress, 1st Session 966 (1981), *reprinted in U.S. Code Cong. & Ad. News* 1328 (Pamphlet 7A, 1981).

87. 42 U.S.C. § 6010(1) (1977).

88. *Id.* § 6010(2).

89. *Id.* § 6010(3)(A).

90. *See* Naughton v. Bevilacqua, 458 F. Supp. 610, 615 (D.R.I. 1978); Halderman v. Pennhurst State School, 446 F. Supp. 1295 (E.D. Pa. 1977), *aff'd in substantial part*, 612 F.2d 84 (3d Cir. 1979) (en banc), *rev'd and remanded*, 451 U.S. 1 (1981) and discussion *infra* at chapter 5.

91. 20 U.S.C. §§ 1401-1420 (1976). *See* J. Gleidman & W. Roth, *The Unexpected Minority: Handicapped Children in America* 173-95 (1980).

92. 29 U.S.C. § 794 (1976).

93. 42 U.S.C. § 1397(4) (Pamphlet No. 4, Dec. 1981).

94. *See* Maxwell v. Wyman, 478 F.2d 1326, 1328 (2d Cir. 1973).

95. *See, e.g.*, Jenkins v. Cowley, 384 F. Supp. 441, 443 (N.D. Tex. 1974) (court reluctant to interfere with decisions of medical authorities in the operation of state mental hospitals).

96. *See* Johnson, "The Constitution and the Federal District Judge," 54 *Tex. L. Rev.* 903, 908-09 (1976); S. Rifkind, "Are We Asking Too Much of Our Courts?" (The Pound Conference), 70 F.R.D. 96, 104 (1976).

97. G. Dybwad, "The Judiciary's Protective Role and the Separation of Powers in the Light of Recent, Consumer-Inspired Court Cases," in *15th Anniversary Symposium on Social Policy* (Heller Graduate School, Brandeis University, 1974).

98. Shelton v. Tucker, 364 U.S. 479, 488 (1960): "Even though the governmental purpose be legitimate and substantial, that purpose cannot be pursued by means that broadly stifle fundamental personal liberties when the end can be more narrowly achieved."

99. *See* H. Turnbull, J. Ellis, E. Boggs, P. Brooks, & D. Biklin, *The Least Retrictive Alternative: Principles and Practices* (1981) [hereinafter cited as H. Turnbull]; Rennie v. Klein, 653 F.2d 836 (3d Cir. 1981) (antipsychotic drugs should pose the least restrictive intrusive infringement on patient).

100. Wyatt v. Stickney, 344 F. Supp. 387 (M.D. Ala. 1972), *aff'd in part and remanded in part sub nom.* Wyatt v. Aderholt, 503 F.2d 1305 (5th Cir. 1974); Welsch v. Likins, 373 F. Supp. 487, 502 (D. Minn. 1974), *aff'd in part and vacated and remanded in part*, 550 F.2d 1122 (8th Cir. 1977); New York State Ass'n for Retarded Children v. Rockefeller, 393 F. Supp. 715 (E.D.N.Y. 1975); Halderman v. Pennhurst State School, 446 F. Supp. 1295, 1319 (E.D. Pa. 1977); Saville v. Treadway, 404 F. Supp. 430, 437 (M.D. Tenn. 1974).

101. Lake v. Cameron, 364 F.2d 657 (D.C. Cir. 1966); Dixon v. Weinberger, 405 F. Supp. 974 (D.D.C. 1975); Woe v. Matthews, 408 F. Supp.

419, 428 (E.D.N.Y. 1976), *remanded in part, dismissed in part sub nom.*, Woe v. Weinberger, 556 F.2d 563 (2d Cir. 1977); Lessard v. Schmidt, 349 F. Supp. 1078, 1096 (E.D. Wis. 1972); Lynch v. Baxley, 386 F. Supp. 378, 392 (M.D. Ala. 1974): "The state . . . shall have the burden of demonstrating that the proposed commitment is to the least restrictive environment consistent with the needs of the person to be committed."

102. *See, e.g.*, Morales v. Turman, 383 F. Supp. 53, 124 (E.D. Tex. 1974), *rev'd and remanded on other grounds*, 535 F.2d 864 (5th Cir. 1976), *judgment of Court of Appeals rev'd and remanded*, 430 U.S. 322 (1977), *remanded for further evidentiary proceedings*, 562 F.2d 993 (5th Cir. 1977). *See also* Morgan v. Sprout, 432 F. Supp. 1130, 1155 (S.D. Miss. 1977).

103. Dixon v. Attorney General, 325 F. Supp. 966 (M.D. Pa. 1971); Eubanks v. Clarke, 434 F. Supp. 1022 (E.D. Pa. 1977); Davis v. Watkins, 384 F. Supp. 1196 (N.D. Ohio 1974); Gary W. v. Louisiana, 437 F. Supp. 1209, 1217 (E.D. La. 1976).

104. *E.g.*, 33 N.Y.2d 161, 350 N.Y.S.2d 889, 892 (1973).

105. 422 U.S. 563, 575 (1975). *See also* Sanchez v. New Mexico, 396 U.S. 276 (1970) (summary action dismissing an appeal from a case rejecting least restrictive principle for want of a substantial federal question); Parham v. J.R., 442 U.S. 584, 620 n.23 (1979) (no need for court to reach question of remedies in less drastic settings).

106. *See* cases cited at notes 101-103, *supra*; Glenn, "The Least Restrictive Alernative in Residential Care and the Principle of Normalization," in *Mentally Retarded Citizen and the Law* 499-514 (1976); Chambers, "Alternatives to Civil Commitment of the Mentally Ill: Practical Guides and Constitutional Imperatives," 70 *Mich. L. Rev.* 1107 (1972); H. Turnbull, *supra*, note 99.

107. 396 F.2d 393 (10th Cir. 1968).

108. 387 U.S. 1 (1967) (right to counsel and other procedural safeguards in juvenile delinquency matters).

109. 396 F.2d 393, 396.

110. *Id.* at 397.

111. *Id.* at 396.

112. Herr, "Civil Rights, Uncivil Asylums and the Retarded," 43 *U. Cin. L. Rev.* 679 (1974); Mason & Menolascino, "The Right to Treatment for Mentally Retarded Citizens," 10 *Creighton L. Rev.* 124 (1976).

113. Wyatt v. Stickney, 344 F. Supp. 387, 396, Standards 3.a. and 7 (M.D. Ala. 1972). Before its modification, Standard 4 had prohibited the admission of mildly retarded persons.

114. *Id.* Standard 3.c. *See, e.g.*, New York State Ass'n for Retarded Children v. Carey, Consent Judgment, para. A.2, *approved*, 393 F. Supp. 715 (E.D.N.Y. 1975).

115. 373 F. Supp. 487, 502 (D. Minn. 1974).

116. 550 F.2d 1122, 1125-26 (8th Cir. 1977).

117. See chapters 5 and 6, *infra*; 393 F. Supp. 715, 717 (E.D.N.Y. 1975); 446 F. Supp. 1295, 1320 (E.D. Pa. 1977); Ferleger & Boyd, "Anti-Institutionalization: The Promise of the *Pennhurst* Case," 31 *Stan. L. Rev.* 717, 731 (1979).

118. 451 F. Supp. 233 (E.D. Pa. 1978); further requests for stay denied (E.D. Pa. Aug. 5, 1981) and (3d Cir. Sept. 2, 1981) (en banc). Petition for certiorari granted, 102 S. Ct. 2957 (1982).

119. *E.g.* Kentucky Ass'n for Retarded Citizens v. Conn, 674 F.2d 582 (6th Cir. 1982).

120. Johnson v. Solomon, 484 F. Supp. 278 (D.Md. 1979); *In re* Guzan, 405 A.2d 1036, 1038 (Pa. Commonwealth Ct. 1979) (right to least restrictive habilitation). *But see* Garrity v. Gallen, 522 F. Supp. 171, 237-39 (D.N.H. 1981) (no constitutional right to habilitation in least restrictive environment); *In re* Borgogna, 175 Cal. Rptr. 588 (Cal. App. 1981) (competent resident's choice of more restrictive setting takes precedence over state law mandating least restrictive alternative).

121. *See* New York State Ass'n for Retarded Children v. Rockefeller, 357 F. Supp. 752, 764 (E.D. N.Y. 1973); Black v. Beame, 419 F. Supp. 599, 607 (S.D.N.Y. 1976).

122. *See* Brewster v. Dukakis, 520 F. Supp. 882 (D. Mass. 1981); Mental Patients Advocacy Project, "Representing Mentally Disabled Persons: Models for Institutional Advocacy and Paralegal Training" (Final Report, NIMH Grant No. 5-T21: MH 13488-[01-03], Aug. 13, 1979).

123. *See* New York State Ass'n for Retarded Children v. Carey, 393 F. Supp. 715 (consent decree at para. W.2) (E.D.N.Y. 1975).

124. New York State Ass'n for Retarded Children v. Rockefeller, 357 F. Supp. 752, 762 (E.D.N.Y. 1973).

125. 446 F. Supp. 1295, 1327-28 (E.D. Pa. 1977), *order modified*, 612 F.2d 84, 113-14 (3d Cir. 1979).

126. Michigan Ass'n for Retarded Citizens v. Smith, 475 F. Supp. 990, 993 (E.D. Mich. 1979).

127. Barbara C. v. Moritz, No. C-2-77-887 (S.D. Ohio Oct. 19, 1981); Evans v. Washington, 459 F. Supp. 483, 488 (D.D.C. 1978). The five consent decrees on the operation of the Massachusetts State Schools, by setting least restrictive alternative standards and putting officials under pressure to bring down institutional censuses, indirectly produced the closing of admissions, except in "critical emergencies." *See, e.g.*, Belchertown State School, Policy No. AB:1 on Admissions (moratorium effective, June 15, 1976).

128. 325 F. Supp. 966 (M.D. Pa. 1971).

129. 349 F. Supp. 1078 (E.D. Wis. 1971).

130. *See* Parham v. J.R., 442 U.S. 584, 627 (1979) (Brennan, J., concurring in part, dissenting in part); Sprecht v. Patterson, 386 U.S. 605, 610 (1967).

131. *E.g.*, Reisner, "Psychiatric Hospitalization and the Constitution," *U. Ill. L. Forum* 9 (1973); Wexler & Scoville, "The Administration of Psychiatric Justice: Theory and Practice in Arizona," 13 *Arizona L. Rev.* 1, 69-71 (1971).

132. 404 F. Supp. 430 (M.D. Tenn. 1974).

133. *Id.* at 432 (citations omitted).

134. 442 U.S. 584 (1979).

135. 404 F. Supp., *supra* note 132, at 442.

136. The George Washington University Institute of Law, Psychiatry and Criminology, *Institutionalization of the Mentally Retarded* (National Ass'n for Retarded Children, 1967); D. Braddock, *Opening Closed Doors: The Deinstitutionalization of Disabled Individuals* 67, 99 (1977); Ellis, "Review of Statutes," *Disabled Persons and the Law: State Legislative Issues* 416 (B. Sales, D. Powell, R. Van Duizend eds. 1982).

137. *See* Hanley-Maxwell & Heal, "Legislative Constraints and Facilitations for Community Integration, *Integration of Developmentally Disabled Individuals into the Community* 163 (A. Novak & L. Heal eds. 1980).

138. New York Mental Hygiene Law [hereinafter M.H.L.], Article 15: Admission of the Mentally Retarded to Schools, §§ 15.01-15.35 (1978).

139. Dybwad & Herr, "Unnecessary Coercion: An End to Involuntary Civil Commitment of Retarded Persons," 31 *Stan. L. Rev.* 753 (1979). According to a high-ranking OMRDD official, less than 100 of New York's 13,000 developmental center residents are formally held as involuntary residents (interview in Albany, Jan. 12, 1982). *See, e.g.*, Massachusetts Gen. Laws Ann. ch. 123 (Michie/Law Coop 1972) (abolishing civil commitment on the basis of mental retardation); Belchertown State School, Policy No. AB:1 on Admissions (permitting admissions only on a "voluntary basis upon application of parent, guardian or self").

140. *Id.* § 1.03(21).

141. *Id.* § 15.01.

142. *See, e.g.*, New York State Office of Mental Retardation and Developmental Disabilities [hereinafter OMRDD], "Memorandum: New Policies Covering Intermediate Care Facilities" (May 9, 1980); Manhattan Developmental Center, "Admission Procedure for Community Clients" (Oct. 1976).

143. *See* S. Sarason & J. Doris, *Psychological Problems in Mental Deficiency* 18-62 (4th ed. 1969). This problem of vague standards, especially the virtually meaningless "in need of care" test, is common to many states. *See, e.g.*, Kinner v. Florida, 382 So. 2d 756 (Fla. App. 2d Dist. 1980), *rev'd*, 398 So. 2d 1360 (Fla. Sup. Ct. 1981) (constitutionality of statute for involuntary commitment of mentally retarded persons upheld).

144. New York State Department of Mental Hygiene [hereinafter DMH] Form 40 (1973).

145. M.H.L. § 29.09(b).

146. Fhagen v. Miller, 29 N.Y.2d 348, 356, 328 N.Y.S.2d 393, 397 (1972) (MHIS as part of "protective shield of checks and balances" should amply protect patient's due process rights).

147. Special Comm. to Study Commitment Procedures of the Ass'n of the Bar of the City of New York, *Mental Illness and Due Process: Report and Recommendations on Admission to Mental Hospitals under New York Law* 14 (1962).

148. *See* M.H.L. § 15.23(a). In response to a legislative proposal to relieve MHIS of the duty to review a patient's suitability for voluntary status, the MHIS argued for keeping that duty, in order to be able "to challenge in court the patient's suitability to remain in a psychiatric center when a developmental center or other program would be more appropriate." MHIS, Statement for Hearings of the New York State Senate Committee on Mental Hygiene and Addiction Control, at 4 (Jan. 12, 1982).

149. New York State Assembly, Ways and Means Comm. Staff Paper, "The MHIS: A Program Review and Suggestions for Reform" 16 (July 31, 1973).

150. *Cf.* 22 NYCRR § 622.2(1) (1975) (First Department Director to inform each patient of his rights to a judicial hearing and to "the services of the Mental Health Information Service including legal representation") *with* 22 NYCRR § 1023.2(a)(1) (1975) (Fourth Department Director to inform patient, *inter alia*, of rights to representation by retained or assigned counsel, and to the assistance of the service).

151. M.H.L. § 29.09(b)(3).

152. Interview with Ronald Soskin, former MHIS attorney, Nov. 15, 1978 (Boston) (quoted with permission).

153. M.H.L. § 15.13(a).

154. When the minor reaches eighteen years of age, he or she can be converted to non-objecting status, if appropriate. 14 NYCRR § 15.4(b)(1) (1977).

155. M.H.L. § 15.19(b).

156. *Id.* § 15.15(a).

157. *See* DMH Form 41 at 1.

158. The applicant's declaration reads:

> I,______, hereby apply for voluntary admission to a school for the mentally retarded. My reasons for requesting care and treatment are stated in Part C below. I have been notified and understand the nature of the voluntary status and the provisions governing release or conversion to involuntary status.
>
> Date________Signature

159. DMH Form 42 (1973).

160. M.H.L. § 15.23(a).

161. *See id.* § 15.17.

162. People v. Durant, 56 A.D.2d 471 (1977) (mental institution and court did not advise patient of right to MHIS legal assistance; *pro se* petitioner denied application for release from mental hospital granted opportunity to make new application and be represented by the MHIS).

163. *In re* Buttonow, 23 N.Y.2d 385, 297 N.Y.S.2d 97 (1968).

164. *Id.* at 105. For an early case finding that no parental authority alone justifies the confinement of "a sane minor in a madhouse," see People *ex rel.* Bebro v. Bond, 104 A.D. 47, 93 N.Y.S. 277 (1905).

165. *Buttonow*, 297 N.Y.S.2d at 104. For analysis of the benefits of commitment hearings to retarded children, see Teitelbaum & Ellis, "The Liberty Interest of Children: Due Process Rights and Their Application," 12 *Fam. L.Q.* 153 (1978).

166. M.H.L. § 15.13(b).

167. On the lack of adequate legal protection under voluntary and minor voluntary admissions, see R. Allen, *Legal Rights of the Disabled and the Disadvantaged* 14 (1964); Murdock, "Civil Rights of the Mentally Retarded: Some Critical Issues," *48 Notre Dame L. Rev.* 133, 156 (1972); Szasz, "Voluntary Mental Hospitalization: An Unacknowledged Fraud," 287 *New Eng. J. Med.* 277 (1972); Mental Health-Retardation Legal Services Project, "Handbook: Legal Principles for Representing the Mentally Different" 114 (American Bar Association, Young Lawyers Section, 1975): "Whatever the label under the conventional admission criteria, the great majority of the institutionalized retarded are, in fact, involuntarily commited." Many cases now adopt this position. *E.g.*, New York State Ass'n for Retarded Children v. Rockefeller, 357 F. Supp. 752, 762 (E.D.N.Y. 1973) ("A 'voluntary' admission on the petition of parents may quite properly be treated in the same category as an 'involuntary' admission, in the absence of evidence that the child's interests have been fully considered."); Aden v. Younger, 57 Cal. App. 3d 662, 674 (1976) (*voluntary* label often only means the patient did not formally protest hospitalization).

168. M.H.L. § 15.25(a).

169. *Id.* § 15.25(c).

170. *Id.* § 15.25(d).

171. *See id.* § 1.03(11).

172. *Id.* §§ 15.01; 15.27(a).

173. Personal observations of the New York State Senate Comm. on Mental Hygiene and Addiction Control, Hearing on Reforming the Mental Health Information Service (Jan. 12, 1982).

174. *See* Matter of Jack T., a person alleged to be a juvenile delinquent, 98 Misc. 2d 16, 413 N.Y.S.2d 957, 961 (Fam. Ct., Kings Co. 1978).

175. 1936 N.Y. Laws, ch. 536, § 124(7) (repealed 1972).

176. M.H.L. § 15.27(b).

177. *See* People *ex rel.* Thorpe v. Clark, 62 A.D.2d 216, 403 N.Y.S.2d 910, 917 (1978); Matter of Jack T., 413 N.Y.S.2d at 961.

178. *Cf.* M.H.L. § 15.05(b) *with* § 9.05(b).

179. *Id.* § 15.27(a).

180. DMH Form 43A (1973).

181. M.H.L. § 15.27(d).

182. DMH Form 43, Part C at 3.

183. OMRDD, Intermediate Care Facility Policy and Procedures, Topic Nos. I.C.F.-2.1, "Admission to a Developmental Center"; I.C.F.-2.2, "Admission to a State-Operated Community-Based ICF/DD; I.C.F.-2.3, "Admission to a Privately Operated Community-Based ICF/DD" (April 1980).

184. *Cf.* 14 NYCRR § 16.1 *with* DMH Form 43A at 2.

185. DMH Form 43 at 4.

186. *See* Fhagen v. Miller, 328 N.Y.S.2d 393, 398 (1972).

187. M.H.L. § 15.29.

188. DMH Form 44 (1973).

189. M.H.L. §§ 33.15, 15.31(a), 15.33(a), 15.35.

190. *E.g., id.* § 15.33(b) (resident must request hearing within five working days of notice of application for continuing retention).

191. *Id.* § 31.19(c).

192. *Id.* § 15.31(c).

193. *See generally* Application of Estes, 75 A.D.2d 451, 429 N.Y.S.2d 514 (1980) (courts have construed statute to require clear and convincing evidence and disclosure of MHIS reports to the attorney of clients seeking release).

194. *Id.* § 15.35.

195. *Id.* § 15.31(c). This provision appears unduly restrictive: charitable group homes, friends or foster parents have been willing to care for committed persons. *See* O'Connor v. Donaldson, 422 U.S. 563, 568-69, 576 (1975); *See generally* Koe v. Califano, 573 F.2d 761, 764 (2d Cir. 1978).

196. Besunder v. Coughlin, 102 Misc. 2d 41, 422 N.Y.S.2d 564, 567 (Sup. Ct., Nassau Co. 1979).

197. *See, e.g.*, People *ex rel.* Anonymous v. Waugh, 76 Misc. 2d 879, 351 N.Y.S.2d 594 (Sup. Ct., N.Y. Co. 1974); Lashway v. Hanes, 78 Misc. 2d 979, 357 N.Y.S.2d 747 (St. Lawrence Co. Ct. 1974).

198. *See, e.g.*, Covington v. Harris, 419 F.2d 617 (D.C. Cir. 1969).

199. 17 N.Y.2d 738, 270 N.Y.S.2d 206 (1966).

200. People *ex rel.* Rogers v. Stanley, 17 N.Y.2d 256, 270 N.Y.S.2d 573 (1966).

201. *Id.* at 577.

202. Usen v. Sipprell, 71 Misc. 2d 633, 336 N.Y.S.2d 848 (Sup. Ct., Erie Co. 1972), *rev'd*, 41 A.D.2d 251, 342 N.Y.S.2d 599 (1973).

203. 342 N.Y.S.2d at 607.

204. Fam. Ct. Act. § 255 (Supp. 1978).

205. 78 Misc. 2d 866, 358 N.Y.S.2d 811 (Fam. Ct., Kings Co. 1974).

206. People *ex rel.* Thorpe v. Clark, 62 A.D.2d 216, 228, 403 N.Y.S.2d 910 (1978) (Family Court may not directly commit to DMH custody, retarded juveniles found unfit to stand trial as delinquents); Matter of Jack T., 98 Misc. 2d 16, 413 N.Y.S.2d 957 (Fam. Ct., Kings Co. 1978) (same juvenile may not be committed where medical certificates do not establish need for involuntary admission to a retardation facility).

207. *See* New York Education Law §§ 4405, 4407 (Supp. 1978).

208. Such cases are part of a national trend. *E.g.,* Gladys J. v. Pearland Independent School District, 520 F. Supp. 869 (S.D. Tex. 1981) (ordering placement of a severely retarded fifteen-year-old child in a private educational facility); Kruelle v. New Castle County School District, 642 F.2d 687 (3d Cir. 1981).

209. 43 A.D.2d 545, 349 N.Y.S.2d 710 (1973), *aff'd*, 36 N.Y.2d 165, 366 N.Y.S.2d 101 (1975).

210. 366 N.Y.S.2d at 104 (further held, that the school was an approved facility because of its accreditation by New Jersey authorities and the DMH rule of approving facilities outside New York licensed by such authorities).

211. *Id.* at 106.

212. Besunder v. Coughlin, 102 Misc. 2d 41, 422 N.Y.S.2d 564 (Sup. Ct., Nassau Co. 1979).

213. *Id.* at 567.

214. Morgan v. State, 319 N.Y.S.2d 151 (Ct. Cl. 1970), *aff'd*, 34 N.Y.2d 709, 356 N.Y.S.2d 860 (1974), *modified*, 34 N.Y.2d 949, 359 N.Y.S.2d 564 (1974), *cert. denied* 419 U.S. 1013 (1974).

215. "If all the psychiatrists and physicians were wrong in their diagnosis, which I cannot accept, the State nevertheless would not be responsible for errors in medical judgment." *Id.* 319 N.Y.S.2d at 161.

216. Ferrucci v. State, 42 A.D.2d 359, 348 N.Y.S.2d 236 (1973).

217. Siegel v. City of New York, 43 A.D.2d 271, 351 N.Y.S.2d 394 (1974).

218. *See, e.g.*, Whitree v. State, 56 Misc. 2d 693, 290 N.Y.S.2d 486 (Ct. Cl. 1968).

219. O'Connor v. Donaldson, 422 U.S. 563, 577 (1975). Plaintiffs will prevail only if defendants knew or reasonably should have known that ac-

tion taken within their sphere of official responsibility would violate the plaintiff's constitutional rights, or if defendants took the action with the malicious intention to cause a deprivation of constitutional rights or other injury to the plaintiff.

220. T. Szasz, *Law, Liberty and Psychiatry* 235 (1963).

5 Rights to Care, Education, and Habilitation

Abandon every hope, ye that enter. —Dante

Abuse thrives in hidden, closed places. The state of Alabama fought long to keep the public from seeing its forgotten people and their stark existence. In a room barely six feet by ten, equipped with only a stained mattress and a coffee can to be used as a toilet, a young man was secluded for at least six years. In the basement of the Women's Cottage, untrained attendants wielded cattle prods on residents. This practice was called behavior modification with "training wands." As many as ninety-seven severely retarded persons, in rags or naked, milled behind locked doors in foul-smelling dayrooms with only two or three attendants present. In barracks, beds were jammed together, reminding one visitor of graveyard lots, where lives passed without privacy or possessions. The sign outside said "Partlow State School and Hospital." But inside, the sights, sounds, and smells announced despair and deterioration.

Our laws had left these regions uncharted. Lacking influence on the political process, retarded people constituted the paradigmatic example of a discrete and insular minority requiring the special solicitude of the judiciary. Yet until the advent of their civil rights movement, instead of solicitude, retarded people confronted a not-so-benign neglect. The history of the legal restrictions they endured, chronicled in chapter 2, is one of state-ratified stigma and debasement.

Once an individual was committed, the legal system's role abruptly ceased. Rights were permanently abrogated by conditions that destroyed any expectation of claiming them. The rule of the superintendent substituted for the rule of law. The courts, like the rest of society, expected the superintendent to act on behalf of residents. Institutions had practically full authority over every aspect of their residents' existence.[1] With virtually nothing to fetter their discretion, institutional staff exercised powers over the individual unique in American life.

For over ten years, an intense human rights struggle has placed these institutions under legal and public spotlights. This chapter analyzes judicial and legislative attempts to secure care, habilitation, and education for residents of public institutions. According to knowledgeable observers, these legal actions have improved the treatment of mental retardation more than any other single factor in recent years.[2] But why did these initiatives have to come from outside the treatment professions? What effects do they have beyond the immediate court decisions? As conditions go from abysmal to merely mediocre, will the legal system sustain its current level of scrutiny? If constitutional rights set a threshold for treating retarded persons with dignity, the professionals involved and the public must surely insist upon and honor higher standards of habilitation.

Dilemmas of Legal Reform

Litigation is an awkward tool for forging a comprehensive remedy to a problem so complex as long-term care. Yet for retarded persons with no political clout, it has sometimes proved the fastest and most economical way to remedy long-standing injustices. Critics had tried to alter the status quo but failed to mobilize the mental retardation profession, the legislature, and the public to deal with these legacies of neglect. Presidential reports, media exposés, National Institute of Mental Health studies, American Association on Mental Deficiency institutional evaluations, sociological reviews of total institutions, and photographic essays had covered these grounds time after time.[3] The documents drew a searing indictment of state inhumanity, but the public's span of attention was astonishingly short. The institutions could absorb an endless array of rhetorical attacks, respond with feeble antidotes or false panaceas (such as unitization, cottage plans, or more staff), and still remain intact. The litigator's dilemma was how to challenge the institutions' more fundamental flaws without shoring up a bankrupt enterprise or just writing off the 200,000 people in those facilities.

Legal reformers confronted at last four interrelated human rights problems. The initial wave of litigation probed the stark realities of what could only be termed human storage. In large state institutions, residents suffered outright neglect, malnutrition, inhumane living conditions, and isolation in damaging environments.[4] Testimony in court revealed a numbing litany of abuse: residents assaulted, straightjacketed, secluded, exploited, and otherwise improperly restrained or handled for the convenience of staff, as well as deaths by scalding, by asphyxiation, by drowning, and by other unnatural causes.[5]

In newer facilities, not yet houses of horror, investigators found patterns of accidents, injuries, brutality, fire hazards, and other threats to basic physical and psychic integrity.[6] Based on his observations of institutions in every U.S. state, Dr. Gunnar Dybwad, Gingold Professor of Human Development at Brandeis University, testified that "individuals who come to institutions and can walk stop walking, who come to institutions and can talk will stop talking, who come to institutions and can feed themselves will stop feeding themselves; in other words, . . . [there is] a steady process of deterioration."[7]

In order to avoid this deterioration and to tap the individual's developmental potential, states were required to provide adequate habilitation in the least restrictive alternative. Thus, the task of defining and achieving such habilitation raised the second major constellation of human rights and service delivery issues. When a state accepts a retarded person into its care, it assumes more than an obligation to feed, clothe, and protect him or her. It assumes parental duties to provide decent education and habilitation. Destructive institutional conditions or the lack of qualified staff were simply inconsistent with those duties. As federal courts had found, the denial of affirmative programming had proved hazardous to "the health, safety and sanity of residents" and a threat to "the very preservation of human life and dignity."[8] And despite the best intentions and conscientious caregiving, staff with institution-oriented practices inflict *dehabilitation*: the resident's learned helplessness and loss of basic personal skills.[9] Though the quality of care and habilitation might vary among and within residential facilities, inadequate treatment and the denial of residents' rights remain national problems, not regional anomalies.

Even as a right to habilitation gained ground, advocates began to promote rights against unwanted, hazardous, experimental, or unduly intrusive habilitation programs. Controlling behavioral technologies involved such matters as coping with excesses of therapeutic zeal and the misuse of medication as punishment or for staff convenience. It meant drawing balances between claims for individual autonomy and the costs and benefits of allegedly efficacious treatments. Legal interventions in this area provoked the greatest controversy since they impinged on the clinician's traditional prerogatives and brought outsiders into what the clinicians perceived as their exclusive domain. But these claims to unfettered discretion were undermined by such dehumanizing practices as involuntary sterilizations, gastrotomies, wholesale tooth extractions, aversive and deprivation behavior modification therapies, overmedication with powerful drugs, nontherapeutic experiments and even lobotomies. With no effective codes of self-regulation, the clinicians had left themselves open to legal scrutiny. As some behavioral professionals acknowledged, the revelations of serious violations of residents' rights proved an unfortunate, but long-overdue stimulus to the creation of guidelines.[10]

The retarded person's right to live in the world posed equally controversial challenges. Increasing numbers of retarded persons sought a measure of control and choice over their destinies. Sometimes with their families' support, and sometimes in opposition, they demanded opportunities to assume reasonable risks and obtain normal life experiences. To achieve this goal meant breaking the institutional monopoly on services, expanding the right to habilitation from the involuntarily institutionalized to the potential consumer of those services who lived in the community.[11] Narrow judicial doctrines might only perpetuate the institution, further concentrating social supports and financial resources on those living in the most restrictive settings. Abrupt deinstitutionalization carried other dilemmas and risks, such as stranding clients in destructive mini-institutions.[12] Without careful planning and a trained staff, custodial-care conditions could easily be replicated in boarding homes and fifty-bed facilities. Programs, principles, and processes were urgently needed in order to satisfy clients' choices, caregivers' cautions, and families' duties. This, in turn, raised novel legal questions of consent, substituted consent, and the assessment of reasonable risks and benefits for those deemed incompetent.[13]

Fighting against human storage and inadequate habilitation were clearly issues of high consensus. But in matters of client autonomy and social integration, the constituency for legal reform dropped sharply. For public officials, there was little political capital to be gained in grappling with such problems. Leaving such disputes to the judicial process was an attractive way out. If courts chose to mandate guidelines, administrators could disclaim responsibility for measures likely to be unpopular with the public, legislators, parents, or clinicians, and plead that their hands were tied by the federal courts.[14] Or they could say, often quite correctly, that the advocate's agenda and their own coincided, and that judicial orders essentially expedited what they had intended to do all along.[15]

The elements of a backlash are now apparent. How far and how long can a court, a legal advocate, and an insular minority compel changes before political pressures build up against new legal norms? As the costs of class-action remedies rise, state legislators are emboldened to challenge federal judges.[16] As overcrowding and "snake-pit" conditions abate, state officials seek to reclaim their traditional standard-setting authority. As the ethical and professional issues become more subtle, clinicians and family members frequently question the competence of courts to settle disputes involving habilitation and expert opinion. After all, it is difficult enough for the legal system to gain acceptance for the concept of "informed and voluntary consent" for the mentally average, let alone the mentally different.[17] Who would then have the legal duty and responsibility for habilitation decisions for persons not capable of making such decisions for themselves?

The Supreme Court and Atrocious Treatment

To human rights conundrums such as these, the United States Supreme Court has issued only fragmentary and equivocal responses. Although the Court has not ruled on whether there is a general constitutional right to treatment, it has watched as federal and state courts throughout the country have repeatedly held that the mentally retarded and others confined under *parens patriae* rationales have a right to individualized care and treatment.[18] Indeed, the philosophy underlying this right is at least as old as the juvenile-court movement and its assertion that the state has a duty to furnish children taken into its custody with proper care and "a real school, not a prison in disguise."[19]

The shorthand phrase *right to treatment* has drawn great popular attention and scholarly support, but lower courts have also ordered substantial relief for retarded residents under right-to-habilitation, protection-from-harm, and right-to-education rubrics. Few of these cases, however, have been appealed, and those reaching the Supreme Court have either ended in denials of certiorari or narrow resolutions of the legal questions presented.[20] Decisions in the last days of the 1981 Supreme Court term, described in the final chapter of this book, have proved no exception.

Since 1972, substantive due process has been the predominant constitutional approach in testing the legitimacy of institutional deprivations. In cases such as *Jackson* v. *Indiana* and *O'Connor* v. *Donaldson* where little or no treatment was proffered, the Supreme Court had little difficulty in finding that the purposes of commitment were not reasonably related to a legitimate governmental objective.[21] *Jackson*, as noted in chapter 4, invited an era of judicial activism for the silent clients who were locked up for treatment but were given no treatment. Yet the Supreme Court in *Donaldson* sidestepped that squarely presented question and preserved its unanimous front by stripping the lower court right-to-treatment decision of its precedental effect.[22]

For retarded persons under the state's control and custody, the arguments for a constitutional right to habilitation are even stronger. Without such a right encompassing basic necessities of life, treatment, and protection, the very survival of a dependent person is threatened. Without habilitation, the severely disabled individual may be helpless to avoid even the hazards of everyday life, for example, recognizing common dangers or learning feeding skills to prevent choking. The adequacy of habilitation in coercive settings is clearly a justiciable issue, for as the *Donaldson* Court noted "[w]here 'treatment' is the sole asserted ground for depriving a person of liberty, it is plainly unacceptable to suggest that the courts are powerless to determine whether the asserted ground is present."[23] But suppose a state should promise only care or protection, can it thereby evade obligations to provide the rest of the package of professionally acceptable habilitation? Though the Supreme Court has not encountered such a case, evasions of this type should be rejected. Instead, courts should recognize that for retarded residents, persons who have "broken no laws, and are not a danger to others,"[24] habilitation is the right and rationale for every commitment. Indeed, since the state has chosen to make these persons its dependents, to assume dominion over their lives, and to isolate them from private and alternative sources of education, care, and support, the state owes them legal as well as moral duties.[25]

To date the Supreme Court has resisted giving a constitutional imprimatur to such broad duties. In a recent decision, the Court also repudiated a federal statutory basis for the right to least restrictive habilitation under the Developmentally Disabled Assistance and Bill of Rights Act.[26] But the legal saga of *Halderman* v. *Pennhurst State School and Hospital* continues: community-directed remedies proceed, as does the search for legal bases upon which to anchor them.

Initially, the district court drew many arrows from the quiver of legal liability. Thus, its 1977 decision invoked no less than five grounds: constitutional doctrines of substantive due process, equal protection, and the ban on cruel and unusual punishment, as well as federal and state statutory rights to nondiscriminatory habilitation.[27] On appeal, the Third Circuit declined to reach these legal questions, and instead affirmed the bulk of the *Pennhurst* remedy on the basis of the federal developmental disabilities statute, a ground not even advanced by the plaintiffs at trial.[28] Although this approach seemed to satisfy the rule against unnecessary decisions of constitutional law, the legal arrow chosen by the Third Circuit—the novel Developmental Disability Act claim—was off the mark. Since its decision on the federal statutory bill-of-rights act was reversed and other claims remanded, the court of appeals has once again upheld all but the institution-closing relief, this time on the basis of an independent state law ground.[29] Thus, the law of the case, as it now stands, is that the right to individualized less restrictive habilitation raises substantial federal questions, is grounded in Pennsylvania law, and is enforceable by a federal court acting under the doctrine of pendent jurisdiction.

This intricate legal handiwork should be sturdy enough to support substantial legal remedies for the *Pennhurst* plaintiff class and their pursuit of community living arrangements. But if, as the district court judge queried, "it is time to sound the death knell for institutions for the retarded,"[30] this Supreme Court will not toll that bell. By a 6 to 3 vote, the Court in the *Pennhurst* case held that Section 6010 of the Developmentally Disabled Assistance and Bill of Rights Act did not, standing alone, create new substantive rights to appropriate treatment in the least restrictive environment.[31] Justice Rehnquist, writing for the majority, found that the act was an exercise not of congressional power to enforce the Fourteenth Amendment, but of its spending power in setting terms for the receipt of federal funds by participating states. Thus, the Court ruled that states cannot be forced to assume "massive financial obligations" when Congress had not given them sufficiently clear notice that the receipt of Developmental Disabilities grants imposed an affirmative mandate to fund certain services.[32] In dictum, five justices also expressed some doubt as to the viability of a private right of action to enforce other provisions of the act.

This narrow decision of statutory construction throws little light on the proper role of courts in enforcing retarded people's rights. Instead, the Court remanded the private-right issues and claims under the state law, federal constitution, and federal Rehabilitation Act. Their decision did not even foreclose judicially enforceable relief when Section 6010 is read together with other parts of the act that require states to make, and the Secretary of Health and Human Services to approve, human rights assurances.[33] Indeed, the secretary must satisfy himself that rights to least restrictive treatment, services, and habilitation—clearly referenced within those state plan assurances—are honored by participating states. Moreover, administrative oversight and funding cutoffs are not the exclusive remedies under this act. The dissenting justices in *Pennhurst* were correct in emphasizing that Congress intended this act and its bill of rights to be taken seriously, and expected the courts and the federally funded protection and advocacy systems to assure respect for its requirements.

Failure to adopt even this modest construction, as Justice Blackmun warned, risks "the odd and perhaps dangerous precedent of ascribing no meaning to a congressional enactment."[34] Further, Congress has recently reaffirmed with even greater precision its intention to confer and ensure a legal right to treatment and habilitation.[35] But after *Pennhurst* and in the current atmosphere of the proposed New Federalism, enforcement of such spending-power legislation is constrained by fresh reminders of the state's option to withdraw from burdensome federal programs, and the declining appropriations and hence worsening cost-benefit ratio to participating states.

Justice Rehnquist's opinion is in step with the current emphasis on states' rights over individuals' rights. It places the informed choice of states in matters of receiving grants above the informed choice of residents and their representatives in matters of receiving habilitation. It puts a higher priority on speculative assertions of the costliness of least restrictive environments for retarded citizens than on the undisputed findings of fact that institutional care can be both abusive and expensive.[36]

With the Supreme Court disinclined to probe deeply into residents' claims of atrocious treatment, let alone inadequate levels of treatment, plaintiffs may increasingly turn to state laws for more congenial forums. This fresh tack is foreshadowed by the United States Court of Appeals for the Third Circuit and its recent reliance on Pennsylvania's Mental Health and Mental Retardation Act to support the right to the least restrictive means of habilitation.[37] Given the Pennsylvania courts' authoritative and independent interpretation of these state law issues, the Third Circuit reinstated its prior order requiring case-by-case determinations of appropriate placement with a presumption in favor of placing individuals in community living arrangements.

Even though this resolution may insulate the substance of the remedy from hostile Supreme Court review, it leaves controversial enforcement questions unsettled. The immediate issue is the scope of federal court monitoring of a remedy that now rests primarily on state court interpretation of state law. The majority opinion's invitation to the state to seek reconsideration of this issue could be a prelude to scaling down judicial intervention in Pennhurst.

Recent Supreme Court decisions have also cast doubt as to the availability of Eighth Amendment protection for those who suffer punitive treatment in supposedly nonpunitive places. Although *Ingraham* v. *Wright* specifically reserved the question of applying cruel-and-unusual-punishment analysis to persons in closed mental institutions, the Court there held that corporal punishment in public schools did not violate the student's Eighth Amendment rights.[38] In 1979, the Court more drastically narrowed the scope of such scrutiny in *Bell* v. *Wolfish,* a case involving conditions of pretrial detention.[39] From this line of decisions, some lower courts have implied that criminal conviction is a precondition for Eighth Amendment protection. But even if correct, the retarded person's constitutional right to protection from harm can still be derived from the Fourteenth Amendment and its ban on state deprivation of life, liberty, or property without due process of law.[40]

Romeo v. *Youngberg* entails no sweet sorrow. Romeo, a thirty-year-old, profoundly retarded man, was involuntarily committed for care and treatment to Pennhurst, a state facility that received him for that purpose. There he was shackled to a bed or chair for long periods, subjected to inadequate treatment, and injured over seventy times, either by himself, other residents, or perhaps even by staff. The human destruction was essentially undisputed: a broken arm, human bite marks, black eyes, scratches, lacerations, a fractured finger, and injuries to sexual organs. Many of these injuries became infected, "either from inadequate medical attention or from contact with human excrement that the Pennhurst staff failed to clean up."[41] Even a prisoner would have a constitutional remedy against such state-inflicted neglect. Yet this incarceration of the retarded, as the court of appeals correctly emphasized, must be judged against a more exacting standard than the Eighth Amendment, and "deliberate indifference to the serious medical needs of the resident."[42]

How stringent a constitutional test should the state and its treatment professionals face when residents' liberty and entitlement interests hang in the balance? The Third Circuit created a complex taxonomy of postcommitment deprivations, varying the burden of proof and the levels of judicial scrutiny with the type of encroachment on constitutionally protected interests.

It reserved "heightened scrutiny" for alleged violations of the right to be free from undue bodily restraint. The rights to personal security and to adequate treatment received lesser legal protection.[43]

These complex legal rules and jury instructions were rejected by the Supreme Court.[44] Though the law remains unsettled, courts in cases of extreme institutional abuse can insist on a constitutional minimum of medical accountability. In theory, state malpractice remedies and internal grievance mechanisms can dispose of most abuse cases. However, the former have been generally unsuccessful and the latter untried. If viable internal mechanisms such as human rights committees or administrative processes functioned, many more least-restrictive-alternative and treatment questions could be settled without litigation.

When state officials attempt to forcibly administer antipsychotic drugs to mental patients, they run the risk of violating due process rights to privacy, bodily integrity, or personal security. Two recent appellate decisions have upheld mental patients' qualified right to reject such medication in nonemergency situations.[45] Residents of facilities for the mentally retarded may also raise similar claims regarding the misuse of psychotropic drugs with dangerous side effects, or other intrusive or painful treatments with unacceptable burden-to-benefit ratios.[46] As demonstrated by a long line of cases and human rights committee reviews, the right to habilitation does not create a corresponding duty on the part of the resident to submit to any habilitation program, no matter how invasive, noxious, or of dubious effectiveness.[47] In this context, the right to decline some forms of habilitation is no more than an element of the right to least restrictive habilitation, and its corollaries of promoting normalization and individual dignity.

The Supreme Court has now ventured into this hotly disputed area of law. *Mills* v. *Rogers* had promised to determine whether involuntary mental patients possess a liberty interest in refusing mind-affecting medications, and, if so, the form of procedural protection to be accorded dissenting patients.[48] Ordinary citizens are clearly free to decide for themselves whether to submit to such drug regimens. Mental patients do not possess, however, an absolute right to refuse such drugs, or the right to dictate their treatment when they are within the shelter of a state hospital. The Court of Appeals for the First Circuit sought to find a pragmatic and principled line that would uphold the hospital's interests in curing and safeguarding its patients, and the competent patients' interests in preserving residual liberty rights to accept or refuse potentially harmful drugs.[49]

In modifying the trial court's ruling, the First Circuit struck a reasonable accommodation of those interests. This permits ad-hoc balancing by qualified physicians of the varying treatment, security, and autonomy interests; and relaxation of the definition of emergency to enable administration of drugs in order to avoid sudden deterioration of the patient's health. Physicians must also make an appraisal of alternative, less restrictive courses of action. On remand, the district court can search for new procedural mechanisms in determining when patient incompetency justifies the exercise of *parens patriae* or police powers to avert difficult-to-predict physical harms. Despite exaggerated reports of violence and chaos resulting from the *Rogers* court orders,[50] the Supreme Court should stay its hand and let state and lower courts seek workable remedies. This would allow the record of exploration and evaluation of nonjudicial safeguards to go forward.

Until now, the courts have strengthened handicapped children's access to educational services. Although there is no constitutional right to education, the absence of some minimum of publicly supported education would surely transgress equal protection standards.[51] However, the Education for All Handicapped Children Act of 1975 established a more stringent standard: provision of a free, appropriate education suited to the handicapped child's unique needs.[52] Application of that standard is especially controversial when sophisticated forms of special education and unusual related services impose high costs on local school districts, from which the child reaps incremental educational advantages.

Amy Rowley v. *Board of Education of the Hendrick Hudson Central School District* poses that atypical case of sorting educational extras from essentials.[53] Amy, a bright eight-year-old child, deaf since birth, attended a regular class. With the aid of supportive teachers and peers and a wireless hearing device to amplify sounds, she achieved above-average academic and social success. Amy's parents wanted a sign-language interpreter in her classroom to enable her to capture more of the classroom discussion, tests having shown only 59 percent of sounds audible through Amy's residual hearing. The school, the district's Committee on the Handicapped, and the State Education Commissioner disagreed, and the Rowleys sued. The district court ruled that a sign-language interpreter was required under the federal statute to give Amy a level of educational opportunity equivalent to that offered her nonhandicapped peers.[54] By a split decision, the Second Circuit affirmed, with the majority expressly limiting its holding to this one particular child.[55]

Despite all these earmarks of an exceptional legal result for a truly exceptional gifted youngster, the Supreme Court chose to review this case. Yet for the young residents of state retardation institutions, *Rowley* should have little legal impact. For example, it will not disturb recent decisions that the dumping of handicapped children into inferior institution-based programs violates their rights to even minimum educational opportunities.[56] Massive legal redress is still required for what is best described as educational malnourishment.

Federal Statutory Rights to Care, Education, and Habilitation

In response to the scandals and the constitutional litigation of the 1970s, federal lawmakers demanded systemic reforms. Instead of piecemeal change through the courts, their legislation proceeded from a new vision of disabled persons and their relationships to the state and to the therapist. To counter dependency, resignation, and isolation, the laws announced new expectations for disabled persons as full citizens and consumers entitled to accountability from therapy providers. The federal government therefore pledged its active involvement in standard setting and the translation of a vague professional consensus into service guidelines. Through procedural as well as substantive requirements, Congress promised retarded persons access to developmental services of decent quality and sufficient quantity. These laws addressed rights to core services and inclusion rather than exclusion of the severely disabled. Thus, the issue would no longer be whether to educate retarded and other disabled children, but how to educate them.

Federal statutes and regulations attacked the barriers that had separated the handicapped from the nonhandicapped. The new civil rights measures placed a premium on activism, risk taking, and self-determination by disabled persons, their families, and other representatives. Individualized planning procedures, due process remedies, and specific, judicially enforceable service mandates became the hallmarks of this statutory approach. Thus the federal government undertook to irrigate barren human-service fields with new funds and a new sense of mission. In a relatively short time, these legal actions have had a profound and positive effect on treatment practices for mental retardation.[57] Paradoxically, their very success has prompted a fierce counterattack from fiscal and organizational conservatives.

The Education for All Handicapped Children Act

Equal educational opportunity remains the driving idea behind the federal role in the education of handicapped children. Practices of classifying retarded children as "ineducable" and excluding them from public schooling, outlawed in the landmark cases of *Mills* v. *Board of Education* and *Pennsylvania Association for Retarded Children (PARC)* v. *Pennsylvania,* blatantly denied such opportunity.[58] These cases, extending to disabled persons the equal-opportunity rights of *Brown* v. *Board of Education,*[59] had a special resonance for children relegated to state schools for the retarded. For here was a segregated dual system of education (and sometimes noneducation) organized on the basis of IQ but imposing additional burdens of residential isolation and profound stigma.

In enacting the Education for All Handicapped Children Act (P.L. 94-142), Congress directly addressed these problems and sought to "assure equal protection of the law" for handicapped children, consistent with *Brown*, *Mills*, and *PARC* rulings. Through planning requirements and the antidiscrimination mandate of Section 504 of P.L. 93-112, Congress made enforceable the goal of providing a "full educational opportunity to all handicapped children."[60] Congressional solicitude was most vividly expressed for those in public residential institutions. These, after all, were children with multiple misfortunes: rejected from the public schools, removed to subhuman conditions of custody, and in too many instances, children "whose families are no longer able to care for them and who themselves have received no educational services."[61] Ironically, just as some progress begins, critics of the act call for diminished federal intervention in the name of simplified administrative requirements and increased local discretion.[62] Behind such bland rationales for the Reagan administration's proposals to trim statutory and regulatory rights is a different reality: attempts to dilute legal obligations to match projected funding cutbacks.[63]

The federal right to "a free, appropriate public education" guarantees more than a token education. Public Law 94-142 codifies the landmark court cases and provides financial aid—totaling $1,042,000,000 in 1982—to states that have a plan and policy in effect of "providing a free appropriate public education for all handicapped children."[64] Only New Mexico has declined to participate.[65] All other states filed the necessary assurances, notwithstanding the breadth of this mandate to provide special education and related services to all handicapped children within prescribed age ranges and timetables.

Along with Section 504, judicial interpretations of P.L. 94-142 have compelled local school districts to make these services available to individual children. For example, cases have sustained a broad definition of related services to include catheterization and residential placement.[66] As a common law on special education and the definition of appropriate education develops, federal courts have walked a middle ground, adopting a standard between the extremes of requiring only minimal education for the child's self-sufficiency and the ideal education for reaching a child's full potential.[67]

Under this law, relatively few disputes as to what constitutes an appropriate education ever reach an administrative appeal, let alone a judicial review. The process of creating an individualized education program (IEP) is a flexible way of defining an instructional program appropriate to a child's unique needs.[68] Thus, each handicapped child is entitled to a written IEP that states the goals, short-term instructional objectives, and specific educational services to be provided. On an annual basis, the special-education supervisor, teacher, parent, and whenever appropriate, the child meet to reconsider and update the IEP.[69] The law encourages and requires a healthy dose of parental participation in this educational planning. Inevitably this favors the more affluent, better educated parents who have the time, skills, and self-confidence to express their views to school personnel. But it establishes a basis for dialogue that potentially benefits all.

When the quest for consensus fails, the act gives powerful leverage to those parents who can invoke due process hearings or tap other statutory remedies. Congress thereby opened a remarkably wide range of questions to administrative and ultimately judicial review: determinations of appropriate education, least restrictive environments, nondiscriminatory diagnostic procedures, and even the length of the school year.[70]

The parent is entitled to written prior notice whenever any local educational agency proposes or refuses to initiate or change the "identification, evaluation, or educational placement of the child or the provision of a free appropriate public education to the child."[71] Parents then have the right to complain of the intended action and to request an "impartial due process hearing." To safeguard this impartiality, the hearing officer cannot be an employee of an agency involved in the education or care of the child.[72]

Contested cases can trigger impressive legal protections. In an administrative hearing, the child's representative has rights to be "accompanied and advised by counsel" and by handicap specialists, to present evidence, and confront, cross-examine, and compel attendance of witnesses, to obtain a written or tape-recorded verbatim record, and to receive written findings of fact and decisions.[73] If still dissatisfied, the representative may appeal to the state education agency, which must conduct "an impartial review" of such findings and decision, and make "an independent decision" based on that review.[74] Final decisions are also subject to judicial review, with the aggrieved party bringing a civil action in any state court of competent jurisdiction or in a United States district court. The act expressly confers jurisdiction on the United States district courts to hear such private actions irrespective of the dollar amount in controversy. Moreover, Congress announced a generous measure of judicial scrutiny: based on the records of administrative proceedings and any additional evidence introduced at a party's request, the court is empowered to make a *de novo* review and to grant such relief as the court determines appropriate.[75]

The concept of *mainstreaming* is central to the act's design and the framing of relief. This refers to integrating children with special educational needs with other children. Although that term does not appear in P.L. 94-142, the statute requires the least restrictive educational environment appropriate to the individual child's needs. Congress was emphatic that recipient states and school districts, to "the maximum extent appropriate" and "practicable," should give handicapped children opportunities to be educated with nonhandicapped children.[76] This principle applied equally to children in public or private institutions or other care facilities. It was intended to eliminate unnecessary segregation. Special classes, separate schooling, or other forms of removal from the regular educational environment were to be limited to children who could not be educated in regular classes even with supplemental and supportive services.[77] Court decisions have upheld this principle, even when the analysis led to costly educational residential facilities.[78] Such results enabled children to avoid even more restrictive total institutionalization.

If the act's pledge of surrogate parents for children without family support were fully implemented,[79] many institutionalized persons who have no one to advocate their rights would benefit. Unfortunately, few states have established meaningful surrogate programs. Without such pressure, institutions often fail to accord their school-age residents the right to least restrictive educational environments.[80]

To remedy such patterns of noncompliance, legal advocates have been forced to bring suit.[81] For example, until a New Hampshire federal court intervened, the Laconia State School had taken few steps to appoint surrogates, to encourage parents and guardians to participate in the IEP process or otherwise comply with P.L. 94-142 requirements.[82] Similarly, New York State altered its exclusionary policies only after federal laws and court decrees required systematic efforts to ensure appropriate special-education and related services. As a matter of state policy, all institutional residents twenty-one years of age or younger are now entitled to six hours of educational programming per day, and to individual educational plans that prescribe, "whenever possible," education in community schools and encourage "maximal contact with non-handicapped peers."[83] In the absence of sustained and substantial participation by parents, surrogates, and other advocates, this policy is unlikely to succeed.

Medicaid and the Regulation of ICF-MR Programs

The Medicaid program similarly requires consumer involvement to achieve its habilitation promise. As explained in the previous chapter, each Medicaid-eligible resident of an approved intermediate care facility for the mentally retarded (ICF-MR) must be provided with an individually structured program of "active treatment."[84] Until 1974, the federal government imposed few specific programming requirements to ensure such treatment, thus permitting millions of Medicaid dollars to subsidize grossly substandard institutions. After the Senate threatened to enact accreditation standards into law and courts began to introduce their own standards, the Department of Health, Education and Welfare (HEW) promulgated detailed regulations as certification standards for facilities receiving Medicaid reimbursements.[85]

The Medicaid regulations were patterned after accreditation standards and the mental-retardation standards developed by the litigants in *Wyatt* v. *Stickney*. These became known as the ICF-MR standards, and covered such areas as admission and release policies, staffing, resident living, resident records, safety, sanitation, and professional programs and services. In keeping with the *Wyatt* standards, HEW barred the seclusion or corporal punishment of residents and limited the use of physical and chemical restraints.[86] Drawing on the Accreditation Council for Facilities for the Mentally Retarded (ACFMR) example, HEW's original standards specified staffing ratios for resident-care staff, but not for professional staff.[87] In contrast to *Wyatt*, the ICF-MR standards did not prescribe educational services or as many civil-rights protections. In lieu of specific ratios, regulations called for appropriately qualified professionals, sufficient in number to meet the residents' needs for training, habilitation, food, and nutrition, as well as medical, nursing, dental, pharmaceutical, occupational-therapy, psychological, recreation, social-work, speech-pathology, and audiology services. Yet ICF-MR facilities clearly had the burden of proving bona fide treatment efforts, and "furnishing documentary evidence" of each resident's progress and response to his or her habilitation program.[88]

These regulations had twin premises: that all retarded persons are capable of habilitation, and that professionals must be accountable for the design and implementation of active habilitation programs. Accordingly, every ICF-MR resident is entitled to training and habilitation services, "regardless of age, degree of retardation, or accompanying disabilities or handicaps."[89] Under the direction of a "Qualified Mental Retardation Professional," an interdisciplinary team is responsible for the delivery of each resident's care, training, and habilitation services. Every resident's individualized plan must include evidence of services designed to meet his or her "training and habilitation objectives."[90] At least once a year, the resident must receive a status review "by all relevant personnel" to consider program recommendations, alternatives to continued institutional residence, and the resident's legal status, including his or her opportunities for the exercise of "civil and legal rights."[91] A resident and his parent, guardian, or advocate are eligible to participate in these reviews; however, this seldom occurs in practice. Here again, retarded persons lack effective means to protest denials of their rights and chronic deficiencies in the quality of their care.

The Developmentally Disabled Assistance and Bill of Rights Act

By 1975, Congress decided the time had come to curb widespread institutional abuses and to provide retarded residents with legal remedies. As the chairman of the Senate Labor and Welfare Committee stressed, little change could be expected "unless substantial legal and advocacy pressure is forthcoming. While much can be said about the lack of funds to improve conditions at these institutions, at some point this country must draw the line. The abuses are too commonplace to point at a single institution or a single abuse and say that it is an anomally."[92]

The Developmentally Disabled Assistance and Bill of Rights Act represented a compromise. Twice the Senate unanimously passed bills virtually incorporating recent accreditation standards into federal law.[93] The Senate Bill of Rights for the Mentally Retarded, a vast opus on their "humane care, treatment [and] habilitation," was inspired, as Senator Javits put it, by the "shocking conditions at Willowbrook in New York, and many other institutions for the mentally retarded throughout the Nation."[94] The Senate but not the House version also provided detailed standards for community programs, including such matters as case-finding and personal advocacy services. The House instead called for planning efforts to eliminate inappropriate placement in institutions and to improve the quality of care and surroundings of institutionalized persons. In conference committee, the Senate gained recognition of essential entitlements and dropped the overly specific standards. Congress intended these rights to be taken seriously, recognizing that those who have "the misfortune to require institutionalization" have "a right to receive appropriate treatment for the conditions for which they are institutionalized," rights that should be "protected and assured by the Congress and the courts."[95]

Title II of the act, captioned "Establishment and Protection of the Rights of Persons with Developmental Disabilities," adopted unique approaches to vindicating these rights. First, Congress articulated a concise bill of rights, expressed as findings and government obligations to ensure the right to appropriate treatment, services, and habilitation in the least restrictive setting. The law also affirmed the obligation of federal and state governments to defund substandard programs.[96]

After the Supreme Court's controversial *Pennhurst* decision, these provisions of 42 U.S.C. § 6010, standing alone, are not judicially enforceable as substantive rights. They do, however, provide a basis for the Secretary of Health and Human Services to deny funds to recipient states that fail to comply with human rights assurances. Indeed, Congress specifically amended the act to link the rights outlined in section 6010 to the condition that states must submit plans satisfying the Secretary that the "human rights of all persons with developmental disabilities (especially those persons without familial protection)" will be protected.[97] At a minimum, states must offer assurances of their fidelity to this federal policy, or forgo financial assistance.[98]

The act's second major approach is to require individual habilitation plans. As an explicitly stated condition for federal financial assistance, states must guarantee that clients receiving residential and other habilitation services have a written, specifically stated habilitation plan in effect.[99] By law, the developmentally disabled person, and/or his parents, guardian, or other representative has the right to review the initial plan and to participate in periodic revisions.[100] A narrow reading of this requirement would confine its application to specific projects funded through the act, while an expansive interpretation would apply to all habilitation programs supported by the designated state administering agency. Yet, as Congress and the federal courts have repeatedly recognized, appropriate habilitation is determined through individual habilitation plans describing goals and services suited to a client's particular needs.[101] Therefore, the state's obligation to provide appropriate habilitation is intertwined with individualized planning.

The most dramatic innovation under this law is the federal funding of systems to protect and advocate the rights of developmentally disabled persons. Congress knew that something tougher than the empty threat of funding terminations was needed to achieve these rights. An independent advocacy system in every state could pursue wider remedies and become a flexible but persistent defender of the rights of those undergoing treatment. Thus, these agencies were authorized to pursue "legal, administrative and other appropriate remedies."[102] With the rights outlined in the act as their starting point, and along with the United States Justice Department and private attorneys, these agencies have sought remedies through judicial actions, information campaigns, and advocacy of administrative and policy reforms. Through impact strategies and individual cases, they attempted to bring state actions in line with the emerging statutory, constitutional, and human rights of developmentally disabled persons.[103]

The Federal Courts and Catastrophic Neglect

If conditions had been less oppressive or legislatures and executives more responsible, the federal courts might not have confronted problem-solving suits for the retarded. Litigants seeking institutionwide or systemwide standards raised novel legal claims requiring complex, ongoing forms of relief. Effective remedies called for invention and large infusions of energy and cash. Dramatic judicial interventions, however, were bound to raise exaggerated expectations of overnight reform from plaintiffs and cries of encroachment from defendants. One certainty was that such cases would prove time consuming and make heavy demands on the calendars, consciences, and capacities of federal judges.

Enlightened treatment professionals welcomed the success of these cases. As a result of courtroom theatre and affirmative decrees, the 1970s witnessed a resounding public affirmation of the rights of retarded people. This could be translated into new jobs, better working conditions, and professionally acceptable training for clients and staff. Even those who criticized undue judicial intrusion, such as Dr. Alan Stone of Harvard Law School, acknowledged that the suits of public interest lawyers represented the decade's most important development in "the quality of life in State institutions."[104] But program administrators still felt something of a love-hate relationship with the judicial process. Though they might welcome a court decree to bolster their appropriation requests, they were often uncomfortable with the increased accountability, paperwork, and exposure risks that go along with adversarial action.

Until *Wyatt* v. *Stickney*, discussions of the right to treatment had ignored retarded people.[105] Psychiatric treatment was the focus of early commentary, and involuntary care was the object of reform.[106] A few courageous judges in the 1960s had found the promise of some treatment implicit in indeterminate civil committal.[107] In *Rouse* v. *Cameron*, the Court of Appeals for the District of Columbia Circuit ruled that the petitioner, a patient in a federal mental hospital, could not be confined without adequate treatment.[108] Chief Judge Bazelon, relying on a District of Columbia statute entitling public mental patients to psychiatric care and treatment,[109] held that involuntarily committed patients had a judicially enforceable right to adequate treatment, and that the hospital had to make a bona fide effort to cure the patient. In dictum, the *Rouse* court acknowledged that serious constitutional questions of due process, equal protection, and cruel and unusual punishment would be presented if the statute were not interpreted to require adequate treatment. It would take six years before a federal court in Alabama would settle these questions and extend similar legal protection to retarded persons.

Wyatt proved a political as well as judicial landmark. Brought on behalf of residents of three Alabama institutions for the mentally disabled, this class action attacked an entire state system. By pioneering techniques of institutionwide standard setting, the *Wyatt* counsel avoided the pitfalls of individual case-by-case adjudication. The constitutional right to adequate habilitation for retarded persons, first affirmed as the law of the Fifth Circuit, soon gained judicial and scholarly support.[110] Most importantly, the facts unearthed in *Wyatt* provoked a national examination of the role of institutions and the services required to free retarded people for community living.

The right to habilitation had its roots in constitutional guarantees of due process, equal protection, and freedom from cruel and unusual punishment. Relying principally upon a substantive due process analysis and its prior holding that civilly committed mentally ill patients have a right to treatment, the *Wyatt* court reasoned that retarded residents were entitled to an analogous right. Chief Judge Frank M. Johnson, Jr., explained that no viable distinction could be made between the mentally ill and the mentally retarded regarding the "right to appropriate care for people civilly confined to public mental institutions."[111] When the state confined such persons on the altruistic theory of satisfying their need for treatment and then failed to provide it, the institution became little more than a prison. According to the court, the mentally retarded person possesses "an inviolable constitutional right to habilitation," and applicable legal principles "clear beyond cavil" require that people involuntarily committed through noncriminal procedures to institutions for the mentally retarded have a constitutional right to receive such individual habilitation as will give each of them "a realistic opportunity to lead a more useful and meaningful life and to return to society."[112]

The real breakthrough at Partlow was the creation of specific standards, thus demonstrating that the right to habilitation posed a judicially manageable dispute. The *Wyatt* opinions had referred to "adequate and effective treatment," "appropriate care," and "individual habilitation." The concept of habilitation was, in fact, broader than treatment, including medical, educational, and other training assistance to raise the level of the retarded person's physical, mental, and social efficiency. By framing minimum standards, the court avoided the pitfalls of case-by-case judicial determinations of the adequacy of each individual's treatment, an impractical task for a plaintiff class with over 8,000 members.

The *Wyatt* standards were the result of extensive consultations between the parties and nationally recognized experts. Initially, the court deferred any injunctive action against Alabama's mental hospitals, granting the defendants' request that they be allowed six months to file a report outlining minimum standards and their progress in implementation.[113] After the Alabama Mental Health Board again failed to promulgate and implement an adequate treatment program, Judge Johnson ordered hearings to allow the parties and *amici* to propose standards that would meet medical and constitutional requirements.

Judicial findings showed the defendants' programs defective in three basic respects: failure to provide a humane psychological and physical environment, insufficient numbers of qualified staff to administer adequate treatment, and lack of individualized treatment plans.[114] The then-amici curiae—the American Association on Mental Deficiency, the American Psychological Association, the American Orthopsychiatric Association, the American Civil Liberties Union, and the United States—were major participants in the trial, the inspections of Partlow, and the preparation of the constitutionally mandated minimum standards. Of the forty-nine standards incorporated in the court's decree as minimum constitutional standards for habilitation, all but four were part of a Memorandum of Agreement, stipulated to by the parties and the *amici*. Based on expert testimony, the court ordered the implementation of these agreed standards as well as the four disputed standards (on seclusion, pharmaceutical services, heating and ventilation, and the creation of a human rights committee).[115] But the court stopped short of more intrusive implementation measures: an advocacy unit, a professional advisory committee, and a special master.

The *Wyatt* standards defined civil-rights protections as well as qualitative habilitation norms. They expressed two dominant goals: the reentry of residents into appropriate community settings, and adequate habilitation programs for each resident to "live as normally as possible" and to "maximize his human abilities and enhance his ability to cope with his environment."[116] Endorsing the principle of normalization and its constitutional counterpart (the doctrine of least drastic alternatives), the standards emphasized the least restrictive conditions necessary to achieve the purposes of habilitation.[117] This included a general presumption favoring the movement of residents to smaller facilities and living units, units fostering more independent living in community surroundings.

In rebuffing Governor George Wallace's attempts to set aside the *Wyatt* orders, the United States Court of Appeals for the Fifth Circuit recognized mentally disabled persons as entitled to levels of rehabilitative treatment, habilitation, and care well beyond the custodial care characteristic of prisons.[118] Writing for a unanimous court, Judge Wisdom rejected the argument that an inability of some mentally disabled persons to care for themselves justified commitment and the provision of mere custody. Governor Wallace's counsel, referring to Erving Goffman, had asserted that the families and friends of the disabled were the true clients of an institutionalization system whose primary function was to relieve families of the burden of care. This misreading of Goffman was rejected. Even if adequate care was a sufficient state purpose, the state had failed to provide it. But on a deeper level, family convenience could not supply a constitutional justification for stripping the residents of "major personal interests" and their basic rights.[119] The appeals court endorsed the propriety of minimum institutional standards. This approach focused not on the merits of individual therapies, but on whether an institution confining persons for purposes of mental treatment had a program "institution-wide in scope" for formulating individual treatment plans. Thus the courts need not guarantee that "all patients will receive all the treatment they need or that may be appropriate to them," but only that the conditions in the state institutions will offer confined patients "a chance to receive adequate treatment."[120]

The defendants' attempt in 1979 to relitigate the *Wyatt* standards and carve out an exception for the "ineducable" severely disabled was a complete failure. Defendants and their experts had proposed dividing institutional residents into those who should receive education and training and the rest: "non-trainables" relegated to a so-called enriched environment. This dichotomy, recalling the two-tiered institutions of the past, was firmly rejected by the courts as an evasion of the constitutional right to habilitation. In reaffirming the centrality of each resident's right to habilitation programming, the court denied defendants' proposed modifications of various standards on rights to suitable education, comprehensive periodic evaluations, monthly record notations of resident's responses to programming, and basic staff ratios.[121] In two areas, however, the battle of expert witnesses yielded relaxation of standards. First, there was a very narrow exception for the admission of mildly retarded persons whose severe "additional handicaps . . . precludes their living in the community." Second, discretion was lodged with qualified mental-retardation professionals freeing them from writing postinstitutionalization plans for certain residents unlikely to be discharged.[122]

The institutional counterattack had fizzled and the basic philosophical premises of the *Wyatt* standards had emerged intact. Although remaining aloof from the professional debate on the benefits of community placement for the profoundly retarded, Judge Johnson clearly ruled that the defendants' failure to move residents from the large institutions to less restrictive settings constituted "substantial and serious noncompliance" with minimum constitutional standards of adequate habilitation. After seven years of failure to meet these and other standards on adequate programming, staffing, privacy, and protection from abuse and overmedication, the Alabama Mental Health Board had run out of excuses, except its own managerial bankruptcy. On October 16, 1979, Governor Fob James conceded as much by petitioning the court to appoint him receiver over all state mental institutions. In granting this extraordinary relief, the court required specific proposals, schedules, and cost estimates for achieving full compliance with the prior orders entered in this case.[123] The judge pointedly reminded the Mental Health Board of its large real-estate holdings as a potential source of financing.

The legacy of Ricky Wyatt and his fellow class members goes well beyond the law books. For all their deficiencies, the institutions of Alabama are decidedly cleaner, better maintained, and more professionally staffed than they were in 1972. Is Ricky Wyatt better off for the court's intervention? The irony is that as an individual he remains a virtually anonymous class representative, simply one of the legions of the displaced who wind up in state institutions.

Wyatt's case, however, cannot be forgotten by state officials who now are well aware of the political peril in permitting deplorably incompetent treatment. As a prophylactic measure, the *Wyatt* standards were widely adopted in psychiatric and retardation programs.[124] Challenges to the constitutionality of institutional treatment for juveniles, mental patients, and mentally retarded residents are now regularly heard by federal courts.[125] In a score of states, suits attacking substandard conditions in retardation institutions are well underway.[126] As the seminal right-to-treatment case, *Wyatt* has been cited with approval in the federal courts of appeals for the First,

Second, Third, Fifth, and Eighth Circuits, and in numerous district and state courts.[127]

To those who dismissed inhuman treatment in Alabama as merely a regional aberration, the evidence uncovered in progressive Minnesota must have been a shock. In 1950, Governor Youngdahl of Minnesota had eloquently pleaded for equal rights for the retarded, and criticized "barbaric" care.[128] David Vail, who led Minnesota's programs, wrote a book in 1966, *Dehumanization and the Institutional Career*, that exposed similar conditions. Eight years later, a federal district court found the residents of Cambridge State Hospital inadequately housed, equipped, fed, cared for, and treated. They had been denied minimally adequate treatment, confined in a a prisonlike atmosphere, and, primarily because of insufficient staff, subjected to inappropriate restraints. According to the testimony presented at a twelve-day trial, residents faced seclusion, excessive physical restraints (some 9,000 hours worth per month), and major tranquilizers used as standard procedure for some 70 percent of the residents.[129] Sadly, these conditions were typical of the six largest state hospitals in Minnesota, as well as those throughout the Midwest.

As in other states with laws granting retarded persons extensive rights, the federal district court in *Welsch* v. *Likins* held that the residents at Cambridge were entitled to adequate care and treatment under both state statutes and the federal constitution.[130] Minnesota law mandated a right to "proper care and treatment" and made references to "contemporary professional standards" of minimizing institutionalization. As a matter of substantive due process, retarded persons committed to state institutions without their consent were constitutionally guaranteed "minimally adequate treatment designed to give each committed person a realistic opportunity to be cured or to improve his or her mental condition."[131] The district court therefore ordered relief patterned after *Wyatt*: constitutional minimum standards on staffing ratios, individualized habilitation plans, a humane environment, and least restrictive settings. Even such physical improvements as carpeting, air conditioning, and removal of heavy wire mesh from windows were not luxury items, the court explained, but were based on testimony of health and safety hazards.

After months of only partial implementation of these remedial orders, Judge Larson sought tough enforcement measures. Enjoining a dozen state funding laws deemed barriers to full compliance, the court found that the people of the state of Minnesota, "despite the loftiest of motives," had continued to impose inhumane and unconstitutional conditions on the plaintiffs. No other forum except the federal judiciary had proved willing to "air their grievances, much less offer them redress."[132] Although the Eighth Circuit upheld the district court's power to enter affirmative injunctive relief, it remanded the case in order to give the Minnesota legislature another opportunity to cure the defaults on the plaintiffs' rights without drastic judicial intervention.[133]

Since then, constitutional confrontation has been avoided by comprehensive consent decrees. These replace earlier judicial orders and set detailed staffing, habilitation, physical-plant, placement, reporting, and monitoring requirements. The first applies to Cambridge State Hospital alone, boosting its complement of state full-time positions by nearly a third.[134] Since the lack of a specific enforcement mechanism had hampered implementation, the decree provides for the appointment of a monitor, empowered as a "neutral officer of the Court" to review compliance, resolve disputes, make findings of facts, and, ultimately, issue judicially enforceable recommendations. The decree also forestalls robbing Peter to pay Paul by prohibiting the state from simply shifting staff positions from other state hospitals to Cambridge, the focal point of litigation. A statewide decree now directly secures parity of treatment for the remaining *Welsch* subclasses.[135]

The *Pennhurst* case again confirms the monumental failure of institutional approaches, and the stubborn difficulties that beset legal reform. The district court ruled that the residents had a right to "minimally adequate habilitation" sufficient to afford them "a reasonable opportunity to acquire and maintain those life skills necessary to cope as effectively as their capacities permit."[136] Under the Pennsylvania Mental Health and Mental Retardation Act, Judge Broderick found a parallel state statutory right and a failure on the part of county and Commonwealth governments to assure the availability of adequate mental retardation programs.[137] But unlike earlier precedents, the *Pennhurst* opinion, in language recalling *Brown* v. *Board of Education*, condemned segregation in isolated facilities as clearly "separate and *not* equal." Even apart from these equal protection claims (which have yet to be adjudicated by appeals courts), Judge Broderick's opinion raised legal and practical doubts as to whether habilitation could truly take place in large, isolated institutions such as Pennhurst. Viewing that institution as counterproductive and "a monumental example of unconstitutionality," the court ordered a planned phaseout of Pennhurst and only modest internal reforms during its supposed interim operation. Instead of detailed standards, judicial injunctions called for certain precautions against abuse, neglect, mistreatment, excessive restraints, and health or safety hazards. Yet as the next chapter will suggest, replacing a large institution with community living arrangements is at best a slow, uncertain process. Given recent appellate decisions, even determined courts may not accomplish this aim in a single judicial stroke.

The prognosis is more favorable in states that have opted for consent decrees instead of court contests. Such settlements reflect a weighing of the precedents supporting the residents' claims,[138] as well as the parties' constructive desire to direct their energies to resolving the human problems rather than just winning lawsuits. This approach can reduce the risk of legislative intransigence to judicially imposed orders, and avert some sensitive questions of federalism. For instance, federal district courts in New York, Massachusetts, Ohio, Nebraska, Tennessee, Michigan, Maine, and West Virginia, have traveled that path, approving broad consent decrees to remedy barren and restrictive institutional conditions.[139] Although contesting those class actions in their initial stages, defendants typically entered consent judgments after motions to dismiss were denied or after damaging evidence was introduced. In granting relief, courts often incorporated the basic elements of the *Wyatt* standards, and issued memorandums affirming the constitutional basis for the remedy.[140] Therefore even in cases resolved without full adjudication, the drive toward recognition of retarded residents' constitutional and other legal rights gathered momentum.

Although the courts have sustained right-to-treatment standards with remarkable uniformity, a few judicial voices have dissented. But courts of appeals for the First, Third, and Fifth Circuits have overruled trial-court dismissals of such constitutional claims of institutionalized mentally ill patients.[141] Other judges, although declining to endorse a constitutional right to habilitation, have ordered massive reforms based on alternative constitutional or statutory theories (such as the Willowbrook and Laconia State School cases).[142] Even in rejecting marginal claims alleging a right to treatment in a particular geographic locale, courts have carefully distinguished claims of constitutional dimension from those aimed at securing the most effective treatment for the mentally retarded.[143]

A new generation of cases emphasize a single critical issue or a more narrowly drawn class of victimized individuals. These discrete class actions are potentially more manageable and less costly and time consuming than the omnibus class actions of the *Wyatt-Welsch-Willowbrook* variety. Individual lawsuits may have similar advantages, although those which pursue novel law-reform objectives or damage remedies often entail protracted legal combat.[144] In contrast to decade-long litigation into the myriad facets of institutional life, the newer cases target such strategic or highly symbolic grievances as sham investigations of abuse,[145] access to advocates,[146] sterilization,[147] the misuse of psychotropic drugs,[148] or denial of vocational programs and social benefits.[149] Whether such focused actions will provide speedier, more thorough relief or simply recycle limited state resources from one group of disabled persons to another is difficult to predict. At a time when the availability of free legal services is dwindling, more narrowly drawn litigation objectives will have obvious appeal.

Access to public education, for example, set the stage for other legal breakthroughs. Under pioneering federal cases, institutionalized retarded children must be afforded educational opportunities similar to their peers. In *Pennsylvania Association for Retarded Children* v. *Pennsylvania*, officials were permanently enjoined from denying or postponing a free public program of education and training to any mentally retarded person between the ages of six and twenty-one, including those institutionalized under the Department of Public Welfare's supervision.[150] *Mills* v. *Board of Education* went even further for a class of school-excluded children, specifically including physically and mentally handicapped plaintiffs who were institutionalized wards of the District of Columbia.[151] On equal protection, due process, and statutory grounds, the district court held that this plaintiff class had been denied their right to suitable publicly supported education. Depriving institutionalized children of this right, according to Judge Waddy, further violated compulsory-school-attendance laws and the custodian's obligation to ensure them regular instruction. If additional funds had not been forthcoming, the school authorities would have been obliged to reapportion their budget.

Although these cases were decided before *San Antonio School District* v. *Rodriguez* rejected education as a fundamental right justifying special constitutional protection under the strict-scrutiny test,[152] this Supreme Court decision would not have changed the outcome in *Mills* and *PARC*. *Rodriguez*, a school-financing case, far from reaching the question of children totally deprived of education, even suggested that some minimally adequate level of educational service might be constitutionally required.[153] Moreover, in *Rodriguez*, unlike the Supreme Court's decision in *Goss* v. *Lopez*,[154] due process issues were not raised concerning the hearing rights of a child threatened with suspension (let alone termination) from public education. A long line of federal and state courts have therefore correctly found Rodriguez no bar to ordering educational opportunities for institutionalized retarded or other disabled students denied appropriate educational services.[155] On constitutional as well as statutory grounds, the law guarantees at least a minimum education for all handicapped children.

Protection from Harm: The *Willowbrook* Case

An evolving body of constitutional, administrative, and common law protects the physical and mental integrity of retarded residents. Courts confronting harmful custodial environments have fashioned remedies that preserve the residents' developmental capacity and ensure affirmative programming to prevent regression. Appellate judges have also upheld decrees enjoining painful behavior-control techniques,[156] prolonged spread-eagling as a disciplinary punishment,[157] and lack of adequate heating.[158] Since retardation facilities must be able to ensure the residents' safety and well-being to perform their habilitative mission, the right to protection from harm can be derived from substantive due process guarantees of the Fourteenth Amendment, rather than the ban against cruel and unusual punishment.

The *Willowbrook* case, formally captioned *New York State Association for Retarded Children and Parisi* v. *Rockefeller*, has come to embody a consensus that both habilitation and protection from harm are best provided in a noninstitutional context. Originally, on March 17, 1972, when public interest lawyers filed two parallel class actions, the Willowbrook State School housed 5,209 residents. It was then the world's largest retardation institution, a desperately overcrowded, antitherapeutic environment. Improperly clothed, often left entirely naked, its residents lay idle, locked on wards giving off an "overpowering stench of sweat, urine, and human excrement."[160] With such appalling sanitary conditions, hepatitis and other infectious diseases were unchecked.[161] Residents lacked any semblance of habilitation: most had no schooling, no individualized programming, no speech therapy, and no means of getting to programs in the community. It was no hyperbole to describe Willowbrook as "at best a custodial warehouse, which provides them with nothing but food and shelter and a place to live until they die."[162] Living there amounted to a one-way ticket to oblivion.

The federal district court granted relief in two stages. On a motion for a preliminary injunction, Judge Orin G. Judd ordered steps to prevent further deterioration and harm to residents: a total prohibition on seclusion; sharp increases in ward attendants, recreation therapists, nurses, physicians, and physical therapists; and periodic reports on implementing health, safety, and care measures.[163] In a subsequent order, the court expressly reserved ruling on the right to treatment and related constitutional claims until necessary evidence and arguments could be introduced at the full trial.[164] At that trial, fifty witnesses (including nationally prominent experts, state employees, and parents) created a three-thousand-page transcript on conditions at Willowbrook, habilitative programming alternatives, and the effects of confining retarded persons in such a barren environment.

Ultimately, the right-to-habilitation issue was avoided by a final judgment on consent. That judgment reflected uncontroverted testimony that Willowbrook was overcrowded, understaffed, and marked by an institutional subculture exposing residents to nontherapeutic and dehumanizing practices. Rather than suffer further adverse publicity and the risk of more stringent judicial remedies, the state of New York agreed to reduce Willowbrook in phases and to furnish residents with habilitation services to prepare them for living in new homes outside the institution. In an opinion approving the consent decree, Judge Judd explained that "protection from harm requires more extensive relief than this court originally contemplated because harm can result not only from neglect but from conditions which cause regression or which prevent development of an individual's capabilities."[165] As the court recognized, no bright line separates the legal rubrics of protection from harm, right to treatment, or right to care.

The Willowbrook Consent Decree

The *Willowbrook* standards were neither optimal nor custodial. As Judge Judd candidly acknowledged in surveying the precedents upholding the treatment and habilitation rights of the mentally disabled, the relief for the *Willowbrook* plaintiffs advanced "the very rights enunciated in the case law."[166] Most notably, the decree set ambitious timetables for the development of new community alternatives, and created elaborate enforcement mechanisms to monitor the proposed community placements as well as the institutional reforms. The court judgment recognized that retarded persons "regardless of the degree of handicapping conditions, are capable of physical, intellectual, emotional and social growth." Yet without "affirmative intervention and programming" that capacity for growth could be lost.[167]

Addressing twenty-three topics, these standards provided a liberal interpretation of this required level of programming. Each resident was entitled to an individual plan of care, development, and services, a plan compiled by an interdisciplinary team, reviewed at least quarterly, and prepared with the "assistance of the resident, his or her parents, relatives or guardian."[168] Unless the resident was specifically exempted for medical reasons, this development plan specified a minimum of six scheduled hours of programming per weekday. With requirements ranging from professional staff to safety, from residents' living conditions to limits on behavior modification or experimentation on human subjects, the *Willowbrook* decree on the whole matched the *Wyatt* standards in breadth and detail.

Its most eye-opening departure was the planned dispersal of the Willowbrook population over a six-year period. Until new community alternatives could be created, Willowbrook's primary function would be to train and educate residents in preparation for future transfers; indeed, to provide "the least restrictive and most normal living conditions possible."[169] But those twin tasks of deinstitutionalization and institutional reform, as chapter 6 documents, frequently proved incompatible. Ironically, the plaintiffs perhaps won too much at the bargaining tables, thereby scattering reform energies in too many directions.

The Willowbrook Review Panel

The creation of a professionally staffed Willowbrook Review Panel represented a striking innovation in monitoring, consulting, and reporting functions. The panel, acting as the eyes and ears of the court, made field investigations and formal and informal recommendations to the parties regarding problems of compliance. With a full-time staff of program monitors and a seven-member panel of leading mental retardation experts, the panel was intended to shoulder the burdens of investigating and acting on day-to-day complaints. Viewing the panel as a cooperative rather than an adversarial device, the court had hoped that amicable resolutions by the panel and parties would minimize its own involvement. Yet in time the relationship between the panel and state officials became a source of friction, as the panel asserted its powers to advise and consult and not merely to criticize after the fact.[170] The state's denial of funding to the review panel, upheld by the Second Circuit, had the result of crippling if not abolishing its functions, and cutting off a potential flow of adverse information. This strategy backfired, however, by forcing the plaintiffs to return to the court to press contempt motions and to again expose deficient care.[171]

Unlike the Partlow Human Rights Committee, hobbled by lack of staff and unclear lines of authority,[172] the Willowbrook Review Panel once had a substantial budget and the will to exercise well-delineated powers. The panel represented a compromise between a special master[173] empowered to oversee implementation of a court decree,[174] and a citizen's human rights (such as Partlow's) that had little more than a watching brief to "ensure that the dignity and human rights of patients are preserved."[175] In conception if not structure, the review panel resembled the court appointment of expert consultants in school-exclusion or desegregation cases to devise remedies.[176] Yet its powers were far wider and included the ability to make binding recommendations to achieve or maintain compliance with the decree. In fact, the panel operated as the core element in an ongoing process of mediation and adjudication.

The Implementation Process: Education and Impacts beyond Willowbrook

Like other omnibus class actions, the *Willowbrook* judgment required full programs of education for residents, including those over the age of twenty-one.[177] Their educational services had to be "generally equivalent" to the special educational services provided in New York City.[178] The decree further specified class-size maximums, year-round educational services (where individually required), provision of teachers' aides, and special programs for the multiply handicapped.[179] All school-age residents were entitled to six hours of instruction per day, with a shorter school day permitted only if a physician certified in writing that the full school day would be "medically harmful" to a resident.[180] Criteria such as toilet training could no longer constitute a precondition to a child's receiving educational services.

Implementing these standards revealed some of the pitfalls of institutional reform. Even among themselves, the defendants and their staff were never quite sure of how to define education. By early 1976, the Willowbrook Review Panel had alerted the court to the problem of insufficient school programs.[181] The panel recommended that the defendants retain an expert consultant to assess the educational needs of all Willowbrook residents and to submit a comprehensive education plan. In upholding that recommendation, Judge Judd warned against further delay and directed preliminary steps to bring the defendants' educational program "into conformity with the Judgment."[182]

Reports of the Willowbrook Review Panel documented the defendants' mixed record of compliance with educational standards. Defining and assessing full compliance raised sharp differences of professional opinion. It was clear, however, that some children received less than six hours of daily education for reasons entirely unrelated to medical harm.[183] The process of implementation was also hampered by the sluggish response of administrators to new responsibilities, such as the requirements to arrange school placements in the public schools and to furnish year-round educational services. But the larger problem was posed by the tension between the goals of making Willowbrook's educational standards equivalent to those of public schools, and of transferring its residents to better, less-restrictive education programs in the community. Although the panel ultimately agreed to set a higher priority on off-campus placement,[184] similar conflicts marked the attempt to reform other habilitative services.

Even with only partial compliance, the *Willowbrook* litigation did much to redirect the delivery of care for retarded persons. As a matter of policy, the state agreed to apply the *Willowbrook* standards to all other institutions and to upgrade their services as soon as possible. Because *Willowbrook* class members transferred to other facilities were still under the consent judgment, any attempt to create a two-tier system of retardation care based on past Willowbrook residence would have proved unworkable and inequitable. Seeking to avoid that result, the state Office of Mental Retardation incorporated many of the *Willowbrook* standards on education and habilitation in the policy directives covering all of its facilities.[185]

These steps were not sufficient to prevent skewed resource allocations. Nor did they foreclose new class actions targeting other large New York institutions posing threats of harm to residents. In a civil rights suit concerning the Wassaic Developmental Center, for example, the New York State Association for Retarded Children argued that the 2,567 residents suffered from overcrowding and a "psychologically destructive atmosphere." Like other parent groups, they sought judicial enforcement of standards matching the *Willowbrook* agreement.[186] The plaintiffs later abandoned their action in return for a three-pronged settlement: an operational plan to establish quality services meeting the residents' needs; a consultative role for plaintiffs' experts in the plan's development; and monitoring of the plan's implementation by the federally funded advocacy agency, plaintiffs' counsel.[187] But in Long Island and upstate institutions, plaintiff groups were not so easily satisfied, and class suits for more thorough community-centered remedies went forward.[188] Perceptions of windfall services for the *Willowbrook* class clearly contributed to the pressure to sue. Widely publicized, the *Willowbrook* case had become a benchmark for reformers and a pilot project for administrators.

The Case for Stricter State Scrutiny

Despite dramatic relief through the federal courts, it is difficult to imagine this judicial surveillance of state mental retardation programs as more than an interim measure. That interim, however, may be a protracted one, unless states are more zealous in protecting the rights of their retarded citizens. Moreover, it is the states' primary obligation to fashion their own specific mechanisms for ensuring quality care and respect for the legal and human rights of the residents of facilities for the developmentally disabled. Notwithstanding state laws that place the general superintendence, regulation, and control of such facilities under state and local governments, those units have been historically lax in enforcing their own care standards. State statutes frequently failed to ensure that retarded persons were protected from discrimination and other practices incompatible with due process.[189] Existing laws on rights to training or treatment were often ignored in practice by state employeees who were, for the most part, misinformed or uninformed of the contents of these laws.[190]

Residents' Rights in New York

Although its laws were more detailed than most, New York was no exception to this pattern. On its face, Article 33 of the Mental Hygiene Law, "Rights of Patients," provides a significant array of rights relating to inpatient care. For example, it guarantees a right to treatment and promises that admission into care shall not deprive any person of his or her civil rights.[191] Every resident of a mental facility is entitled to receive "care and treatment that is suited to his needs and skillfully, safely and humanely administered."[192] Such individualized treatment must be provided with full respect for the resident's "dignity and personal integrity." By law, each patient must have at least an annual periodic review; medical, dental, and mental evaluations and reevaluations; entry of all written treatment plans, periodic examinations, and individualized treatment programs in the patient's clinical record; and treatment based on the order of a staff member "operating within the scope of a professional license" and "appropriate examination." Section 33.03 also codifies the common-law requirement of patient consent for surgery, major medical treatment "in the nature of surgery," shock treatment, or the use of experimental drugs or procedures.[193] In addition, statutory provisions define the rights of institutional residents to education, to be free from uncompensated involuntary labor, and to the writ of habeas corpus.[194]

Although these rights apply to mental patients and retarded residents, the New York Office of Mental Retardation and Developmental Disabilities (OMRDD) has specific responsibility for ensuring that residents of state-provided or state-licensed facilities receive quality care and treatment, and that their personal and civil rights are protected.[195]

Consistent with the state policy of providing retarded individuals "appropriate care and treatment close to their families and community,"[196] the OMRDD commissioner must conduct comprehensive programs of care, treatment, rehabilitation, training, and education. But despite that mission, the bulk of the OMRDD's direct care and treatment services is still delivered in remotely located facilities (twenty-one developmental centers for the care, treatment, training and education of the mentally retarded).

Without distinction as to legal status or mode of admission, each resident has statutory and regulatory rights to care, treatment, and related habilitative services. Facility directors are responsible for supervising the residents' care and treatment, ensuring their humane treatment, and investigating every case of alleged resident abuse or mistreatment.[197] Administrative regulations and policy statements outline standards of care and treatment that reflect the areas of concern enumerated in *Wyatt* v. *Stickney*: a humane environment, a qualified and sufficient staff to administer adequate treatment, and individualized treatment plans.[198] Each client has the "right to adequate care, treatment and rehabilitation" in a "physically safe, sanitary, convenient and comfortable" facility.[199]

The problems arise in enforcing such standards. Under the New York constitution and the Mental Hygiene Law, the commissioner or his representative must visit and inspect all public and private facilities for the care, treatment, and rehabilitation of the mentally disabled.[200] When conducting onsite reviews, inspectors must review restraint and seclusion records, legal admission documents and procedures, medication procedures, staffing patterns, and other specific matters.[201] This quality control has been undermined, however, by the state's inability to impose meaningful financial penalties on substandard programs or to take effective license-revocation action when residents are endangered. Moreover, though the statute specifies that licensed facilities shall be inspected at least twice each year (once without prior notice), there is no requirement as to the frequency of inspection for departmental facilities.[202] Given a shortage of inspectors and a statutory scheme requiring inspections as part of a licensing procedure, inspectors tend to concentrate on private facilities. Yet, ironically, some developmental centers cannot meet the regulatory standards that the state imposes on private service-providers.

Each state developmental center has a Board of Visitors, but these volunteers are no substitute for a rigorous inspectorate. Appointed by the governor, the seven-member boards are to consult, advise, and work with the institutional directors on such matters as facility conditions, programs, and activities.[203] At least once every three months, a board member or committee of members must make a facility inspection, and annually they submit recommendations and an assessment of conditions. Empowered to investigate all cases of alleged resident abuse or mistreatment, the Board of Visitors can interview residents and employees, subpoena witnesses and compel testimony under oath.[204] But given the directors' primary responsibility in such cases, boards tend to simply defer to directors. According to a state Senate report, "At their worst, they are social clubs whose members have accepted honorariums from the governor, not infrequently because of a political relationship. They gather bi-monthly to nod assent to the director's activities and explanations of conditions."[205] At Willowbrook and elsewhere, they had failed to sound an alarm.

By 1977, New York's lawmakers recognized the need for greater accountability and stronger oversight agencies. The state Commission on Quality of Care for the Mentally Disabled was therefore created to perform monitoring and advisory functions. Its statutory purposes include aiding the governor in ensuring a "uniformly high standard" of care; fashioning procedures for "effective investigation" and speedy, impartial review of resident abuse and mistreatment allegations; inspecting facilities; and making written findings and recommendations on investigative matters referred to its attention.[206] Although the commission has the power to place its staff as monitors in any mental facility deemed "an imminent danger to the health or safety" of the residents, this power has yet to be used. Within the commission, the New York legislature also established a Board of Visitors Advisory Council to orient board members and increase their capabilities to make site reviews. The Mental Hygiene Medical Review Board, established to investigate unusual deaths of facility residents, has also been organized under the commission. Through investigations of some five hundred of the three thousand reported deaths, these agencies have questioned poor staff training, failure to use community hospitals, unnecessary surgery, and other systemic breakdowns.[207]

At a consumer's level, the legislature also mandated steps to inform patients and their representatives of their rights. It directed the OMRDD and OMH commissioners to prepare and distribute separate manuals in clear language describing the rights of mental patients and retarded residents.[208] At the time of admission, residents (as well as persons authorized to act on their behalf) are to receive a manual informing them of their rights and describing the institution's educational and rehabilitative services.

The State Right to Treatment

Although the state right to treatment is a counterpart to federal constitutional due process, its remedial outcomes have been far more limited. In *Kesselbrenner* v. *Anonymous,* the New York Court of Appeals held that a civilly committed mental patient as a matter of constitutional law is entitled to a confinement under conditions that are therapeutic and not punitive.[209] Similarly, for juveniles adjudicated as Persons in Need of Supervision (PINS), that court has twice construed a care and protection statute as requiring a right to adequate individualized treatment as a matter of due process.[210] Indeed, as the Second Circuit Court of Appeals and New York's highest court have made clear, the state constitutional right to reasonable care and treatment, though relying on leading federal cases, represents a parallel but independent ground of action.[211] The fulfillment of that right, as state courts have explained, demands the presence of a bona-fide treatment program, entailing adequate staff, facilities, and each client's periodic reassessment.[212]

Retarded persons placed in the custody of state institutions clearly have analogous needs for and rights to adequate treatment and supervision. In *Renelli* v. *Department of Mental Hygiene,* a New York supreme court held that when the state undertakes responsibility for the institutional care of a retarded person, it must provide a program of adequate care and treatment.[213] The evidence demonstrated that Adrienne Renelli, a twenty-two-year-old Willowbrook resident, had markedly deteriorated because of the lack of a structured habilitation program. Relying on *Wyatt* and statutory treatment, care, training, and education provisions, the trial judge held the state in violation of the resident's right to adequate treatment under both the U.S. Constitution and the New York Mental Hygiene Law. Finding that Adrienne's institutional caretakers had "made no meaningful attempt" to improve her condition, the court ordered the Department of Mental Hygiene to devise a specific habilitation program that would afford her the opportunity to learn basic life skills. Though Renelli was listed as a voluntary resident since her parents had placed her in the institution, this did not limit her right to treatment. When mentally disabled persons have little or no effective choice, courts have upheld their treatment rights, notwithstanding a nominal voluntary status.[214] In New York State developmental centers where only 45 of the 14,067 residents have involuntary status, any other result would be manifestly unjust.[215]

Toward a Unitary Educational System

Education law is still in transition from a dual to unitary system of accommodating handicapped children. The New York constitution long recognized the state's obligation to provide a system of free schools "wherein all the childen of this state may be educated."[216] But education laws, by exempting children classified as unable to "benefit from instruction," had created loopholes and exclusions eventually evoking strong judicial criticism.[217] By 1976, under pressures of new federal legislation and a mounting number of state-court decisions ordering special education for handicapped individuals, the New York legislature enacted Article 89 of the Education Law, an inclusive approach to identifying, evaluating, and placing all handicapped children in need of special services.[218]

In every school district, a Committee on the Handicapped must review each handicapped child's condition and recommend placement for a "free appropriate public education." Before changing the child's educational placement, the committee must give the parents prior written notice. Each district board of education then has the duty to furnish the individual handicapped child, directly or by contract, with "suitable educational opportunities."[219] Any parent or guardian who objects to the local board's determination has the right to administrative proceedings before an impartial hearing officer, and can ultimately appeal to the State Commissioner of Education. Children in local school districts thus draw upon the resources of a well-articulated education system. If educational services close to home are unavailable, they may obtain, if necessary, free transportation, tuition, and maintenance expenses while attending a residential school.

Children in institutions for the retarded, in contrast, primarily look to the OMRDD commissioner for their educational fare. Although the Mental Hygiene Law required equality of educational opportunity for those in state-run facilities, generations of institutionalized children had been cruelly deprived of necessary education. The state developmental centers, struggling to fulfill even basic care responsibilities, had great trouble mounting full-scale educational programs.

Under scattered legislation, the outline of a unitary educational system can be glimpsed. Recent state laws authorize the admission of some institutionalized children to local school programs. The cost of those educational services thereby becomes a charge on the child's home school district and the local Committee on the Handicapped can now review and evaluate the status of each handicapped child placed from their district into a state facility.[220] Article 89 empowers boards of education to contract for special programs and services, including private residential and nonresidential schools deemed "reasonable and appropriate," for children for whom public education programs are unavailable.[221] To prevent unnecessary placement in residential state facilities, the law places a priority on appropriate nonresidential schools, and even bars the state commissioner of education from considering the state's residential facilities when approving contractual services for a child in private school. These directions are positive; however, they fall far short of the full transfer of educational responsibilities for mentally disabled children from mental-health to education authorities, a divestiture that has been undertaken in the United Kingdom and elsewhere.[222]

Litigation thus often focuses on the costs of placing handicapped children in residential schools. In *Levy* v. *City of New York,* the Court of Appeals upheld the constitutionality of education laws requiring parents of some handicapped children to contribute to maintenance costs incidental to residential schooling, while blind or deaf children receive free maintenance in boarding schools.[223] Although all children are entitled to free tuition or transportation expenses when compelled to attend special-education programs lacking in the public schools, the court refused to invalidate this legislative differentiation between the blind or deaf and other handicapped persons. The logic of *Levy* has since been followed in a challenge to a statute imposing maintenance fees for care in state retardation institutions. However, in *State Department of Mental Hygiene* v. *Schneps,* the parent was relieved of any obligation to pay these fees, since his daughter had received "little or no care" and "grossly inadequate maintenance" during her three-year stay at the Willowbrook State School.[224]

Subsequent legislation rejects a parental-means test for school-age residents. The New York Education Law, for example, imposes the maintenance expense for placing a handicapped child in a residential school upon the county or municipality.[225] Recent amendments to the Family Court Act no longer impose parental contribution for these incidental expenses.[226] With these legislative changes, the state has come into compliance with federal regulations requiring that educational programming (including nonmedical care, room, and board) should be furnished without cost to the parents when a private or public residential program is necessary to provide special-education and related services to the handicapped child.[227]

Resident Abuse and Administrative Law

The abuse of helpless residents by staff members remains one of the most vexing legal problems. Despite mounting public concern over the volume of incident reports, administrators still encounter serious obstacles to removing employees implicated in misconduct. The Mental Health Information Service, at the direction of the New York legislature, reported on internal procedures for handling patient abuse, and documented "serious deficiencies" that threatened the "rights of patients to humane treatment."[228] Their investigation revealed unreported incidents of patient abuse, lack of notice to the statutory-empowered watch-dog agencies, inadequate internal investigation of charges, "overly informal" disciplinary arbitration hearings, and only limited protection of the patients' interests in those hearings. Though employees were represented by able union lawyers, the DMH's ad hoc investigative system failed to uncover or present the relevant facts. The distinct interests of injured patients or residents are seldom directly represented. Those interests are compromised by more than simply the state's ineffective presentations of its cases. Under the arbitration process then in force under the union contract, only 18 percent of the arbitrated cases of alleged patient abuse resulted in employee terminations, compared to a 50-percent termination rate under former procedures. Not surprisingly, patients are reluctant to report abuse incidents; some are even advised by staff members to forget serious charges because such charges often result "in more trouble for the patient than the employee."[229]

Some courts have come to the aid of residents victimized by employee assaults. In *Brown* v. *Ristich,* the New York Court of Appeals held that unsworn testimony in administrative proceedings is admissible from retarded witnesses possessing rudimentary testimonial capacity.[230] A twenty-two-year-old Willowbrook resident with an IQ of 43 and a mental age of four to six years old complained that an attendant had struck her in the head with a broom handle causing a serious laceration. Following a hearing at which the complainant and another eyewitness were permitted to testify without being sworn, the attendant was dismissed. The hearing officer had heard a psychologist's evidence that the two residents were competent to give testimony and knew the difference between telling the truth and telling a lie. Nonetheless, the Appellate Division summarily annulled the administrative determination because of its reliance on unsworn testimony. The Court of Appeals reversed and reinstated the employee's dismissal, explaining that the lower court had failed to distinguish between the concept of testimonial capacity and the ritual of a formalistic oath. The court reasoned that such administrative proceedings were not meant to be governed by technical rules of evidence, that even in criminal proceedings children under the age of twelve unable to understand the oath can give unsworn testimony, and that policy considerations of protecting residents' rights provided a subordinate and valid motivation for its holding.

Firing the wrongdoer can provoke hard-fought legal battles to the state's highest court. These cases reveal patterns of abuse in retardation institutions across the state.[231] Hearing officers have often recommended only fifty-dollar fines or short suspensions,[232] but the directors, with final authority to determine employee misconduct, have sought more stringent penalties.

Yet employees dismissed for resident mistreatment often retain their jobs as a result of the institution's own procedural errors. In *Simpson* v. *Wolansky,* a ward aide accused of sexual intercourse with a resident could not be fired since the director's initial dismissal determination was partially based on considerations outside the hearing record, and his second determination was not supported by substantial evidence.[233] The director stated that he had considered every aspect of such a case, even if it did not appear in the hearing transcript. This, the Court of Appeals held, violated the rule that an administrative agency may not base a decision of an adjudicatory nature, where there is a right to a hearing, upon evidence or information outside the record. In another case of a provisional employee who could have been dismissed without a reason and without a hearing, a court vacated a dismissal determination because a finding of physical abuse of a resident involved the employee's "good name or reputation," thus entitling him to a due process hearing.[234] Other firing attempts have failed in instances where a director denied a rehearing to an attendant seeking to introduce subsequently discovered alleged inconsistencies in the statements of a retarded eyewitness, and where posthearing communications between the hearing officer and the DMH employee prosecuting a charge contravened fundamental fairness.[235] As these cases suggest, state facilities must have access to effective investigators and counsel if they are to remove incompetent or abusive employees and deter a violent institutional subculture.

Negligence Actions

Given these notorious conditions, it is curious to find so few civil actions for damages and almost no criminal prosecutions initiated by or on behalf of the residents of these facilities.[236] In the past, the legal process put such little value on the lives of retarded residents that recovery was impossible; for example, an action for the wrongful death of a twenty-eight-year-old man was denied on the ground that the decedent had no reasonable prospect of release from the institution if he had lived.[237] In repudiating this pessimistic philosophy, the postwar Court of Appeals spoke of New York's duty to treat and care for "its mental defective wards, with an eye toward returning them to society more useful citizens."[238]

Negligent supervision of retarded residents, in part because of inadequate staffing, has led to serious injuries to residents and breaches of this duty. For example, in 1965, the Court of Claims ruled that a mentally retarded resident should recover damages when institutional attendants, knowing that he was mentally agitated, failed to exercise extremely careful supervision.[239] The court further held that the plaintiff, because of his retardation, could not be found contributorily negligent for smashing his hand through two unscreened windows. In *Doty* v. *State,* the court reaffirmed that a state school for the retarded owed its residents the duty of "every reasonable care" to protect them from self-inflicted or other injury, the degree of such care to be measured by the resident's known physical and mental ailments.[240] In that case, the claimant had lost an eye as a result of having a knife thrown at him by another resident working in the institution's kitchen.

Severely retarded persons face special problems in winning a recovery. Appellate cases have reversed or reduced damage awards in claims involving inadequate medical treatment to retarded residents.[241] Although a 1968 New York case awarded damages to a mental patient confined under custodial care for fourteen years without adequate medical treatment,[242] no similar case has been brought on behalf of a retarded resident. Evidentiary problems are part of the explanation. In *Rodriguez* v. *State,* a nonambulatory five-year-old Willowbrook resident had suffered a fractured leg under unexplained circumstances.[243] Since the child could give no account of the cause of her injury, the court attempted to apply the doctrine of *res ipsa loquitur* to overcome the problems of proof. Taking judicial notice of the overcrowding and inadequate staffing documented in the *Willowbrook* case, the court cited the state's affirmative statutory duty to provide high quality care and treatment, and went on to apply the *res ipsa loquitur* doctrine, since the state DMH had control over the probable instrumentalities causing the injury and the injury was presumed to result from the act of an attendant or a resident. In reversing the judgment awarding the child $3,000 for her pain and suffering, the Appellate Division dismissed the case on the basis that no showing had been made of the state's negligence.[244] According to the panel, this doctrine could only be invoked after the introduction of evidence demonstrating a probability that the accident could not have occurred in the absence of negligence.

Damage actions have clearly not been a meaningful deterrent to inadequate care and treatment within state retardation facilities. Since 1973, the Mental Hygiene Law no longer contains any extraordinary impediment to such damage claims against departmental employees.[245] But this legal change hardly matters, when even the few residents and their families who are aware of possibilities for bringing such actions have well-grounded fears of either violent or subtle victimization.[246] Collecting and presenting evidence is also a difficult task in closed institutions where infirm residents, although competent to testify, have little ability to withstand stern cross-examination. Potential claimants are likely to encounter a barrage of affirmative defenses: that a judicial declaration of incompetence or commitment to a state mental institution does not preclude contributory negligence;[247] that the claim is barred by the lapse of time since its accrual;[248] that an action against the state and against other defendants cannot be prosecuted in the same court; or that negligent professional judgments by the state are not actionable under the government-immunity doctrine.[249] Even if the retarded resident can surmount the practical and legal obstacles to establishing liability, a substantial damage award is seldom obtained. The resident may have little or no earning capacity, and may already receive free medical care, board, and other services. Furthermore, because of the statutory indemnification of state employees and other persons rendering professional treatment services to OMRDD clients[250] or otherwise acting within the scope of public employment duties,[251] the rare monetary judgment has little pocketbook impact on the caretakers.

Conclusion

Unless the state's performance can come closer to its promises, private legal actions will become more common. Changes in due process now give clients and their representatives the right to object to care and treatment received. When there is disagreement with a hearing officer's findings at the local level, clients can appeal to the OMRDD commissioner. In an era when parents and advocates no longer go hat in hand to the authorities, the grievances not satisfactorily resolved in administrative chains of command will surely spill over into the courts.

It is a depressing but accurate reflection of the current law that New York State is neither alone nor most recalcitrant in responding to institutional scandals. Indeed, as of 1981, the average annual cost of care for an institutionalized mentally retarded person in New York was $53,200. The rapid escalation of these costs nationally is partly a result of effective legal reforms and the attention thereby drawn to the historic negation of retarded people's rights. But precisely because of this new visibility and heightened civil rights expectations, the gap between declared rights and their implementation seems ever wider. Measured against the evolving legal framework identified in this chapter, developmental centers and state schools in the United States are costly anachronisms. Though the rights to care, habilitation, and education exist, the means of their delivery are inchoate. Pressure from costs and courts may, however, speed a community solution.

Notes

1. *See* H. Best, *Public Provisions for the Mentally Retarded in the United States* 250 (1965).

2. *E.g.*, M. Maloney & M. Ward, *Mental Retardation and Modern Society* 297 (1979).

3. *E.g.*, D. Vail, *Dehumanization and the Institutional Career* (1967); U.S. President's Comm. on Mental Retardation [hereinafter P.C.M.R.] *MR 69: Toward Progress* (1969); G. Rivera, *Willowbrook* (1972).

4. P.C.M.R., *MR 71: The Decisive Decade* 1 (1971); P.C.M.R., *Residential Services for the Mentally Retarded: An Action Policy Proposal* v (1970); P.C.M.R., "A Renewed National Commitment," in President's Comm'n on Mental Health, IV *Appendix: Task Panel Reports* 2022, 2023-29 (1978); National Ass'n for Retarded Children, *Policy Statements on Residential Care* (1968); National Ass'n for Retarded Citizens, *Residential Services* 4 (1976).

5. Wyatt v. Stickney, 344 F. Supp. 387, 393-94 n.13 (M.D. Ala. 1972). *See* Halderman v. Pennhurst State School and Hospital, 446 F. Supp. 1295, 1308-10 (E.D. Pa. 1977) [Hereinafter cited as *Pennhurst*] (resident killed by another in pushing incident; in one month alone, 833 minor and 25 major injuries reported).

6. *See, e.g.*, Michigan Ass'n for Retarded Citizens v. Smith, 475 F. Supp. 990 (E.D. Mich. 1979).

7. Record, Partlow Hearing at 24, Wyatt v. Stickney, 344 F. Supp. 387 (M.D. Ala. 1972).

8. New York State Ass'n for Retarded Children v. Rockefeller [hereinafter cited as *Willowbrook*], 357 F. Supp. 752 (E.D.N.Y. 1973); Wyatt v. Stickney, 344 F. Supp. 387, 394 (M.D. Ala. 1972).

9. *See generally* DeVellis, "Learned Helplessness in Institutions," 15 *Mental Retardation* 10 (Oct. 1977).

10. *See* Thompson & Grabowski, "Ethical and Legal Guidelines for Behavior Modification," in *Behavior Modification of the Mentally Retarded* 511 (2d ed. T. Thompson & J. Grabowski 1977).

11. *See, e.g., Pennhurst*, 446 F. Supp. 1295 (E.D. Pa. 1977), *aff'd in part*, 612 F.2d 84 (3d Cir. 1979), *rev'd*, 451 U.S. 1 (1981), *aff'd on other grounds*, 673 F.2d 628 (3d Cir. 1982), *cert. granted*, 102 S. Ct. 2956 (1982) (right to least restrictive habilitation for class of current, as well as potential residents of the institution). *But see* Sundheimer v. Blum, 79 A.D.2d 512, 433 N.Y.S.2d 456 (1980) (reversing supreme court order on equal protection claims to family care payments for parents of retarded persons living in their own homes).

12. *See generally* A. Scull, *Decarceration: Community Treatment and the Deviant—A Radical View* (1977).

13. For discussion of one such controversy, see *Mental Retardation and Sterilization: A Problem of Competency and Paternalism* (R. Macklin & W. Gaylin eds. 1981).

14. *E.g.*, Wyatt v. Hardin, Civ. No. 3195-N (M.D. Ala. June 26, 1975); United States v. Codina, Crim. No. 75-10-N (M.D. Ala. June 26, 1975) (ad-

ministrators and doctors found not guilty of criminal contempt of court, even though doctors had administered hazardous treatment in violation of the standard of "express and informed consent after consultation with counsel or interested party of the patient's choice").

15. See Greenblatt, "Class Action and the Right to Treatment," 25 *Hosp. and Community Psychiatry* 449 (1974).

16. New York State Ass'n for Retarded Children v. Carey, 492 F. Supp. 1110 (E.D.N.Y. 1980), *rev'd*, 631 F.2d 162 (2d Cir. 1980) (state legislature can "de-fund" Willowbrook Review Panel); Halderman v. Pennhurst State School, 673 F.2d 628 (3d Cir. 1982) (legislature acted improperly in denying funds for court-appointed masters, by failure to seek a modification of the order).

17. *See generally* Mickenberg, "The Silent Clients: Legal and Ethical Considerations in Representing Severely and Profoundly Retarded Individuals," 31 *Stan. L. Rev.* 625 (1979); American Ass'n on Mental Deficiency, *Consent Handbook* (1977); R. Burt, *Taking Care of Strangers* (1979).

18. *See, e.g.*, Nelson v. Heyne, 491 F.2d 352, 360 (7th Cir. 1974), *cert. denied*, 417 U.S. 976 (1974); Burnham v. Dep't of Public Health, 503 F.2d 1319 (5th Cir. 1974), *cert. denied*, 422 U.S. 1057 (1975).

19. Mack, "The Juvenile Court," 23 *Harv. L. Rev.* 104, 114 (1909).

20. *In re* Philip B., 92 Cal. App. 3d 796 (1st Dist. 1979), *cert. denied sub nom.* Bothman v. Warren B., 445 U.S. 949 (1980); New York State Ass'n for Retarded Children, Inc. v. Carey, 596 F.2d 27 (2d Cir. 1979), *cert. denied*, 444 U.S. 836 (1979); S-1 v. Turlington, 635 F.2d 342 (5th Cir. 1981), *cert. denied*, 454 U.S. 1030 (1981) (expulsion of mentally handicapped student for misconduct triggers statutory due process).

21. 422 U.S. 563, 569 (1975) (Donaldson's "milieu therapy" a euphemism for confinement in a mental hospital); 406 U.S. 715, 728 (1972) (no treatment or training available for Jackson's condition as a deaf mute with limited communication skills).

22. 493 F.2d 507 (5th Cir. 1974), *vacated and remanded*, 422 U.S. 563 (1975), remanded, 519 F.2d 59 (5th Cir. 1975). Since Donaldson had requested treatment or release, the Supreme Court recast his claim as a right to liberty.

23. O'Connor v. Donaldson, 422 U.S. at 574 n.10.

24. Halderman v. Pennhurst State School and Hospital, 612 F.2d 84, 92 (3d Cir. 1979), *rev'd and remanded on other grounds*, 451 U.S. 1 (1981).

25. For a so-called right-to-life analysis of habilitation, see Garvey, "Freedom and Choice in Constitutional Law," 94 *Harv. L. Rev.* 1756, 1791-92 (1981).

26. 42 U.S.C. §§ 6000-6081 (Supp. 1982), discussed at text and notes 92-103, *infra*.

27. 446 F. Supp. 1295 (E.D. Pa. 1977).

28. 612 F.2d 84 (3d Cir. 1979) (en banc) (case-by-case determination required as to the appropriateness of an improved Pennhurst for each resident).

29. Halderman v. Pennhurst State School and Hospital, 673 F.2d 647 (3d Cir. 1982) (en banc).

30. Judge Raymond J. Broderick questioning a witness in the *Pennhurst* trial, quoted in Ferleger and Boyd, "Anti-Institutionalization: The Promise of the *Pennhurst* Case," 31 *Stan. L. Rev.* 717, 718 (1979).

31. 451 U.S. 1 (1981).

32. *Id.* at 17.

33. For the link between 42 U.S.C. § 6063(b)(5)(C) and 42 U.S.C. § 6010, see text and notes 97-98, *infra.*

34. 451 U.S. at 32 (concurring opinion).

35. H.R. Rep. No. 97-208, 97th Cong., 1st Sess. 800 (1981) (legislative history reemphasizes that developmentally disabled persons "truly have a right to habilitative services in a setting least restrictive of their personal liberty").

36. On the deterioration of the physical, intellectual, and emotional skills of Pennhurst residents, see 446 F. Supp. 1295, 1308-12 (E.D. Pa. 1977) and 451 U.S. 1, 7 (1981).

37. *Pennhurst*, 673 F.2d 647 (3d Cir. 1982), *relying on* Pennsylvania Mental Health and Mental Retardation Act of 1966, 50 Pa. Stat. Ann. § 4201 (Purdon 1969).

38. 430 U.S. 651, 669 n.37 (1977).

39. 441 U.S. 520 (1979).

40. *See* New York State Ass'n for Retarded Children v. Carey, 393 F. Supp. 715 (E.D.N.Y. 1975).

41. 644 F.2d 147, 155 (3d Cir. 1980).

42. *See* Estelle v. Gamble, 429 U.S. 97, 106 (1976).

43. 644 F.2d at 164-70.

44. The recent decision in Youngberg v. Romeo, 102 S. Ct. 2452 (1982) is analyzed in chapter 8, *infra.*

45. Rogers v. Okin, 478 F. Supp. 1342 (D. Mass. 1979), *aff'd in part and rev'd in part*, 634 F.2d 650 (1st Cir. 1980); Rennie v. Klein, 462 F. Supp. 1131 (D.N.J. 1978), *aff'd in part*, 653 F.2d 836 (3d Cir. 1981).

46. *See, e.g.*, Superintendent of Belchertown State School v. Saikewicz, 373 Mass. 728, 370 N.E.2d 417 (1977); Wyatt v. Stickney, 344 F. Supp. at 400; *Pennhurst*, 446 F. Supp. at 1307 (E.D. Pa. 1977), *aff'd and modified*, 612 F.2d at 93; Wouri v. Zitnay, No. 75-80-SD (D. Maine July 14, 1978) (consent decree includes medication standards).

47. *See* Knecht v. Gillman, 488 F.2d 1136 (8th Cir. 1973) (aversive therapy); Kaimowitz v. Dep't of Mental Health of Michigan, No. 73-19434

AW (Cir. Ct., Wayne Co. July 10, 1973) (psychosurgery); Guardianship of Roe, 421 N.E.2d 40 (Mass. S.J.C. 1981) (noninstitutionalized ward may not be forced to take antipsychotic medication without judicial review), and cases cited in note 46, *supra. See generally* P. Schrag, *Mind Control* (1978).

48. Mills v. Rogers, *cert. granted*, 101 S. Ct. 1972 (1981). For discussion of the result, see chapter 8, *infra.*

49. See Rogers v. Okin, 634 F.2d 650 (1st Cir. 1980).

50. *See* Brooks, "The Constitutional Right to Refuse Antipsychotic Medications," 8 *Bulletin of the American Academy of Psychiatry and the Law* 179, 205 (1980).

51. *See* San Antonio Independent School District v. Rodriguez, 411 U.S. 1 (1973).

52. 20 U.S.C. § 1412 (1978).

53. Board of Ed. of Hendrick Hudson Central School District v. Rowley, 102 S. Ct. 3034 (1982), discussed in chapter 8, *infra.*

54. 483 F. Supp. 528 (S.D.N.Y. 1980).

55. 632 F.2d 945 (2d Cir. 1980).

56. *E.g.*, Garrity v. Gallen, 522 F. Supp. 171 (D.N.H. 1981); Colorado Ass'n for Retarded Citizens v. Colorado, No. 80-K-563 (D. Colo. May 20, 1981).

57. *See* M. Maloney & M. Ward, *Mental Retardation and Modern Society* 297 (1979).

58. 348 F. Supp. 866 (D.D.C. 1972); 334 F. Supp. 1257 (E.D. Pa. 1971), *modified*, 343 F. Supp. 279 (1972).

59. 347 U.S. 483 (1954).

60. 20 U.S.C. § 1412(2)(A)(1)(1978); 29 U.S.C. § 794 (1976).

61. S. Rep. No. 168, 94th Cong., 1st Sess. at 9 (1975).

62. Letter from Secretary of Education T.H. Bell to Speaker of the House of Representatives Thomas P. O'Neill, Jr. (March 1982).

63. *Id.*, "A Bill to amend the Education of the Handicapped Act . . . cited as the Education of the Handicapped Amendments of 1982."

64. 20 U.S.C. § 1413(a)(2)(1978).

65. New Mexico Ass'n for Retarded Citizens v. New Mexico, 495 F. Supp. 391 (D.N.M. 1980), *rev'd and remanded*, 678 F.2d 847 (10th Cir. 1982) (failure to provide free appropriate public education to handicapped children may violate § 504).

66. North v. District of Columbia Bd. of Ed., 471 F. Supp. 136 (D.D.C. 1979); Kruelle v. New Castle Cty. School District, 642 F.2d 687 (3d Cir. 1981); Tatro v. Texas, 625 F.2d 557 (5th Cir. 1980).

67. *See* Springdale School District v. Grace, 656 F.2d 300, 305 (8th Cir. 1981); Battle v. Pennsylvania, 629 F.2d 269, 277 (3d Cir. 1980).

68. 20 U.S.C. § 1402(19).

69. 34 C.F.R. § 300.343(d) (1981).

70. *See, e.g.*, Battle v. Pennsylvania, 629 F.2d 269 (3d Cir. 1980), *cert. denied sub nom.* Scanlon v. Battle, 452 U.S. 968 (1981) (policy limiting school year to 180 days held inconsistent with individualized process requirements).

71. 20 U.S.C. § 1415(b)(1)(c). The term *parent* also refers to guardians or surrogates.

72. *Id.* § 1415(b)(2).

73. *Id.* § 1415(d).

74. *Id.* § 1415(c).

75. *Id.* § 1415(e)(2). Courts may, however, first require exhaustion of administrative remedies, unless it would be futile to do so. Riley v. Ambach, 508 F. Supp. 1222 (E.D.N.Y. 1980), *rev'd*, No. 80-7600 (2d Cir. May 19, 1981); Lombardi v. Ambach, 522 F. Supp. 867 (E.D.N.Y. 1981).

76. 20 U.S.C. §§ 1412(5)(B), 1414(a)(1)(C)(iv).

77. Sen. Conference Report No. 94-455, 94th Cong., 1st Sess. at 30 (1975).

78. *E.g.*, Gladys J. v. Pearland Independent School District, 520 F. Supp. 869 (S.D. Tex. 1981).

79. 20 U.S.C. § 1415(b)(1)(B).

80. *See* Miller, Miller, & Repp, "Are Profoundly and Severely Retarded People Given Access to the Least Restrictive Environment?" 16 *Mental Retardation* 123 (April 1978).

81. Tina A. v. Shedd, No. H-80-462 (D. Conn. 1980) (settlement under P.L. 94-142 and Section 504 to provide a statewide system of surrogate parents).

82. Garrity v. Gallen, No. 78-116-D (D.N.H. Nov. 16, 1981) (implementation order).

83. New York State Dep't of Mental Hygiene Directive: Policies and Procedures for Mental Retardation, Items No. 7.13.5, 7.13.3 (May 1977).

84. 42 U.S.C. § 1396d(d)(2)(1974).

85. Standards for Intermediate Care Facility Services in Institutions for the Mentally Retarded, 39 Fed. Reg. 2220 (1974) (codified in 42 C.F.R. § 449.13).

86. 42 C.F.R. §§ 442.437(c)(1),(3); § 442.438-40 (1981).

87. 42 C.F.R. §§ 449.13(b)(5)(ii)(A)-(C) (1974).

88. 42 C.F.R. § 442.499(a)(2) (1981).

89. *Id.* § 442.463(a).

90. *Id.* § 442.463(d).

91. *Id.* § 442.422.

92. 121 *Cong. Rec.* S9361-62 (daily ed. June 3, 1975). On the denial of adequate habilitation, see Mentally Ill and Handicapped Children: Hearings Before the House Comm. on the District of Columbia, 92d Cong., 2d Sess. 19, 323-53 (1972); Developmentally Disabled Assistance and Bill of

Rights Act, 1974: Hearings on S.3378 Before the Subcomm. on the Handicapped of the Senate Comm. on Labor and Public Welfare, 93d Cong., 2d Sess. 389 (1974).

93. S. 3373, 93d Cong. (passed Oct. 1, 1974); S. 462, 94th Cong. (passed June 2, 1975).

94. 121 *Cong. Rec.* S16,549 (Sept. 23, 1975) (remarks of Sen. Javits).

95. H.R. Rep. No. 473, 94th Cong., 1st Sess. 43 (1975).

96. 42 U.S.C. § 6010(3) (1977).

97. Rehabilitation, Comprehensive Services, and Developmental Disabilities Amendments of 1978, 42 U.S.C. § 6063(b)(5)(C).

98. The Supreme Court left open the possibility of a private right of action to enforce these assurances. However, a district court's choice of remedy may be limited to prospective orders to force states to comply with duties incident to the receipt of federal funds, or termination of further funding. *See* Pennhurst State School v. Halderman, 451 U.S. 1, 51-54 (1981).

99. 42 U.S.C. § 6011.

100. *Id.* § 6011(c). Advocates, including representatives of protection and advocacy systems, can have a role in development of individual plans. U.S. Dep't of HEW, Developmental Disabilities Office, *Guidelines on Individualized Habilitation Plans* 3 (Sept. 23, 1977).

101. *See, e.g.*, Sen. Rep. 94-455, 94th Cong., 1st Sess. at 39 (1975) (written statement of individualized education program defines appropriate education); Rehabilitation Act, 29 U.S.C. § 722 (1975) (individualized written rehabilitation program); Social Security Act, 42 U.S.C. § 1396(d)(2) (1974) (individual habilitation plan defines active treatment); Wyatt v. Stickney, 344 F. Supp. 387, 397 (M.D. Ala. 1972).

102. 42 U.S.C. § 6012(a)(2)(A).

103. *See* S. Herr, *Advocacy under the Developmental Disabilities Act* (1976).

104. *Civil Rights of Institutionalized Persons: Hearings on S. 1393 before the Subcomm. on the Constitution, Senate Comm. of the Judiciary*, 95th Cong., 1st Sess. 400 (1977) (remarks of Dr. Alan A. Stone, Professor of Law and Psychiatry, Harvard Law School).

105. 325 F. Supp. 781 (M.D. Ala. 1971), 334 F. Supp. 1341 (1971), 344 F. Supp. 387 (1972), *aff'd in part sub. nom.* Wyatt v. Aderholt, 503 F.2d 1305 (5th Cir. 1974).

106. Birnbaum, "The Right to Treatment," 46 *A.B.A.J.* 499 (1960); Robitscher, "The Right to Psychiatric Treatment: A Social-Legal Approach to the Plight of the State Hospital Patient," 18 *Vill. L. Rev.* (1972); Symposium, "The Right to Treatment," 57 *Geo. L. J.* 673 (1969).

107. *See, e.g.*, Ragsdale v. Overholser, 281 F.2d 943, 950 (D.C. Cir. 1960); Sas v. Maryland, 334 F.2d 506, 517 (4th Cir. 1964).

108. 373 F.2d 451 (D.C. Cir. 1966).

109. D.C. Code § 21-562 (Supp. V, 1966).

110. That literature is collected in *Pennhurst*, 446 F. Supp. 1295, 1315 n.51 (E.D. Pa. 1977) and notes 126-127, 139, *infra*.

111. Wyatt v. Stickney, 344 F. Supp. 387, 390 (M.D. Ala. 1972).

112. *Id.*

113. 325 F. Supp. 781, 784-85 (M.D. Ala. 1971).

114. 334 F. Supp. 1341, 1343 (M.D. Ala. 1971).

115. Wyatt v. Stickney, 344 F. Supp. 387, 400-05 (M.D. Ala. 1972) (standards 23, 22(e)-(g), 38(i)(2), 24).

116. *Id.* at 396 (standard 2).

117. *Id.* (standard 3).

118. Wyatt v. Aderholt, 503 F.2d 1305, 1314 (5th Cir. 1974).

119. *Id.* at 1313.

120. *Id.* at 1316.

121. Wyatt v. Ireland, No. 3195-N (M.D. Ala. Oct. 25, 1979).

122. *Id.* Order of Oct. 25, 1979 (standards II 4, III 10).

123. *Id.* Order of Jan. 15, 1980 (Alabama governor appointed as receiver, and human rights committees replaced by court-approved monitor).

124. "'Wyatt Standards' Found to be Widely Observed," *Psychiatric News* at 1 (Oct. 21, 1977).

125. McRedmond v. Wilson, 553 F.2d 757, 762 (2d Cir. 1976).

126. In addition to the Alabama, Michigan, New Hampshire, New York, and Pennyslvania cases previously cited, see Connecticut Ass'n for Retarded Citizens v. Thorne, No. H78-653 (D. Conn., filed Dec. 6, 1978); Evans v. Washington, 459 F. Supp. 483 (D.D.C. 1978); Florida Ass'n for Retarded Citizens v. Graham, No. 79-418 (M.D. Fla, filed Aug. 22, 1979); Kentucky Ass'n for Retarded Citizens v. Conn, 674 F.2d 582 (6th Cir. 1982); Gary W. v. Louisiana, 437 F. Supp. 1209 (E.D. La. 1976); Wuori v. Zitnay, No. 75-80-SD (D. Maine July 14, 1978); United States v. Solomon, 419 F. Supp. 358 (D. Md. 1976), *aff'd*, 563 F.2d 1121 (4th Cir. 1977); Welsch v. Likins, 373 F. Supp. 487 (D. Minn. 1974); Caswell v. Califano, No. 77-0488 CV-W-4 (W.D. Mo., filed June 30, 1977); Doe v. Hudspeth, No. J. 75-36(N) (S.D. Miss. Feb. 19, 1977); United States v. Mattson, 600 F.2d 1295 (9th Cir. 1979); Horacek v. Exon, 357 F. Supp. 71 (D. Neb. 1975); Davis v. Watkins, 384 F. Supp. 1196 (N.D. Ohio 1974); Barbara C. v. Magnone, No. C-2-77-887 (S.D. Ohio Oct. 19, 1981); Sidles v. Delaney, No. C75-300A (N.D. Ohio April 26, 1976); Iasimone v. Garrahy, No. 77-0727 (D.R.I. April 29, 1982); Saville v. Treadway, 404 F. Supp. 430 (M.D. Tenn. 1974); Washington Ass'n for Retarded Citizens v. Thomas, No. C-78-168 (E.D. Wash., filed June 16, 1978); Medley v. Ginsberg, 492 F. Supp. 1294 (S.D. W. Va. 1980).

127. Gomes v. Gaughan, 471 F.2d 794, 800 (1st Cir. 1973); New York State Ass'n for Retarded Children v. Carey, 596 F.2d 27, 39 (2d Cir. 1979);

Romeo v. Youngberg, 644 F.2d 147, 161 (3d Cir. 1980); Dilmore v. Stubbs, 636 F.2d 966, 969 (5th Cir. 1981); Welsch v. Likins, 550 F.2d 1122, 1128 (8th Cir. 1977); Nelson v. Heyne, 355 F. Supp. 451, 459 (N.D. Ind. 1972), *aff'd,* 491 F.2d 352 (7th Cir. 1974), *cert. denied,* 417 U.S. 976 (1974); Pena v. New York State Div. for Youth, 419 F. Supp. 203, 207 (S.D.N.Y. 1976); Morgan v. Sprout, 432 F. Supp. 1130, 1136 (S.D. Miss. 1977); Patients v. Camden County Board of Chosen Freeholders, No. L 33417-74 P.W. (N.J. Super. Ct., Camden Co. July 19, 1976); Brown v. Ristich, 36 N.Y.2d 183, 192, 366 N.Y.S.2d 116, 124 (1975).

128. Address by Governor Luther Youngdahl, National Ass'n for Retarded Children Convention (Sept. 29, 1950).

129. Plaintiff's Post-Trial Memorandum at 16-17, Welsch v. Likins, No. 4-72 Civ. 451 (D. Minn. Oct. 1, 1974).

130. 373 F. Supp. 487 (D. Minn. 1974), *subsequent orders aff'd in part and vacated and remanded in part,* 550 F.2d 1122 (8th Cir. 1977).

131. 373 F. Supp. at 499.

132. Welsch v. Likins, No. 4-72 Civ. 451, slip op. at 3 (D. Minn. July 28, 1976).

133. 550 F.2d 1122 (8th Cir. 1977).

134. Welsch v. Dirkswager, No. 4-72 Civ. 451, consent decree, para. 14 at 2 (D. Minn. Dec. 1977).

135. Welsch v. Noot, No. 4-72 Civ. 451 (1981).

136. 446 F. Supp. 1295, 1318 (E.D. Pa. 1977) *aff'd in part,* 612 F.2d 84 (3d Cir. 1979).

137. 50 Pa. Stat. Ann. § 4201 (Purdon 1969).

138. *See* National Ass'n of Attorneys General, *The Right to Treatment in Mental Health Law* at ii (1976).

139. The *Willowbrook* case, discussed at text and notes 159-185, *infra;* Brewster v. Dukakis, No. 76-4423-F (D. Mass. Dec. 7, 1978); Ricci v. Greenblatt, No. 72-469F (D. Mass. Nov. 12, 1973); McEvoy v. Stevens, No. 74-2768-T (D. Mass. July 12, 1977); Massachusetts Ass'n for Retarded Citizens v. Dukakis, No. 75-5023-T (D. Mass. July 12, 1977); Davis v. Watkins, 384 F. Supp. 1196 (N.D. Ohio 1974); Sidles v. Delaney, No. C 75-300A (N.D. Ohio April 26, 1976); Horacek v. Exon, 357 F. Supp. 71 (D. Neb. 1973); Saville v. Treadway, 404 F. Supp. 430 (M.D. Tenn. 1974); Michigan Ass'n for Retarded Citizens v. Smith, 475 F. Supp. 990 (E.D. Mich. 1979); Wuori v. Zitnay, No. 75-80-P (D. Maine Sept. 18, 1981); Medley v. Ginsberg, No. 78-2099 CH (S.D. W.Va. Oct. 8, 1981).

140. *E.g., Willowbrook*, 393 F. Supp. 715 (E.D.N.Y. 1975); Davis v. Watkins, 384 F. Supp. 1196 (N.D. Ohio 1974).

141. Harper v. Cserr, 544 F.2d 1021 (1st Cir. 1976); Scott v. Plante, 532 F.2d 939 (3d Cir. 1976); Burnham v. Dep't of Public Health, 349 F. Supp.

1335 (N.D. Ga. 1972), *rev'd,* 503 F.2d 1319 (5th Cir. 1974), *cert. denied,* 422 U.S. 1057 (1975).

142. Garrity v. Gallen, 522 F. Supp. 171 (D. N.H. 1981); *Willowbrook,* 393 F. Supp. 715 (E.D.N.Y. 1975).

143. *E.g.,* Bettencourt v. Rhodes, No. C 77-12, slip op. (N.D. Ohio Sept. 14, 1977).

144. O'Connor v. Donaldson, 422 U.S. 563 (1975); Youngberg v. Romeo, 102 S. Ct. 2452 (1982).

145. *See, e.g.* Amended Complaint, McBride v. Okin, No. 81-0268-S (D. Mass., filed April 8, 1981) (failure of Dep't of Mental Health to follow its own rules for adjudicating clients' individual complaints).

146. Brewster v. Dukakis, 520 F. Supp. 882 (D. Mass. 1981); Developmental Disabilities Advocacy Center v. Melton, 521 F. Supp. 365 (D.N.H. 1981), vacated and remanded, (1st Cir. Sept. 22, 1982) No. 81-1727; Becker v. Hobby Horse Ranch School, No. 79-303 (D. Ariz. Dec. 17, 1979) (consent decree on access to privately owned residential facility).

147. *E.g.,* Ruby v. Massey, 452 F. Supp. 361 (D. Conn. 1978); *In re* Grady, 85 N.J. 235, 426 A.2d 467 (1981).

148. *E.g.,* Rennie v. Klein, 653 F.2d 836 (3d Cir. 1981); Naughton v. Bevilacqua, 458 F. Supp. 610 (D.R.I. 1978), *aff'd,* 605 F.2d 586 (1st Cir. 1979).

149. *E.g.,* Dixon v. Stanton, 466 F. Supp. 335 (N.D. Ind. 1979).

150. 343 F. Supp. 279 (E.D. Pa. 1972).

151. 348 F. Supp. 866 (D.D.C. 1972).

152. 411 U.S. 1 (1973), *rehearing denied,* 411 U.S. 959 (1973).

153. *Id.* at 37. *See* Fialkowski v. Shapp, 405 F. Supp. 946, 958 (E.D. Pa. 1975) (court will hear equal protection claim of retarded pupils to a minimum level of education).

154. 419 U.S. 565 (1975) (school pupil entitled to due process before disciplinary suspension).

155. *In re* G.H., 218 N.W.2d 441 (N.D. Sup. Ct. 1974); Frederich L. v. Thomas, 419 F. Supp. 960, 970-72 (E.D. Pa. 1976), *aff'd,* 557 F.2d 373 (3d Cir. 1977); Lora v. New York City Bd. of Ed., 456 F. Supp. 1211 (E.D.N.Y. 1978), *vacated in part, aff'd in part,* 623 F.2d 248 (2d Cir. 1980); Jose P. v. Ambach, 70 Civ. 270 (E.D.N.Y. 1979), *aff'd,* 669 F.2d 865 (2d Cir. 1982).

156. Wyatt v. Stickney, 344 F. Supp. 387, 400-03, 407 (M.D. Ala. 1972), *aff'd sub nom.* Wyatt v. Aderholt, 503 F.2d 1305 (5th Cir. 1974).

157. Wheeler v. Glass, 473 F.2d 983, 987 (7th Cir. 1973) (two mentally retarded residents bound and spread-eagled to a bed for over 77 hours).

158. Rozecki v. Gaughan, 459 F.2d 6 (1st Cir. 1972).

159. No. 72-C-356/357, 357 F. Supp. 752 (E.D.N.Y. 1973), *consent decree approved sub nom.* N.Y.S.A.R.C. v. Carey, 393 F. Supp. 715 (1975) [*Willowbrook*].

160. *Willowbrook*, Complaint at 22.

161. *See* N.Y.U. Medical Center, Proceedings of the Symposium on Ethical Issues in Human Experimentation: The Case of Willowbrook State Hospital Research (Urban Health Affairs Program, May 4, 1972).

162. *Willowbrook*, Complaint at 27.

163. 357 F. Supp. at 768-69.

164. Order of May 23, 1973, at 2.

165. 393 F. Supp. at 718.

166. *Id.* at 716 (referring to *Wyatt, Welsch*, and *Donaldson*).

167. *Willowbrook*, Consent Judgment of April 30, 1975, at para. 1.

168. *Id.* Appendix "A", Steps, Standards, and Procedures at para. D.1.

169. *Id.* para. A.1.

170. *See* 409 F. Supp. 606, 608 (E.D.N.Y. 1976).

171. *Willowbrook*, slip op. (E.D.N.Y. April 28, 1982) (noncompliance with the consent judgment requires appointment of a special master). For further discussion, see chapter 6, *infra.*

172. *See* Mahan, Maples, Murphy, & Tubb, "A Mechanism for Enforcing the Right to Treatment: The Human Rights Committee," *Law and Psychology Rev.* 131, 145-49 (Spring 1975).

173. F.R. Civ. Pro., Rule 53.

174. *See, e.g.*, Mills v. Bd. of Ed., No. 1939-71 (D.D.C. June 9, 1975); Halderman v. Pennhurst, 446 F. Supp. 1295 (E.D. Pa. 1977); Davis v. Watkins, No. 73-205 (N.D. Ohio April 30, 1976); Gary W. v. Louisiana, 441 F. Supp. 1121 (E.D. La. 1977), *aff'd*, 601 F.2d 240 (5th Cir. 1979).

175. *Wyatt*, 344 F.Supp. at 376.

176. *See, e.g.*, Hart v. Community School Bd. of Brooklyn, 383 F. Supp. 699, 758 (E.D.N.Y. 1974), *aff'd*, 497 F.2d 1027 (2d Cir. 1974); Knight v. Bd. of Ed. of the City of New York, 48 F.R.D. 115, 117-18 (E.D.N.Y. 1969).

177. Consent Judgment, *supra* note 167, para. F.1; *Wyatt*, 344 F. Supp. at 396-98 (Standards 5, 9, and 12); *Pennhurst*, 446 F. Supp. at 1308-10 (E.D. Pa. 1977); Gary W. v. Louisiana, 437 F. Supp. 1209, 1225-26 (E.D. La. 1976). *See also* Morgan v. Sprout, 432 F. Supp. 1130, 1150-52 (S.D. Miss. 1977); Green v. Johnson, 513 F. Supp. 965, 968 (D. Mass. 1981) (incarcerated status of youth offenders does not negate their right to a free and appropriate special education).

178. Consent Judgment, para. F.2.

179. *Id.* at paras. F.4, F.9, F.3, and F.6.

180. *Id.* at para. F.4.

181. Hearings in *Willowbrook* case (Feb. 10, 1976).

182. *Willowbrook*, slip op. at 13 (E.D.N.Y. March 10, 1976).

183. *See* Willowbrook Review Panel, Report to the Court at 39 (June 1978); Willowbrook Review Panel, Report to the Court 8-9, 70-94 (Dec. 1975).

184. Willowbrook Review Panel, Report to the Court 49-50 (Dec. 1978).

185. N.Y. Office of Mental Retardation and Developmental Disabilities (OMRDD), Directive: Policies and Procedures for Mental Retardation, Item 7.13.1-5 (1977).

186. New York State Ass'n for Retarded Children v. Carey [Wassaic], 76 Civ. 2860, complaint at paras. 57-59 (S.D.N.Y., filed Nov. 23, 1976).

187. *Id.* stipulation of voluntary dismissal (Nov. 9, 1977).

188. Philipp v. Carey, 517 F. Supp. 513 (N.D.N.Y. 1981); Society for Good Will to Retarded Children v. Carey, No. 78-C-1847 (E.D.N.Y., filed Aug. 23, 1978).

189. President's Comm. on Mental Retardation, *Report to the President, Mental Retardation: Century of Decision* 65, 133 (1976).

190. R. Allen, "Law and the Mentally Retarded," in *Psychiatric Approaches to Mental Retardation* 585, 594 (F. Menolascino ed. 1970); R. Newman, ed., Institutionalization of the Mentally Retarded: A Summary and Analysis of State Laws Governing Admission to Residential Facilities, and Legal Rights and Protections of Institutionalized Patients 4-5, 141 (The George Washington University, Institute of Law, Psychiatry and Criminology, 1967).

191. N.Y. Mental Hygiene Law [M.H.L.] §§ 33.01, 33.03 (1978).

192. *Id.* § 33.03(a).

193. *Id.* § 33.03(b)(4).

194. *Id.* §§ 33.11, 33.09(b), 33.15.

195. *Id.* § 13.07(c).

196. *Id.* § 13.01.

197. *Id.* § 13.21(a)-(b).

198. *Cf.* 14 NYCRR § 27.1(b)-(c) (1977) *with Wyatt*, 344 F. Supp. at 375.

199. N.Y. State Dep't of Mental Hygiene, Principles and Policies for Insuring Citizen Rights and Increasing Citizen Participation in Mental Hygiene Programs at 4 (May 20, 1973); *Accord*, N.Y. OMRDD *Comprehensive Plan for Services to Mentally Retarded and Developmentally Disabled Persons in New York State, 1981-1984* at 59 (Oct. 1980); 14 NYCRR § 150.7 (1973).

200. N.Y. Const. art. 17, § 4.

201. 14 NYCRR § 71.3 (1972).

202. *See* M.H.L. § 31.07.

203. *Id.* § 13.33(a),(g).

204. *Id.* § 13.33(h).

205. N.Y. State Senate, Select Comm. on Mental and Physical Handicaps, *Violence Revisited! A Report on Traditional Indifference in State Mental Institutions toward Assaultive Activity* 24-27 (1976).

206. M.H.L. § 45.07.

207. N.Y. State Comm. on Quality of Care for the Mentally Disabled, *Annual Report 1980-1981* 16-18, 22-24 (Feb. 1982).

208. 1977 N.Y. Laws, ch. 16.

209. 33 N.Y.2d 161, 165, 350 N.Y.S.2d 889, 892 (1973).

210. Lavette M. v. Corporation Counsel, 35 N.Y.2d 136, 359 N.Y.S.2d 20 (1974); Matter of Ellery C. v. Redlich, 32 N.Y.2d 588, 347 N.Y.S. 2d 51 (1973).

211. *E.g.*, McRedmond v. Wilson, 533 F.2d 757 (2d Cir. 1976); *Lavette M., supra.*

212. *Id.* 35 N.Y.2d 136, 142, 359 N.Y.S.2d 20, 24 (1974).

213. 73 Misc. 2d 261, 340 N.Y.S.2d 498 (Richmond Co. 1973). Even the early cases had recognized that persons in such institutions were entitled to legal protection from unconsented surgery, or misclassification with "offensive inmates of low mentality." *In re* Thomson, 103 Misc. 23, 169 N.Y.S. 638, 644 (Sup. Ct. 1918); People *ex rel.* Cirrone v. Hoffmann, 255 A.D. 404, 8 N.Y.S.2d 83 (1938).

214. Medley v. Ginsberg, 492 F. Supp. 1294, 1302 (S.D. W.Va. 1980); Naughton v. Bevilacqua, 605 F.2d 586 (1st Cir. 1979); *Pennhurst*, 446 F. Supp. 1295, 1310-11 (E.D. Pa. 1977) (voluntariness an "illusory concept" in the institutional context); Wyatt v. Stickney, 344 F. Supp. 387, 390 n.5 (M.D. Ala. 1972) (high burden upon state to show any resident is in fact voluntarily confined).

215. N.Y. OMRDD, "Statistical Table 3429—Clients in State Developmental Centers—Year Ended March 31, 1981" (July 30, 1981).

216. N.Y. Const. art. XI § 1.

217. *See* N.Y. Educ. Law § 4407 1. (1981); *In re* Leitner, 40 A.D.2d 38, 337 N.Y.S.2d 267, 272 (1972).

218. N.Y. Educ. Law §§ 4401-4409 (1981). *See* Matter of Kaye, 54 A.D.2d 907, 388 N.Y.S.2d 620 (1976); *In re* Jessup, 85 Misc. 2d 575, 379 N.Y.S.2d 626 (Fam. Ct., N.Y. Co. 1975).

219. N.Y. Educ. Law § 4402(2) (1981).

220. N.Y. Educ. Law § 3302(c)(2); 1977 N.Y. Laws, ch. 470, § 18.

221. N.Y. Educ. Law § 4402(2)(b)(1).

222. *E.g.*, Education (Handicapped Children) Act, 1970, c. 52 (England); Education (Mentally Handicapped Children) Act, 1974, c. 27 (Scotland).

223. 38 N.Y.2d 653, 382 N.Y.S.2d 13 (1976).

224. 95 Misc. 2d 828, 408 N.Y.S.2d 980 (Sup. Ct. 1978). For the archaic dichotomy between treatment and education as a basis for a contrary result, see State Dep't of Mental Hygiene v. Dolan, 392 N.Y.S.2d 980, 983 (Civ. Ct., N.Y. City 1977).

225. N.Y. Educ. Law § 4405(1)(a) (1981).

226. N.Y. Fam. Ct. Act § 236 (Supp. Pamp. 1982).

227. 34 C.F.R. § 300.302 (1981). *See* Matter of Scott K., 92 Misc. 2d 681, 400 N.Y.S.2d 289 (Fam. Ct. N.Y. Co. 1977); Matter of Gano, 105 Misc.2d 740, 432 N.Y.S.2d 764 (Fam. Ct., Delaware Co. 1980).

228. 1976 N.Y. Laws, ch. 334; MHIS, Report on the Adequacy of the Current Grievance and Disciplinary Procedures of the Department of Mental Hygiene in Safeguarding the Rights of Patients Involved in Incidents of Abuse and Mistreatment, at 7 (1976).

229. *Id.* at 13.

230. 36 N.Y.2d 183, 366 N.Y.2d 124 (1975).

231. *See, e.g.,* Smart v. Francis, 43 A.D.2d 623, 349 N.Y.S.2d 803 (1973), *rev'd,* 35 N.Y.2d 872, 363 N.Y.S.2d 953 (1974) (Sunmount State School resident assaulted by attendant, causing laceration over left eye); Traber v. Feinstein, 39 A.D.2d 643, 331 N.Y.S.2d 150 (1972), *aff'd,* 32 N.Y.2d 860, 346 N.Y.S.2d 529 (1973) (West Seneca School resident struck by attendant; a second resident choked due to positioning; Merriman v. Dep't of Mental Hygiene, 52 A.D.2d 726, 382 N.Y.S.2d 165 (1976) (therapy aide at Rome State School punched residents in the head, face, back and stomach, and ground the heel of his shoes on the tops of a resident's feet); Blackmon v. Feinstein, 39 A.D.2d 642, 331 N.Y.S.2d 137 (1972) (attendant dropped and struck West Seneca School residents); Merchant v. Dep't of Mental Hygiene, 41 A.D.2d 588, 340 N.Y.S.2d 214 (1973) (attendant struck children at Rome State School in three separate incidents).

232. *Blackmon, supra* (fine of $50 recommended); *Traber, supra* ($50 fine); *Smart, supra* (five-day suspension); *Merriman, supra* (two-month suspension, notwithstanding findings of malicious abuse).

233. 38 N.Y.2d 391, 380 N.Y.S.2d 630 (1975), *determination annulled sub nom.* Simpson v. Director of Letchworth Village, 56 A.D.2d 631, 391 N.Y.S.2d 883, 884 (1977).

234. Cohen v. Dep't of Mental Hygiene, 48 A.D.2d 697, 368 N.Y.S.2d 50, 51 (1975).

235. Boone v. Ristich, 48 A.D.2d 833, 368 N.Y.S.2d 276 (1975); Avery v. Rechter, 56 A.D.2d 963, 392 N.Y.S.2d 714 (1977).

236. *See* N.Y. Penal Law § 260.25 (1980) (endangering the welfare of an incompetent person a misdemeanor offense, but no reported cases construing it). Ward supervisors are reluctant to report incidents even for internal disciplinary proceedings. *See* Williams v. Dep't of Mental Hygiene, 52 A.D.2d 727, 382 N.Y.S.2d 167 (1976) (demotion of supervisor who observed

slapping incident without reporting it). Even after a state policeman (working undercover as a ward aide) testified as to an employee's repeated and malicious assaults on residents, only an administrative action resulted. *Merriman, supra.*

237. Grasso v. State, 177 Misc. 690, 31 N.Y.S.2d 398 (Ct. Cl. 1941), *aff'd*, 264 A.D. 745, 34 N.Y.S.2d 440 (1942), *aff'd,* 289 N.Y. 552, 43 N.E.2d 530 (1942).

238. Excelsior Insurance Co. v. State, 296 N.Y. 40, 69 N.E.2d 553 (1946).

239. Surprenant v. State, 46 Misc. 2d 190, 259 N.Y.S.2d 306 (Ct. Cl. 1965).

240. 33 Misc. 2d 330, 226 N.Y.S.2d 901 (Ct. Cl. 1961).

241. *Accord,* Zajaczkowski v. State, 189 Misc. 299, 71 N.Y.S.2d 261, 263 (Ct. Cl. 1947) (unattended seven-year-old badly burned by contact with exposed radiator valve; state negligent in leaving 66 retarded children under the care of two attendants); Davis v. State, 35 A.D.2d 762, 315 N.Y.S.2d 82 (1970) (failure to perform operation for removal of cataracts of Willowbrook resident was not negligent, and no state liability for erroneous medical judgment); Santana v. State, 28 A.D.2d 576, 279 N.Y.S.2d 253 (1967) (damages reduced from $6,000 to $3,500 for a child's death a few weeks after state school admission; lack of evidence of pecuniary loss, possibilities of physical recovery, or conscious pain and suffering).

242. Whitree v. State, 56 Misc. 2d 693, 290 N.Y.S.2d 486 (Ct. Cl. 1968).

243. 355 N.Y.S.2d 912 (Ct. Cl. 1974).

244. 50 A.D.2d 985, 376 N.Y.S.2d 685 (1975).

245. *See* 1972 N.Y. Laws, ch. 251, § 9.11 (repealed 1973); Gorgoglione v. Contreras, 41 A.D.2d 644, 340 N.Y.S.2d 845 (1973).

246. *See* National Ass'n for Retarded Citizens, *Residential Services* 13 (1976).

247. Young v. State Dep't of Social Services, 92 Misc. 2d 795, 401 N.Y.S.2d 955, 957 (Ct. Cl. 1978).

248. *See* Boland v. State, 30 N.Y.2d 337, 333 N.Y.S.2d 410 (1972).

249. Bartlett v. State, 52 A.D.2d 318, 383 N.Y.S.2d 763, 767-69 (1976).

250. M.H.L. §§ 7.35, 13.35 (1978).

251. N.Y. Public Officers Law § 17(2)(b), (3)(a) (Supp. 1981).

6 Rights to Community Reintegration

A quiet legal revolution and a protracted scandal are slowly emptying the old asylums. In the past, scant attention was paid to transfer and discharge procedures; judges viewed commitment to a retardation institution as tantamount to a life sentence.[1] Even when a prisoner serving a life term could expect release in ten or fifteen years, a resident of a state school for the retarded remained an average of twenty-one years.[2] If the terrible overcrowding had not fueled a crisis of conscience, many of those residents might have spent their entire lives in institutions. This chapter examines a response to that crisis: the rise of judicial and legislative mandates to restore retarded people to lives as close to normal as possible.

Yet many states still pursue the paths of least resistance, transinstitutionalization rather than community reintegration of their dependent wards. An estimated 100,000 to 175,000 developmentally disabled persons reside in nursing homes, many diverted from state institutions and receiving no active treatment.[3] Construction of new 250-bed facilities results in mini-institutions that fail to assure the residents of quality care or a less restrictive life-style. Attrition is another factor in census reductions, with annual death rates for the institutionalized retarded reported at between 1.6 to 1.98 percent.[4] As cavernous buildings are depopulated, states have seized upon an alternative use for their mental institutions. In unconscious mimicry of civil libertarians' complaints, New York officials have already begun moving prisoners into living units that formerly housed mental-care clients.

Roadblocks to an Exodus

Until the drive for legal rights, states had resettled only a handful of residents in normalized community alternatives. Despite state schools swollen to 165 percent of their rated capacities, there were no plans for a mass exodus. For example, the New York Department of Mental Hygiene (DMH), with the nation's largest institutionalized population (28,875 at its all-time high in 1965),[5] did not begin to implement Operation Exodus, its attempt to resettle some Willowbrook residents, until late 1972, but by then, the institutions could not be permitted the "luxury of only slowly moving ahead."[6] Courts and advocates could no longer wait for new managed communities, group homes, or fostering arrangements to materialize.[7] Despite the critical need for domiciliary and other supportive services, the DMH lacked such programs to draw people out of retardation institutions or prevent their initial entry.

Even the more intellectually capable residents were trapped in place by their own inexperience and the system's institutional bias. Many mentally alert persons spent the better portion of their developmental years in retardation institutions through misdiagnosis, stunted expectations, staff discouragement, and even the state's legal opposition to alternative living arrangements.[8] Bernard Carabello, for instance, endured sixteen years in Willowbrook even though he was not retarded and desperately wanted to live somewhere else. After his release, he said,

> Everyone in the outside world has equal rights but in Willowbrook the residents have no rights. Normal kids reach out for their mother's love and get it, but in Willowbrook the residents are reaching out in desperation to be loved and no one gives it to them. People think we are animals but we have feelings too.[9]

Family members sometimes reacted to the prospect of a relative's community placement with well-intentioned but misdirected anxieties. Some mythicized the institution as a safe, snug haven from an outside world of perils. Yet in the words of Professor Gunnar Dybwad, former executive director of the National Association for Retarded Citizens, "imprisonment in our institutions for the mentally retarded is often vastly more uncomfortable, vastly more restrictive, and vastly more interfering with personal integrity than in institutions for juvenile delinquents."[10] Other parents of retarded people viewed institutionalization as the poor man's guardianship, a way of assuring their child's care after their own deaths. As a result of faulty medical advice, they had been led to believe that once admitted into state custody, their children would never leave the institution.[11] Not surprisingly, families were often skeptical or unresponsive to the state's efforts to elicit their interest in alternative placements.[12] Indeed, they had genuine worries: that state agencies might try to dump their retarded members on their doorsteps, or in inferior care settings, or in marginal neighborhoods, or in underfunded community agencies that might one day collapse. Without legally enforceable pledges of quality community care, parents were thus reluctant to barter the reassurance of brick-and-mortar institutions for the new and complex world of normalized, community-based habilitation.

Courts should intervene, however, when families unreasonably insist upon permanent institutionalization. Even after a child reaches the age of eighteen and has capacities for choice, some parents are surprised, shocked, and angered that their right to block a transfer from an institution is less than absolute. Minors may also fall martyrs to such thinking. In 1981, in a nationally publicized case, a California court overruled a so-called parental-rights objection to a foster-home placement for a fifteen-year-old boy with Down's Syndrome.[13] In transferring the guardianship of Phillip Becker from his natural parents to his "psychological parents," the Superior Court acknowledged Phillip's constitutional and statutory rights to habilitation, specifically the right to be given "a realistic opportunity to lead a more useful and meaningful life and to return to society."[14]

The case turns on a stark choice: authorizing habilitation and life-prolonging surgery, or "consigning Phillip . . . to rust away in permanent congregate care."[15] Applying a substituted-judgment analysis, Judge Fernandez held that Phillip would opt for life and custody in the home of the "psychological parents" who had regularly visited him in a board-and-care facility since he was five years old. In urging recognition of a developmentally disabled child's right to choose his own destiny by some process of substituted judgment, the court sustained Phillip's best interests and endorsed the least detrimental alternative. The question of unreasonably withheld medical treatment is unusually poignant, and *Guardianship of Becker* suggests a broader truth: that the legal system has an obligation to intervene on behalf of a retarded child whose parents deem his life of no value.

For a small minority of parents with unreasonably low expectations of their handicapped children, plans to offer their child a home substitute may evoke strenuous opposition. Of the many impediments to community placement, the unwritten rule of honoring such parental vetoes is especially disturbing. As a matter of informal policy, tacitly reaffirmed by state commissioners, state workers generally will not place a resident out of an institution over a parental objection. Thus the state ignores the judgments of its own clinicians and refuses to contest decisions of great detriment to its clients. For every resident who gains his or her release through a legal hearing, scores of other candidates for community placement remain in limbo.[16] Given highly politicized systems of care, local politicians can effectively block a transfer at a constituent's request.

Lack of clear due process for residents in postinstitutionalization planning also adds to frustration. Besides a fuzzy terminology of least restrictive alternatives, participants face uncertainty as to who decides exactly what, how, and when. It is unclear, for instance, how an emancipated child, an abandoned child, or a child coming of age can revoke a so-called voluntary admission or have some say as to where he or she will live as an adult. Courts sometimes assume that retarded children as a matter of law will gain this right at the age of majority, but the practice is often to the contrary.[17] Automatic review procedures, with the assistance of advocates and mentors, are still the exception rather than the rule.

Although foster programs for retarded people have been in existence for over a half century, state judges and other officials have rarely used foster homes and scarcely considered adoption possibilities.[18] In the past, family courts often shared the view of welfare agencies that mentally retarded children were simply not adoptable.[19] With changing child-welfare practices, specialists report considerable success in New York and elsewhere in finding adoptive homes for hard-to-place retarded children.[20] They warn that hundreds of such children are unnecessarily institutionalized because social workers write these children off with blanket exclusionary practices or lack of awareness of the special services available to adopted retarded children. With this new knowledge, agencies and courts should undo the discrimination against those retarded children in need of substitute homes.

By far the dominant obstacle to deinstitutionalization is the absence of a coherent budget strategy to support long-term noninstitutional care for retarded persons. Since states maximize their receipt of federal Medicaid dollars, current funding patterns perpetuate perverse incentives to use the most costly and restrictive levels of care. The states aggravate this imbalance by spending five dollars on institutional care for every dollar of community care, and by new institutional construction.[21] Federal officials are well aware of the consequences of this skewed funding—the over institutionalization of persons not requiring hospital-type care, the inappropriate retention of mildly and moderately retarded children who should not have been admitted in the first place, and the violation of judicially determined constitutional rights.[22] Task forces of federal consultants forcefully urged remedial steps, such as clarifying Medicaid ICF-MR regulations to subsidize relocation of residents in less restrictive care settings and the phasing down of institutions as part of "plans for correction."[23] But such federal action has been halting and state officials continue to pump scarce resources to institutional renovations rather than to move ahead in managing and monitoring a truly comprehensive community-care delivery system. Nor has the legal advocates' indirect strategy of raising standards and hence costs led to the closing of antiquated institutions. States such as Alabama and Minnesota have lowered their censuses and clung to the convenience of keeping the remaining residents in large, central facilities.

States also face counterpressures against further deinstitutionalization. Labor unions, for example, fear that transfers of residents to foster homes, schools, or private care could lead to layoffs and loss of jobs. Some labor leaders made no secret of their campaigns to discredit community care, and spread stories that played on parental fears.

Certainly there were legitimate concerns that state officials not replicate past errors, such as the dumping of large numbers of mental patients into unprepared communities or the transfer of retarded residents to inappropriate nursing homes. In New York, the ill-managed release of thousands of mental patients had stirred neighborhood resistance, contaminated the political atmosphere for other community-care programs, swelled the ranks of the homeless, and provoked doubts as to state-government intentions and capabilities.[24] Advocates for retarded people wanted the state to do something better than abandon the ex-resident to an indifferent society or create small, custodial total institutions in decaying neighborhoods. Unless planning, quality control, and aftercare responsibilities were more clearly defined, deinstitutionalization could degenerate into a cost-shifting exercise, a massive population shuffle from one kind of institution to another.

Fencing in the Mentally Disabled: Supreme Court Responses

Cases before the High Court offer glimpses of the overprotectiveness and public animosity that have isolated mentally disabled people from society. In 1966, the United States Supreme Court held that a New York mental patient had been unconstitutionally confined in a security hospital, a decision that ultimately triggered the administrative reclassification and transfer of hundreds of similar patients to less restrictive surroundings. In *Baxstrom* v. *Herold*, the Court held that the patient was denied equal protection under a statutory procedure permitting his civil commitment at the expiration of a penal sentence without the safeguards available to all other civilly committed persons.[25] The Court found two distinct defects in the New York procedure. Unlike other patients civilly committed, the petitioner had no right to *de novo* review on the question of his sanity. Furthermore, Baxstrom's civil commitment to a hospital maintained by the Department of Corrections was made without a judicial determination that he was dangerously mentally ill, a procedure required before any other civil patient could be detained in a secure hospital. As the Court explained: "Equal protection does not require that all persons be dealt with identically, but it does require that a distinction made have some relevance to the purpose for which the classification is made."[26] Since New York had created functionally separate institutions for the mentally disabled, it could not classify patients for involuntary commitment on a totally arbitrary basis, and Baxstrom, like other civil patients in Dannemora, would be entitled to a judicial hearing on the issues of his sanity and his dangerousness.

Arbitrary administrative processes and scant legal aid also contributed to the petitioner's long incarceration. Because of his indigence, Baxstrom had no counsel and no independent psychiatric testimony to rebut the state's claims at his original commitment proceeding. This was true of his equally unsuccessful habeas corpus attempts. Despite the testimony of the state's psychiatrists that Baxstrom could be transferred to a civil mental hospital, the Department of Mental Hygiene made its own *ex parte* determinations barring him from such a hospital. As a result Baxstrom stayed in Dannemora for five years, a period twice as long as his already completed criminal sentence.

In the after math of the Supreme Court's decision, events demonstrated that treatment professionals had imposed more restrictive forms of mental care and custody than necessary. The case touched off Operation Baxstrom, a review of the status of all similarly confined persons and the transfer of almost one thousand inmates from maximum-security to ordinary civil state hospitals. Some professionals had feared that the transferred patients would prove disruptive to the nonsecure receiving hospitals. Yet one year after these Operation Baxstrom transfers had taken place, only seven patients had been returned to maximum security institutions.[27] By 1970, the vast majority of Operation Baxstrom patients were thoroughly integrated into the receiving civil hospitals, and more than one-third had been discharged by those hospitals.[28] This experience and the results of a similar Pennsylvania case[29] provoked criticism of staff biases toward overuse of maximum-security mental facilities.

Institutional staffs overconfine because of various pressures extraneous to the clients' best interests. However, as the Court stated in *O'Connor* v. *Donaldson*, the state's agents may not "fence in the harmless mentally ill" or incarcerate the "physically unattractive or socially eccentric" to save the public from discomfort or to appease intolerance.[30] Similarly, the liberty and associational rights of retarded persons cannot legitimately be denied unless the state can prove a constitutionally valid purpose. The recent decision in *Youngberg* v. *Romeo* marks the provision of "minimally adequate training" related to safety and freedom from restraints as one such purpose.[31] There the justices reserved questions of least restrictive alternatives and broader habilitation rights for appropriate future cases.

The Supreme Court has, however, begun to probe the due process issues of transfers between institutions. *Vitek* v. *Jones* explored the risks of misclassification and other "grievous loss" to an individual transferred to a mental facility.[32] It held that prisoners have a state-created liberty interest in procedural protections when they face involuntary transfer to a mental hospital. As the justices recognized, even felons may suffer "qualitatively different" and adverse consequences when moved to an institution for the treatment of "mental disease or defect." The harms identified by the Court were substantial—the stigmatizing consequences of transfer for involuntary mental treatment, the imposition of mandatory behavior-modification programs, and other restrictions on freedom of action and personal security.

Retarded persons suffer comparable losses when moved to facilities with more restrictive conditions of confinement. Threatened with an equally imposing litany of harms, they should be entitled to constitutional procedures substantially similar to those outlined in *Vitek*. Those safeguards include notice of the proposed transfer; an opportunity to challenge the contemplated action at a hearing before an independent decision maker; and rights to call, confront, and cross-examine witnesses. Drawing on civil commitment precedents, the majority opinion recognized that the "medical nature of the inquiry, however, does not justify dispensing with due process requirements. It is precisely '[t]he subleties and nuances of psychiatric diagnoses' that justify the requirement of adversary hearings."[33]

Independent and zealous advocacy assistance should be available to disabled clients in this transfer process. The issue in contention, however, is whether a state must supply free legal assistance for all indigent prisoners subject to removal to mental institutions. Although four justices in the *Vitek* majority would compel this right to counsel, Justice Powell, concurring in part, concluded that the necessity for the appointment of a licensed attorney should be determined on a case-by-case basis. Thus, five of the justices believed that constitutional law requires that the state provide no less than qualified, competent, and independent assistance in those transfer proceedings. Whether that demands a free lawyer or trained lay advocate will depend on such factors as the complexity of the dispute and the capability of the alleged mentally disabled person to protect his or her own interest.

In contrast with procedural claims, the Supreme Court has difficulty resolving cases on the rights of people to enter societal mainstreams. For instance, in its only Section 504 decision to date, the Court declined to rule on whether handicapped persons have an implied private cause of action to sue under this federal antidiscrimination law.[34] Yet they did permit a deaf applicant for admission to a college's nursing program to pursue her legal claims, albeit on a narrower basis. The result is that recipients of federal assistance, such as schools of higher education, need not take affirmative action under Section 504, which would set lower standards, although an unreasonable refusal to modify an existing program can still constitute discrimination against the handicapped.[35] So far, the Supreme Court has not settled the question of a state's affirmative obligations to assist institutionalized retarded persons in their quest for more independent living. Nor does the Court seem eager to enter this constitutional thicket or to engage in sharper line drawing under the Rehabilitation Act.

Municipal zoning barriers are another form of discrimination that can strand retarded persons in harmful institutions. Such exclusionary zoning has not yet been tested in the Supreme Court, but some of its earlier opinions are relevant. *Arlington Heights* v. *Metropolitan Housing Corporation*, for example, proscribed intentional discrimination in withholding zoning permission for racially integrated low- and moderate-income housing.[36] In determining whether an invidious discriminatory purpose barred housing for retarded people, courts under this standard can look to such factors as the background of the challenged decision, departures from normal procedures, contemporary statements of decision makers, and a pattern of disproportionate impact on the injured class. While *Village of Belle Terre* v. *Boraas* held that groups of transient unrelated students can be excluded from single-family residential zones, the Court reasoned that zoning boards may do so to establish "zones where family values, youth values, and the blessings of quiet seclusion and clean air make the area a sanctuary for people."[37] Since retarded people are entitled to no less a sanctuary, this decision does not bar stable group homes for retarded persons from ordinary neighborhoods. As the functional equivalent of a biologically related family, the lower courts have frequently upheld these small-scale community living arrangements over municipal objections.[38]

Congress and the Community-Care Consensus

This approach is consistent with the national policy of reintegrating severely disabled persons into normal residential and service patterns. As has been shown, the congressional mandate establishes a powerful preference for community-based and home-based care. Thus, laws such as the Social Security Act, the Developmental Disabilities Act, and the Education for All Handicapped Children Act reveal a recurrent theme: preventing the disabled individual's inappropriate institutional retention and instead offering mainstreaming and other forms of less restrictive habilitation. By foiling the presidential administration's attempts to replace habilitation programs with block-grant legislation, Congress has reaffirmed this goal.

Particularly at a time of budget austerity, federal laws should be administered to encourage rather than discourage more independent community-based living. Unfortunately, bureaucratic barriers have kept many retarded persons unnecessarily institutionalized because affordable and appropriate care is not made available in their home communities. These patterns are both costly and illogical. As Secretary of Health and Human Services (HHS) Schweiker recently conceded, "It makes no sense to keep a disabled individual institutionalized just to get help in paying medical bills."[39] Although Schweiker commendably adopted a temporary rule to permit Medicaid eligibility in extraordinary cases to fund home-based care, this step will foster only very limited deinstitutionalization. The regulation takes narrow aim at the deeming rules of the Supplemental Security Income (SSI) program, whereby a family's income is considered in determining SSI eligibility for a child or a spouse living at home, but not for the same individual living in an institution. Since Medicaid hinges on SSI eligibility in many states, the regulation provides a new method for exercising the Secretary's long-standing discretion to modify the deeming rules in inequitable circumstances. Accordingly, he has now delegated this power to an internal departmental board under the following conditions: Medicaid eligibility for home care will result in future savings to the Medicaid program, and the quality of medical care will be maintained for the deinstitutionalized client.[40]

Clearly this is a stop-gap measure until states develop Medicaid-waiver plans for home- and community-based services to individuals still in mental facilities and denied "other benefits of deinstitutionalization."[41] Unfortunately, current Reagan administration strategies fall far short of the frequently reiterated congressional goal of securing "the right to appropriate treatment and related services" for clients of mental disability services in settings and under conditions "most supportive" of the individual's personal liberty.[42]

Section 504 of the Vocational Rehabilitation Act must therefore remain a vital tool for providing access to such less restrictive services. Frequently termed the civil rights act for disabled Americans, it broadly prohibits discriminatory actions against persons with physical or mental impairments such as mental retardation. Section 504 states that

> No otherwise qualified handicapped individual in the United States . . . shall solely by reason of his handicap, be excluded from the participation in, be denied the benefits of, or be subjected to discrimination under any program or activity receiving Federal financial assistance or under any program or activity conducted by any Executive agency or by the United States Postal Service.[43]

Detailed regulations emphasize the integration thrust of this cryptic provision. For example, HHS regulations seek to eliminate unduly separate services "unless such action is necessary to provide qualified handicapped persons with aid, benefits or services that are as effective as those provided to others."[44] Although the concept of access to equally effective services does not require equal outcomes, it does require that handicapped persons be afforded "equal opportunity to obtain the same result, to gain the same benefit . . . in the most integrated setting appropriate to the person's needs."[45] For instance, in meeting the needs of minors institutionalized because of a handicap, state and local authorities are obligated to provide an appropriate education that maximizes contact with nonhandicapped minors. In interpreting Section 504, courts also have ordered less restrictive, community-based settings for institutionalized retarded persons,[46] and home health-care services for a quadriplegic adult at risk of institutionalization.[47]

Efforts to dilute Section 504 and its enforcement are short-sighted. For example, proposals by the Reagan administration would strip the 504 regulations of the guarantees of free appropriate public education to handicapped children, and would weaken other equal-access provisions in health and social services, recreational programs, employment, and program accessibility. Yet when this same administration sought an effective federal response to the denial of lifesaving medical care to baby Doe of Bloomington, Indiana, and similarly endangered defective newborns, it invoked the authority of Section 504. Baby Doe died as a result of lack of nutrition and parental opposition to surgical efforts to repair an esophageal defect, and that death aroused the federal government to action.[48] Threatening possible termination of federal funds, HHS put the nation's health-care providers on notice of the unlawfulness of withholding sustenance or medical treatment based on the fact or belief that an infant is mentally retarded or otherwise handicapped.[49]

The continuous isolation of many handicapped persons in unnecessarily costly, dependency-fostering, and separate institutions is further evidence of the need for strong and effective regulatory programs. For the most part, claims under Section 504 can be satisfied without counterproductive burdens. Indeed, only a tiny proportion of discrimination complaints based on handicap ever become the subject of federal administrative action. Still fewer are subject to federal court review. For the one in ten Americans with disabilities, this is a small price to pay for fairness.

Even with Section 504 remedies intact, handicapped persons in mental institutions and other congregate-care facilities have special difficulties in preserving their rights. Congressional enactments acknowledge that reality. Focusing on reports of inadequate, unsafe, and unsanitary conditions in some community residences, Congress adopted Social Security amendments in 1976 covering certain institutions, foster homes, and group-living arrangements.[50] This required each state to develop and enforce regulations covering any community residence in which an SSI recipient may live. Yet for facilities serving the mentally retarded, these regulations appear to give too little weight to habilitative programs and other civil rights of clients.[51]

In 1980, Congress passed a tougher measure to vindicate the constitutional and statutory rights of persons in mental institutions, juvenile facilities, nursing homes, and prisons. Under the Civil Rights of Institutionalized Persons Act, the Attorney General is authorized to sue state or local public officials where there is "a pattern or practice of resistance to the full enjoyment" of the residents' federal rights.[52]

Although the impetus for this act came from suits by the United States against restrictive retardation institutions,[53] the Department of Justice has so far made only limited use of its newly granted authority. Partly because of the act's unwieldly prelitigation investigation and negotiation requirements, the United States has not filed any cases as the sole plaintiff and entered only two cases by intervention.[54] As a result, the prosecution of deinstitutionalization-related suits is largely in the hands of so-called private attorney generals.

Federal Courts and Resident Resettlement

Current litigation reflects a shift in emphasis by government and private lawyers alike. Disenchanted with institutional reform, litigants have come to demand more specific assurances of client transfers to community-based alternatives. This direction is scarcely unique to the field of mental retardation, as public-interest lawyers seek foster care, group homes, and halfway houses for neglected children, persons in need of supervision, juvenile delinquents, mental patients, pretrial detainees, and even prisoners.[55] However, the pressure is most intense in mental-disability contexts as courts insist that state authorities locate or develop less restrictive alternatives. This result is now common in cases testing civil commitment statutes,[56] requiring release or transfer from illegal detention,[57] or relieving overcrowding and unconstitutional conditions of confinement.[58] This latter group of cases is responsible for dramatic reductions in the censuses of retardation institutions. In the jargon of professionals, these so-called structural class actions offer vehicles for *communitization*, the process of progressive integration of disabled individuals into communities.[59] Some actions pursue an ambitious objective of a judicially supervised mass resettlement of residents from institutions to nurturing, home-like environments.

Even where a state concedes its past defaults, it may contest the legitimacy of a court's continuing jurisdiction. The issues are legion: What level of review is appropriate for a federal judge and his agents in the deinstitutionalization process? Who is to pour content into abstract phrases such as *adequate habilitation* and *least restrictive setting appropriate to the individual's needs*? Assuming that clinical professionals are the primary decision makers at the individual level, what safeguards should govern the exercise of their discretion when a client is proposed for transfer or release? For many of these questions the case law provides little guidance.[60] To make matters worse, the answers may distinguish between remedies that are products of litigation settlements or adjudications.[61] But where federal judges bring new procedures and standards into being, they have a special legal obligation to ensure compliance with constitutionally based requirements. In the next pages, four broad legal approaches to community placement are identified.

The first approach is exemplified by lawsuits that challenge the adequacy of transfer or retention procedures, and are generally the least intrusive. Because they impose only limited additional costs, parties frequently are willing to reach stipulated settlements. These may call for elaborate procedural checks and balances such as periodic reviews, access to legal counsel, and clinically independent psychiatric assessments for minors treated as inpatients in mental facilities.[62] For adult residents previously admitted by third parties to retardation facilities, judicial reviews have tested less restrictive residential placements.[63] On the basis of constitutional deficiencies, courts have also invalidated procedures for summary revocations of conditional leaves or discharges.[64] Cases dealing with attempts to block transfers or release can be relatively straightforward. As a discrete rather than recurrent event, the dispute may affect a single individual or a type of assignment.[65] For example, a group of New York parents prevented officials from removing their autistic children from an out-of-state residential school. Relying on the Education for All Handicapped Children Act, the court restrained state officials from removing the students from an environment in which they were learning to state developmental centers, reasoning that a prior hearing was required for children who had already been "shuttled from pillar to post by an uncaring society."[66] By temperament and training, judges are especially comfortable in settling such claims of procedural irregularity.

A second more diverse set of cases seek ad-hoc relief in establishing community-based facilities. Their target may be a highly specific injury, such as a discriminatory regulation or conspiracy aimed at preventing mentally disabled persons from living in a particular area. In one noteworthy federal civil-rights conspiracy suit, the New York Attorney General, acting in a *parens patriae* capacity on behalf of mentally disabled citizens, prevented Long Island residents from defeating the sale of a house to a state agency for the purpose of a group home for eight to ten moderately retarded adults.[67] Ruling that the plaintiffs' equal protection claims were substantial, Judge Mishler held, on the basis of pendent jurisdiction, that the state had demonstrated the discriminatory impact of defendants' conduct in denying housing accommodation to mentally retarded citizens in violation of a state human rights law.[68] The defendants, eighteen neighbors, had bought this single-family house only after public notice that the OMRDD planned to purchase it and establish a community residence for the retarded.

Nor was this the first time a federal court had intervened to give mentally disabled persons who might otherwise remain stuck in institutions a chance to lead more normal lives. In declaring unconstitutional a local zoning ordinance excluding persons requiring continuous medical or psychiatric care from living in hotels or rooming houses, a district judge struck down a thinly disguised attempt to keep ex-patients out of the community.[69] But when class actions are geared to institutional reconstruction, unsystematic consent decrees give scant attention to community program development. Such "shopping-list" decrees may thereby enable states to compromise the residents' right to receive a suitable less restrictive residential environment within a reasonable amount of time.[70]

Standards cases, a third legal approach, aim at a comprehensive remedy to strike a balance between interim internal reforms and deinstitutionalization goals. The classic examples of such cases—*Wyatt, Welsch*, and *Wuori*—were nothing less than attempts to change an entire service-delivery system. Despite differences in legal theory, the centerpiece of this approach was a broad set of standards, sufficiently specific and enforceable, to require settings for normalized habilitation. These decrees forced states to develop new community resources and overcome the status quo. Yet neutral, general standards had their drawbacks, *inter alia*—selective implementation, distorted priorities, and undue preoccupation with cleaning up institutions. District judges were often reluctant to enter into the "complex web of relationships" involved in creating new facilities.[71] These cases made a bow toward least restrictive alternatives, but more specific plans, timetables, and monitoring were needed.

Even with broader agendas, results were often slow in coming. For example, *Wuori* v. *Zitnay*[72] represented an important step beyond *Wyatt* as the first decree to provide detailed standards for the care and treatment of mentally retarded persons discharged into the community, along with standards for those still in a central facility. Yet two years after that decree, the state lacked even the data base to assess unmet needs for new homes, programs, and services.[73]

A new generation of cases builds upon these precedents and rejects the wisdom of investing scarce public dollars in institutional reform. Sometimes this stance is reflected in the very definition of the injured class. Thus, the plaintiffs in one recent suit are all retarded persons under age twenty-three "unable to live in their homes due to lack of resources in their homes or in their home communities" because of the state's failure to "provide foster homes or other community facilities."[74] In a consent decree with only sparing references to institutional conditions, the West Virginia class members are guaranteed "the least restrictive placements appropriate to the resident's needs," timetables for removals from specified wards and hospitals, and the benefits of individual and statewide planning to fund new community-based services.

The Minnesota class action, now captioned *Welsch* v. *Noot* (*Welsch II*) has evolved toward a parallel objective. Ten years ago, with its focus on a subclass of Cambridge State School residents, *Welsch I* recognized the constitutional doctrine of the least restrictive alternative. However, the court's orders stopped short of an obligation to create new programs and essentially applauded the defendants' community-care proposals. By 1980, with those efforts slowing, plaintiffs went back to trial, demanding census reductions and assurances of small residential settings and placement of class members in community programs which appropriately meet their individual needs. Rather than contest those claims, the defendants agreed to a statewide consent decree, a massive document that gives priority to reductions in population at eight institutions.[75] Thus, *Welsch II* responds to misgivings that litigation of this type not become a device to resurrect obsolescent institutions.[76] As Neil Mickenberg, one of the counsel for the *Welsch* plaintiffs in the original proceedings, has said:

> In framing that case, we did not pay adequate attention to its "least restrictive alternative" aspects. I would never bring that same type of case again. The implementation of its community care parts was pretty weak. I would not try to improve institutional conditions, but I'd rather try to close it or drastically reduce its size. I just don't see a need to keep mentally retarded people in institutions. It also diverts resources that could go to support community services. I've come to the view that institutions are inherently bad places, and as much as you do to change them and no matter how much resources you pour into them, they're still crummy places. Now the Macombs Regional Center [in Michigan] provides short-term respite care, back-up services to foster families, and group homes; I could live with that. But the institution as we know it today is an anachronism. I just wouldn't do anything to improve it.[77]

Out of similar perceptions and experiences has come the fourth, more radical litigation strategy: *total institutional evacuation.* Based on equal protection and statutory legal foundations, lawyers first applied this approach to close an institution for dependent children.[78] The *Pennhurst* case looked to similar principles and objectives. Although the court of appeals overturned the district court's ruling on closing that institution, it left the door open for indirectly accomplishing the same result.[79] Since few if any residents require institutionalization to survive, the appellate mandate for determining each individual's least restrictive environment will drive Pennhurst's size down. At some point the state will find it both cheaper and better to care for the residual population elsewhere.

Drastic deinstitutionalization is now a dominant national theme in these class-action suits. In Massachusetts, for instance, under a final consent decree in *Brewster* v. *Dukakis,* the state was obligated to evacuate the Northampton State Hospital in stages over a three-year period and replace it with community residential and day programs.[80] The court entered the decree to fulfill the rights of the 380 mentally ill and retarded residents and over 5,000 other class plaintiffs at risk of future institutionalization. As a product of a detailed planning process among the parties' representatives, the *Brewster* decree is a binding blueprint for the creation of a comprehensive system of appropriate, less restrictive treatment, training, and support services. Although the court retained jurisdiction to issue further orders on the interpretation, implementation, enforcement, or modification of the decree, defendants have recently won appeals narrowing the plaintiffs' ability to compel the state to furnish additional funds.[81]

In the field of mental retardation, the Plymouth Developmental Center decree has gone even further. Under court-approved deadlines, Michigan authorities agreed to reduce the census to one hundred residents by 1983, to increase community residential, day, and management services, and to phase out the institution completely by 1984.[82] Inspired by these successes, litigators in Texas, Florida, Washington, and other states are pursuing remedies to develop community homes in lieu of institutions.[83] Yet the fate of these newer suits may well depend on the lessons and legal limits drawn from the bellwether cases of *Wyatt, Pennhurst*, and *Willowbrook*. Although strikingly different in legal theory, these epic cases display many similarities in aspiration and ultimate effect. Table 6-1 summarizes these and other leading cases in terms of their census reductions and targets.

Wyatt: The Pioneering Experience

This Alabama right-to-habilitation suit has spurred both institutional reform and community-based care. A historic precedent, it recognized that mentally retarded residents in institutional custody possessed a right to the least restrictive alternative appropriate to their individual needs. Residents were thereby entitled to programming designed to help them live outside Partlow's walls. Seven out of forty-nine standards in the *Wyatt* decree concerned the residents' right to "the least restrictive conditions necessary to achieve the purposes of habilitation."[84] Each resident's habilitation plan had to include a statement of the least restrictive setting to achieve the individual's habilitation goals, criteria for release to that setting, a projected date for discharge, and postinstitutionalization plans.[85] The parties further agreed that borderline or mildly retarded persons should not be institutionalized and that all institutional residents should receive an interdisciplinary screening to determine their appropriate placement. The defendants bound themselves to make "every attempt" to move residents to smaller living units and facilities, and to provide living arrangements allowing each resident to live as independently and as "normally as possible."[86] With this *Wyatt* opinion cited as precedent in over ninety court cases, it is no surprise that similar language should appear elsewhere.

The Alabama defendants, however, had little expertise or enthusiasm for meeting this community objective. Having relied for so long on institutional responses to retardation care, the Department of Mental Health was unprepared to change this pattern. It was two years after the entry of the *Wyatt* decree before the state even assigned someone the task of writing a statewide plan for deinstitutionalization of the developmentally disabled.

Their problem was a classic self-fulfilling prophecy. Despite the fact that the Partlow State School's budget had more than tripled since the 1972 trial, community-based care limped along on meager rations. Although the Partlow census, virtually static in the prelitigation years, dropped by over one thousand persons, this reduction was primarily through transfers to

Table 6-1
Census Reductions in Institutions under Litigation

Lawsuit	*Site*	*Year Initiated*	*Census at Time of Filing*	*Latest Census*	*Projected Census*
Wyatt v. *Stickney*	(Partlow) Ala.	1971	2,204	800	Tentative projections 275-550
NYSARC v. *Rockefeller*	(Willowbrook) N.Y.	1972	5,343	1,369	250 (1985)
Welsch v. *Noot*	Minnesota system	1972	4,186	2,395	1,850 (1987)
	(Cambridge)		862	517	No projection
Halderman v. *Pennhurst*	Pennsylvania	1974	1,944	776	No projection
Ricci v. *Okin*	(Belchertown) Mass.	1972	1,076	454	257 (1984)
McEvoy v. *Stevens*	(Fernald) Mass.	1974	1,649	953	664 (1984)
Gauthier v. *Benson*	(Monson) Mass.	1975	851	629	476 (1984)
Mass. ARC v. *Dukakis*	(Wrentham) Mass.	1975	1,406	853	504 (1984)
Mass. ARC v. *Dukakis*	(Dever) Mass.	1975	1,336	731	318 (1984)
Brewster v. *Dukakis*	(Northampton) Mass.	1975	590	215	50 (1981)
Wuori v. *Zitnay*	Maine	1975	986	347	325 (1982)
Iasimone v. *Garrahy*	Rhode Island	1976	750	450	210 (1985)
Barbara C. v. Magnone	Ohio	1977	2,000	979	575 (1985)
Michigan ARC v. *Smith*	Michigan	1978	837	220	0 (1983)
Garrity v. *Gallen*	New Hampshire	1978	620	460	270 (1985)

Source: Unpublished court documents and interviews.

smaller institutions. Starting from scratch, the Alabama defendants as of 1977 still had only fifteen group homes serving less than one hundred retarded persons for the entire state. The state's failure to give higher priority to creating such alternatives had stymied compliance with the decree.

In fairness, assessing compliance was never an easy task. The Human Rights Committee at Partlow began with no staff, no reporting procedures, and no instruments for measuring implementation progress. Acting on a part-time basis, they had difficulty enough being Judge Johnson "eyes and ears" within the institution, let alone his monitors of compliance in satellite facilities. Even more frustrating were efforts at prodding the central office to implement effectively the community-oriented requirements of the decree.[87] Though the defendants produced voluminous reports, the plaintiffs and *amici* had to reopen discovery to obtain truly useful data.[88] Moreover, the court's own pronouncements were ambiguous as to what constituted full compliance with minimum constitutional standards of adequate habilitation.[89]

Seven years after his original judgment, Judge Johnson found that the defendants' failure to move residents from the large institutions to less restrictive settings was one of the areas of "substantial and serious noncompliance."[90] In criticizing the very slow development of community facilities and services, the court emphasized evidence of residents identified as ready for but still awaiting these services. Taking no position on the basic debate—community versus institutional care—Judge Johnson characterized the beneficial effects of community placement as implicating treatment ideals rather than constitutional minimums. His opinion expressed reliance on the good-faith efforts of qualified professionals to make decisions regarding the appropriateness of community placement "when an individual's habilitation demands such treatment."[91] Although it relaxed the requirements for mandatory discharge and postinstitutionalization plans, the court's modification left the basic premises of the 1972 standards unchanged. Habilitation, as the court observed, is not always defined as deinstitutionalization. However, the district judge firmly rejected residential segregation which would defeat the purposes of habilitation. The defendants had wanted judicial endorsement of their assertion that "community living is an unrealistic goal" for the majority of Partlow's residents,[92] but *Wyatt II* did not provide it.

If *Wyatt* propelled Alabama out of the dark ages of mental care, it fell short of ushering residents into the promised land of community living. Its impact on mental-disability budgets had been dramatic: in the first three years, the state's spending per resident patient soared from forty-ninth to thirty-eighth in the nation.[93] The bulk of these cash infusions went to Alabama's institutions. When measured against the "bad old" days, there were improvements in the quality of care within Partlow, Bryce, and Searcy hospitals, but not enough to eliminate serious deficiencies. Deinstitutionalization gains, at least in terms of numbers, were also impressive. By July 1982, the total population of these three institutions had dropped from 9,116 to 2,670 persons. Many of these class plaintiffs, however, were former mental patients released to the community with limited aftercare, or retarded persons transferred to newer institutions.

But in a strange twist, the defendants now seem on the verge of doing in practice what they so vigorously protested in court. *Wyatt II* had left the planning of future deinstitutionalization to the discretion of qualified professionals. Although the defendants had requested that the Partlow Human Rights Committee be replaced by four separate human rights committees, the court instead dissolved the human rights committee and appointed as its monitor a former state judge who had chaired the Bryce Human Rights Committee. As an agent of the court, his duties were to review the receivership administration of the governor, "monitor all operations of the Alabama mental illness and retardation facilities," and make periodic reports and recommendations to the court.[94] Although the monitor selected an advisory committee with community-oriented specialists, it was the state's own Plan of Compliance that promised to develop additional community-based residential alternatives. In a hopeful new direction, the Department of Mental Health has begun to place lower functioning, multiply disabled clients into community settings. Concepts it stoutly argued were unrealistic and unjust in 1979, it has begun to embrace. For example, their most recent plans contemplate reducing Partlow's population (now less than 800 residents) from a target census of 550 to half that number.

Even with this progress, further rounds of litigation lie ahead. *Wyatt* created standards that the defendants a decade later perceive as singling out Alabama for unique burdens. The state has therefore abandoned its efforts at further modifications of those standards,[95] seeking to replace them with private accreditation standards for mental hospitals and Medicaid standards for retardation facilities. Although Medicaid-funded group homes have altered the state's opposition to community care, it is clear that the *Wyatt* standards and the court's continued use of a receiver still play a major role in eliciting affirmative professional responses.[96] Similar plans have been introduced before, but realization of such plans has always taken steady judicial prodding.

Pennhurst: The Polarization of Parties

At first look, the *Pennhurst* case in Pennsylvania seems a triumph of consensus. All parties and their many experts endorsed normalization as the "most beneficial method of habilitating a retarded person."[97] At the trial, the state reiterated its policy in favor of deinstitutionalization, and announced its intention to close Pennhurst in the early 1980s. Yet five years later, the closing of Pennhurst and the end of this litigation remain elusive goals.

Throughout multiple appeals and two Supreme Court reviews, Judge Raymond J. Broderick has steered a consistent course. His remedial orders are based upon evidence that habilitation of a retarded person can best be accomplished through community living arrangements. After a trial of thirty-two days, the record documented that "given appropriate community facilities, all the residents at Pennhurst, even the most profoundly retarded with multiple handicaps, should be living in the community."[98] In a far-reaching legal conclusion, Judge Broderick declared that the plaintiffs' segregation in Pennhurst violated their rights to nondiscriminatory habilitation under the equal protection clause and Section 504 of the federal Rehabilitation Act of 1973. On the record of this case, the defendants had a stark dual system: extensive community-based education, training, and residential care for other retarded persons of all ages and degrees of retardation, while institutional residents were isolated from less-separate services.

The court's original remedial order contained neither detailed standards nor timetables. Instead, its broad injunctive decree required state and county officials to provide suitable community living arrangements for Pennhurst residents, a monitoring system, and correction of serious health and safety hazards pending Pennhurst's prompt replacement. In appointing a special master to preside over a planning process, the court intended to assure class plaintiffs of the "least separate, most integrated, least restrictive community settings," along with adequate care in the meantime.[99] To avoid inappropriate transfers, the court relied heavily on a detailed process of individual habilitation planning to precede community placement, including the creation of a friend-advocate program to represent class members.

Efforts to shut down the institution by judicial fiat failed. Opposition escalated after a 1979 order included a timetable that would have emptied Pennhurst within a period of two and one-half years.[100] In rejecting the district court's total prohibition against placement at Pennhurst, the Third Circuit Court of Appeals instead upheld a strong presumption in favor of deinstitutionalization.[101] While remanding for individual determinations by the court or by the special master of appropriate least restrictive environments, it recognized that some transfers could result in harm, but implied that only a small minority of residents would be unable to adjust to life on the outside.[102]

If a flat rule against institutionalization was beyond the court's power, individual reviews could still spur wholesale movement. Under requirements to fulfill the dictates of individual habilitation plans (IHPs) fashioned by the parties and approved by the special master, the defendants have a duty to create new community services. Whereas the court-appointed Hearing Master previously conducted hearings to determine the voluntariness and appropriateness of the placements approved under these so-called temporary IHPs, these reviews and the involvement of the masters in this process have been scaled down.[103]

As the court of appeals has twice held, the use of masters by the district court is central to monitoring the "complex and lengthy process" of providing each Pennhurst resident with an appropriate habilitation plan.[104] But that role creates its own tensions, particularly in a period of Supreme Court pronouncements decrying the second-guessing of state professional opinion by federal courts. This was underscored when the Supreme Court agreed to again hear the *Pennhurst* case and determine the appropriateness of a special master enforcing a federal decree based upon an independent state-law ground.[105] Given the individual rights at stake and the record of foot-dragging by *Pennhurst* defendants, the district court's circumscribed use of a master is justified.

The implementation history of the *Pennhurst* decree has been marked by halting compliance. Compared with prelitigation levels, the rates of community placement actually fell in the years after the decree was ordered.[106] The court therefore resorted to more specific remedial orders. Class members of school age, for example, were given highest priority in the allocation of community placements.[107] Yet by March 1981, with the movement of institutional residents to community residences almost at a standstill, the court ordered more stringent relief: timetables for the placement of ninety residents.[108] When county defendants lagged in their compliance, the plaintiffs brought a contempt motion that evoked a great spurt of activity and thereby produced substantial compliance with this order.[109] But when a state defendant urged legislators to cut off funding for the special masters, the court struck back with contempt findings and a daily fine of $10,000 for each day that the special masters' monthly expenses of $67,746 were not paid. The court of appeals has upheld these penalties.[110] Having failed by political means to eliminate the masters, the defendants' strategists filed legal challenges against what they contend is a duplicative and intrusive surveillance of their administrative operations. Even though evidence shows that the special master has narrowed her role to urging the defendants to comply with the court's orders and advising the court on the status of compliance,[111] defendants' legal resistance continued.

Notwithstanding the unceasing legal battle, Pennhurst residents continue to leave and to record developmental gains. From 1977 to 1981, 226 residents moved to community living arrangements.[112] Those who have moved are slightly younger, and more highly functioning than those who have stayed behind. But according to matched samples of seventy institutionalized and seventy former Pennhurst residents, only the deinstitutionalized group showed significant developmental growth as measured in improved adaptive behavior.[113] Consistent with other research studies, those who had moved from the institution were not only better off in developmental terms; they also enjoyed advantages over their institutionalized peers when criteria of family satisfaction, family involvement, and perceived client happiness were taken into account.[114] Against this backdrop and the expressed commitment of all parties to bring superior community care to more class members, a settlement, in theory, is still attainable. Yet as the parties continue to maneuver for the equivalent of a legal knockout, opportunities to shift from adversarial to problem-solving stances are frittered away.

Willowbrook: Escalating Judicial Intervention

Structural-reform litigation often brings cycles of cooperation and conflict. The parties to the Willowbrook Consent Judgment began with two assets of incalculable value: clearly defined, pragmatic objectives and strong political support for attaining them. They also had federal judges willing to give the case highest priority and to insist on faithful adherence to the decree's spirit as well as letter. Although the court could remind state officials that these were reforms to which they had consented, the defendants' resentment grew as the implementation process dragged on. Moreover, as the emphasis shifted from goals to methods, Judge Bartels became embroiled in programmatic and ideological debates.

Although the *Willowbrook* case began with aims modeled after *Wyatt*, the movement of residents to noninstitutional alternatives is now its dominant note. During the settlement negotiations, the plaintiffs and the United States, acting as *amicus curiae*, had jointly called for a three-year plan for phasing out Willowbrook entirely.[115] Ultimately, a compromise was reached: over a six-year period, Willowbrook would be reduced to an institution of two hundred fifty or fewer beds, solely for Staten Island residents requiring such care. Willowbrook's primary goal would be to "ready each resident . . . for life in the community at large."[116]

This constituted judicially supervised relief on a heroic scale. In 1975, there was no precedent for depopulating a major retardation institution and resettling so many residents with severe physical as well as mental impairments. The implementation details were left to a planning process under the auspices of the court's deputies, the Willowbrook Review Panel. The consent judgment specified that the panel, in close collaboration with the parties, would produce a comprehensive community placement plan outlining the necessary types and numbers of community facilities and programs.[117] As initial goals, the state agreed to develop and operate at least two hundred new community placements for class members in the first year, and to request or reallocate $2 million in legislative appropriations to finance such residential facilities.[118] In a standard of great importance, community placement was defined as living in a noninstitutional residence in the community with fifteen or fewer beds, such as a hostel, halfway house, group home, or foster-care home for mildly retarded adults, or a residence of ten or fewer beds for any other class member.[119]

To avoid sending Willowbrook residents from frying pan to fire, the judgment erected precautions against ill-considered transfers. With the class defined to include all 5,209 persons who were residents of Willowbrook on March 17, 1972 (the day the complaint was filed), class members, even after movement out of the institution, retained the protection of the decree. Thus, they had an entitlement to services suited to their needs. Pledges, audits, and individualized procedures were all part of that protection. Before a resident could be placed in the community or in another state institution, Willowbrook's director had to certify that the proposed placement offered the individual "better services, an opportunity for personal development, and a more suitable living environment than Willowbrook."[120] The defendants also agreed to create new procedures to safeguard the rights of individuals who were denied a requested less restrictive setting, or who were proposed for transfer to a residential placement outside Willowbrook. Finally, the Willowbrook Review Panel was given broad evaluation responsibilities, including the task of auditing community and other placements to ensure that ex-residents received adequate day and residential services.

From the outset, the community provisions attracted greatest attention. In approving the consent judgment, the court acknowledged that the dispersal of Willowbrook's residents was better than "other possible alternatives."[121] Of all the provisions and procedures incorporated in the judgment and judicially approved as securing the plaintiffs' constitutional right to protection from harm, Judge Judd quoted only those relating to deinstitutionalization. Though the parents' group of one satellite Willowbrook facility, fearing its closure, had submitted an objection, the court ruled that the issue was prematurely raised. The judgment itself called for the review panel to evaluate the Keener Unit's appropriateness as a receiving facility for transferred class members. Although the panel could screen the district court from some hearings on complex disputes of fact and professional opinion, the court would ultimately have to settle the tough interpretative questions. And the toughest of those questions involved the remedy beyond Willowbrook.

The parties tried to strike the right balance between immediate improvements for residents on the inside and new resources to bring more residents out. But Willowbrook was not a salvageable proposition. Even the defendants' expert consultant had described it as based on "the wrong concept in the wrong place with the wrong plan."[122] Yet attempts at institutional reform were made and when their results proved disappointing, the parties, the panel, and the court reexamined whether the residents' lives could be significantly improved in institutions. Over time, the court and its panel redirected their energies to movement out of Willowbrook, a shift that promised real benefits for the residents.

This approach was fully consistent with the consent judgment. Under it, the New York Department of Mental Hygiene was required to provide each resident with the least restrictive living conditions and to devote an increasing proportion of its "budget, resources and expenditures" for Willowbrook class members to community rather than institutional programs.[123] The Community Placement Plan represented a striking departure from the old institution-centered care system. This plan reflected a commitment to several basic principles: 1) comprehensive community services so that retarded persons need not leave, or could return to their home communities for necessary services; 2) services individually tailored to fit the person's needs; and 3) local offices established as the "major fixed point of responsibility for services to the mentally retarded in each community."[124] By December 1976, the defendants had accepted these principles, along with the plan's forty-two specific recommendations and the decentralized service delivery proposal for Boro Developmental Services Offices.

Before long, the monitoring process was turning up deficiencies in the state's compliance with the consent judgment. On the basis of the review panel's early audits, the plaintiffs filed a motion to have the defendants held in contempt. In partial settlement of that motion, the parties agreed to a stipulation, signed by the court, effectively widening the defendants' obligations. In admitting noncompliance with portions of the consent judgment, the defendants agreed to "a substantial increase and redirection of efforts to achieve compliance with the Consent Judgment."[125] The Stipulation and Order on Consent added interim goals, increasing the monthly rate for community placements. Its most striking innovation, however, was to require the takeover of five of Willowbrook's twenty-seven buildings by a private organization.

This 1977 consent order marked a turning point. It amounted to a clear recognition that better care could be obtained by releasing residents to competent private or other community-care providers than by retaining them in the state facility.[126] It demonstrated the seriousness with which all parties viewed attainment of the consent judgment's basic goal. In separating priority objectives from the morass of compliance details, the parties signaled an allocation of greater resources to the community aspects of the case.

But the Stipulation and Order on Consent was also paradoxical: if the defendants had not met community-placement timetables in the past, why would they be able to satisfy accelerated rates of community placement? The defendants' confidence stemmed from several factors—the competence of the Metropolitan Placement Unit's director, the personal commitment of Governor Carey to the consent judgment's success, and the full cooperation of the governor and legislature in ensuring the full and timely financing of this stipulation. Yet even with all these advantages, the defendants could not meet their obligations.

By 1978, the drive toward full implementation was faltering. In approving a modification in the placement timetable, the court reduced the schedule of projected placements to 550 placements over a 9-month period, and required the defendants to submit a new plan for projected placements "relating to the depopulation of Willowbrook."[127] As part of those efforts, the defendants promised to fund new recreation and socialization programs; assure the availability of sex education, psychological, medical, and other professional services for class members in the community; develop a $350,000 community-education campaign to counter neighborhood opposition; initiate comprehensive training programs for case managers, family-care providers, natural parents, and group-home staff; and operate six new homes. This package of relief followed a familiar pattern in Willowbrook negotiations: the plaintiffs compromised on timetables in exchange for additional specific obligations. Yet the defendants continued to fall behind even this relaxed schedule.[128]

While the Willowbrook Review Panel was designed to make judicial review a measure of last resort,[129] the court repeatedly issued opinions to spur compliance or uphold controversial recommendations. Of the panel's more than two dozen formal recommendations, the majority dealt with community placement, such as the closings of various institutional units. A formal recommendation was deemed *prima facie* proper and correct, but if an objecting party could show some impropriety, the burden of proof shifted to the panel to establish the correctness and propriety of its recommendation.[130]

The fight over moving Willowbrook residents to a new transitional facility was a preview of larger confrontations. The defendants sought to overturn a ban on using the Bronx Developmental Center as a residential facility for members of the Willowbrook class. The consent judgment permitted the defendants to transfer Willowbrook residents to other institutions as transitional steps to community placements, but the 1977 Stipulation had sharply restricted such intermediate transfers.[131] On June 10, 1977, the court upheld the review panel's recommendation that the Bronx Center, a recently built 384-bed facility, not be used as a residence for members of the Willowbrook class. As Judge Bartels wrote, the parties had agreed on normalization as the ultimate goal and community care as the ultimate placement for class members.[132] On the evidence presented, the benefits that might be derived from improved institutional care were outweighed by the risks that such transfers would create a "loss of present improvement and also of delay in community placement, where the only real improvement in the handicapped and the retarded can be expected." This ruling, however, was not inflexible: DMH could still accept transfers to the Bronx facility at the request of a parent or guardian. Given the trade-offs between continued stays at Willowbrook and better care in transitional facilities, this decision was a resounding endorsement of social integration and community placement. According to the expert testimony, such placement offered the soundest hope for eliminating "the indifference and negligence which have characterized the institutional care of the retarded and handicapped for many years."[133]

In condemning that negligence, the *Willowbrook* court drew the hostility of some state professionals and unions. Furthermore, in reviewing union objections that the United Cerebral Palsy (UCP) takeover of five Willowbrook buildings infringed state employees' rights, the court held that UCP, as an independent contractor furnishing services to the state, was not bound by civil-service laws.[134] Even before that stipulation to remove residents from inferior state-school custody, the court had warned the union not to hinder the state's "constitutional obligation to provide minimum care for the mentally retarded Willowbrook class members and to protect them from harm."[135]

Some transfers to large private-care providers brought only incremental gains, however. When Gouverneur, a Willowbrook satellite facility, was closed, 152 multiply handicapped class members were transferred to Flower Fifth Avenue Hospital in New York City. When the parties later repudiated the wisdom of that move, they entered a consent order to transfer those residents again to valid community facilities of no more than three or six beds.[136] If class members were not to be shuffled from place to place, the transfer process would require a more searching investigation for permanent placements.

By necessity, the *Willowbrook* litigation served as a laboratory for innovation. The creation of due process procedures for institutional residents moving to other living arrangements is a prime illustration. Once the state committed itself to wholesale movements of residents, ad-hoc procedures were no longer adequate. The consent judgment therefore required the defendants to promptly prepare a plan for adequate hearing procedures. It specified "appropriate due process safeguards," including written notice to the Mental Health Information Service, and to parents, relatives, or legal guardians at least thirty days prior to a resident's transfer; interdisciplinary team consultation with the individual resident and parents or guardians in setting a projected date for "progress to a community setting"; and surrogates for friendless residents through the Consumer Advisory Board (CAB) and its designees.[137]

After nearly fifteen months, the state submitted its plan. Unfortunately, the end product was repetitive, unduly complex, and in parts nearly incomprehensible.[138]

Resident movement from a state facility to a community placement or another state facility was to involve a three-stage process. At a Team Case Conference, the facility staff must draft a placement plan with the participation, if possible, of the resident and/or the resident's family or representative. Thirty days prior to placement, the resident and/or representative and the MHIS must receive written notice. Steps are then taken to obtain parental consent and/or the consent of a competent adult resident (a person eighteen years or older "capable of understanding the nature and implications of the move").[139] If a transfer is denied or a proposed transfer is refused, a resident or his representative can invoke administrative hearing and appeal remedies.

Transfers are subject to stringent safeguards. Consistent with the *Willowbrook* judgment, the basic standard requires the proposed placement to offer the client better services, an opportunity for personal development, and a more suitable living environment than the client's present setting. Furthermore, the placement must be the least restrictive environment possible and in the client's best interests.[140] There are several options for the recipient of such written notice: accept the proposed placement, visit the site and obtain further information, or request an administrative hearing before a hearing officer with experience in developmental programs for the mentally retarded. If the resident is unrepresented or no one responds to the notice, the CAB or the parental advisory group of the facility can file an objection and thus trigger a hearing on behalf of the resident. In theory, a parent or surrogate has no absolute veto over a satisfactory community placement. Yet a determined objector, exhausting all administrative proceedings, can stall a placement for at least half a year. Given the cost and strain of contested procedures, state officials are reluctant to take up such battles.

The OMRDD voluntarily extended the transfer procedures to their clients throughout the state. This litigation was also a catalyst for other statewide transfer procedures. On this basis, OMRDD adopted new processes concerning movement from a community placement to a more restrictive environment (such as psychiatric or developmental centers); movement from one community placement to another; and respite care for those already in a community placement. These procedures following the *Willowbrook* lead, attempt to place and maintain residents in as normal and homelike a setting as possible. Yet as the Willowbrook experience demonstrates, procedural rights are hollow without advocates for individuals and additional homes for groups.

With the recent appointment of a special master,[141] the *Willowbrook* case has entered another period of adversarial confrontation. As the case enters its second decade, the battle lines are sharply drawn. The judge and the plaintiffs are committed to the superiority of small-scale community living arrangements in 4-, 6-, 10- and 15-bed residences (with the size limits depending upon the class members's degree of disability). In language reminiscent of *Brown* v. *Board of Education,* the court commands the defendants to comply with the consent judgment "with all deliberate speed." But unlike *Brown,* there is a specific deadline for these integration provisions. By April 1, 1985—four years beyond the original target—community-placement provisions must be fulfilled.

Willowbrook may have changed its name, but the recent hearings prove that it has not changed its fundamental nature. Reviewing conditions at Willowbrook, now called the Staten Island Developmental Center, and other institutions housing class members, the court's opinion deplores the "totally unsatisfactory" sanitation, "glaring maintenance inadequacies," inexcusable clothing, and "low quality" programming. According to the evidence, a resident's life in the large metropolitan institutions is "sterile, dreary and one of enforced idleness."[142] The results can be tragic: a resident, for example, choked to death because of an improper diet and a poorly trained staff.

Against this portrait of unrelieved gloom, small community residences stand out as places of hope and rescue. In rejecting defendants' motion to modify their earlier agreements so as to authorize 11- to 50-bed facilities, the court canvassed an extensive array of professional opinion and factual testimony in this 25-day trial. It concluded that nearly all the class members, including individuals with multiple handicaps, behavior problems, and serious medical problems, can be placed in small community settings. In the battle of expert witnesses, the court was persuaded that the needs of the *Willowbrook* class members are better met in small group homes than in "institutions larger than 10 beds" that do not provide "as good care and as normalized an environment."[143] The evidence of this superiority was marshalled not only in terms of better care, but of exposure to normal every-day living, avoidance of stigma, and reduction of neighborhood opposition to new settings. In buttressing this conclusion, the court referred to the Bronx Developmental Center litigation and the tendency of such "transitional" facilities to become long-term placements that retard the individual's growth. Despite defendants' assurances that this would not happen, over two-thirds of the class members transferred to that center since 1977 still await community placement.

A significant portion of the *Willowbrook* class now receives personalized care. In some way nearly all are better off today than in 1972, but the greatest gainers are the more than two thousand persons resettled in decent community care. This includes 1,108 ex-Willowbrook residents placed in small community residences, and 580 placed in family care. Another 730 persons discharged from state supervision have also, for the most part, found lives of greater dignity and independence.[144] The *Willowbrook* case has demonstrated that even severely handicapped, profoundly retarded people and others badly damaged by years of custodial neglect can be placed in family-scale residences and can obtain support services outside an institution. For these ex-residents and their families, getting out of Willowbrook has overwhelmingly improved the quality of their lives.

For the remainder still awaiting placement, there is a bitterly learned lesson. Neither boundless financial resources nor the immense energies stimulated by a consent order can transform a custodial institution into an authentic center for habilitation. Of the original class, 1,369 people still live on the Willowbrook grounds, 999 have been transferred to other state and private institutions, and 557 have died. The annual cost per resident for care at Willowbrook exceeds $50,000. Even with abundant legislative appropriations and administrative good will, the state has only succeeded in turning a wretched institution into a deficient one. Although uncrowded, the Staten Island Developmental Center, like other institutions of its type, still remains an unhappy holding point until appropriate substitutes can be created. At the current rate of placement, the defendants assert that it will take twenty years to find community placements for the rest of the class.[145] In imposing a 1985 deadline, the court has rejected such a pace, characterizing many of the obstacles to swifter compliance as of the state's own making. To have done otherwise would have sanctioned an unconscionable wrong, a deinstitutionalization by inches and by attrition.

The Impact of Federal Decrees

Whether in Alabama or New York, Minnesota or Pennsylvania, class-action remedies helped to fill a legal and political vacuum. They often provided powerful and necessary stimuli to the planned reduction of giant institutions and the simultaneous development of community residences and day-care resources. At last, here was a potent response to gross overcrowding, to improper confinement, and to the misuse of mental institutions as old-age homes and human dumping grounds. Until the courts turned watchful eyes on departments of mental retardation, state professionals had barely skimmed the surface for potential candidates for transfer to homelike settings. Under class-action scrutiny (or the expectation of it), the same professionals adopted a different set of expectations, thus enabling more severely disabled individuals to gain community placements than had been previously imagined. To those who criticized such judicially triggered reform, Judge Frank M. Johnson, Jr. noted the breakdowns in "conscientious, responsible leadership" by other branches of government charged with protecting individual rights and freedoms: "As long as government officials entrusted with responsibility for constitutional governance disregard that responsibility, the judiciary must and will stand ready to intervene to the extent necessary on behalf of the deprived."[146]

State Law: Potentials and Pitfalls

In the 1980s, state law is the critical frontier for the growth of community-care options. These provisions basically determine who gets out of institutions, by what procedures, and with what assurances of aftercare services. The structure of those laws can entrench or eliminate financial incentives for unnecessary institutional care.[147] Moreover, federal courts are likely to rely increasingly on state laws as an independent legal basis for deinstitutionalization orders. State law remedies are not only important in themselves, but their exhaustion can sometimes be a precondition for federal judicial review.[148] This statutory framework can therefore be both an impediment to and a source of positive prescription for community-based care. This section concentrates on New York, where plans to reduce its institutional census from 19,309 residents in 1975 to 10,139 in 1982 have been described as the single largest community-placement effort in the United States.[149] Those plans lag well behind schedule, in part because of legal problems that are typical in many states.

Mandates for Least Restrictive Alternatives

State statutes can give rise to an enforceable right to least restrictive care for institutionalized persons. They can create a presumption in favor of integration, rebuttable "only upon a showing that the individual's service needs cannot be met successfully through generic or integrated services."[150] Several federal courts have adopted similar readings of state law.[151] This approach is also shared by the courts of Pennsylvania, which have fashioned foster-care plans for residents of retardation facilities.[152] Statutory commands that dictate such exploration and development of less restrictive care plans are increasingly found in the laws of rural as well as highly industrialized states.[153]

These laws require governments to take proactive rather than reactive postures. The state of Illinois, for example, facing a U.S. Justice Department investigation of the 800-bed Dixon Developmental Center, decided to close that rural facility and disperse its residents to more habilitative settings. Reversing the typical scenario, the state is defending the legality of that transfer process against a suit by a parents' group and has called upon the federal government's expert witnesses to testify as to the conditions in Dixon and the necessity for this evacuation.[154] Given progressive laws and administrations, other states may soon witness similar institutional closings.[155]

Discharge by Judicial Action

Unfortunately, New York's law is an outmoded patchwork, reflecting neither present-day realities nor contemporary professional norms. Provisions of mental hygiene law on discharging residents by judicial action derive from a 1927 statute.[156] They take aim at an evil of that age of segregation: freeing from involuntary detention the person who is not mentally retarded or not in need of retention.[157] But such trials by jury or judge, like petitions for habeas corpus, have virtually disappeared. Even for the Willowbrook population of the early 1970s, 73 percent of whom were involuntarily confined and many who expressed a desire to leave,[158] these procedures were useless.

Discharge by Administrative Action

In lieu of indeterminate institutionalization, the legal system now relies upon durational limits, periodic reviews, and administrative discretion to determine a resident's release. The Mental Health Information Service (MHIS) also had a nominal role in the annual reviews of the suitability of retaining voluntary and other residents,[159] but the real control always remained with the clinical staff. According to state regulations, interdisciplinary staff reviews, conducted on a semiannual basis, were supposed to protect the resident's civil rights by ensuring treatment in "the least restrictive setting possible," including community placements in "the most independent residential accommodation" appropriate to the individual's needs.[160] Despite these general principles, and the more specific overlay of OMRDD policies and Medicaid requirements, thousands of mentally disabled people remained in overly restrictive state institutions and private mini-institutions.[161] State law had become a weak symbol rather than an effective instrument for securing their rights.

Transfers and Conditional Releases

The gaps in this law are especially glaring for people in transit from institutional to community lives. The OMRDD commissioner's broad power to order transfers to another appropriate facility was subject only to the limitations of obtaining the consent of a voluntary resident, or the parent's or guardian's consent for a minor.[162] But the statute lacked criteria for such transfers and failed to describe the circumstances in which officials could override an unreasonable refusal to consent.

Conditional release laws, added to assuage public alarm over unsupervised mental patients, posed another gray area for civil liberties and mental care. Discharge terminated a facility's legal responsibility for a patient, but the more restrictive conditional-release status rendered the patient subject to the vaguely worded recall authority of the facility director.[163] Another statute unsuited to the needs of severely retarded persons required state institutions to provide a discharged resident only with "suitable clothing," and, in necessary cases, no more than $50 to "reach his relatives or friends, or find employment to earn a subsistence."[164] Ex-residents with chronic mental and physical disabilities, however, needed aftercare services and could not survive so drastic a separation from alternative public supports.

Discharge and Aftercare

Even though discharge did not preclude a resident or his family from applying for residential care in the future, families quite rightly feared discharge as a one-way street. Recent legislation on aftercare has done little to alleviate those risks and concerns. Prior to being discharged, a resident must have a written service plan, specifying any need for aftercare services.[165] This can include medical and psychiatric care, and vocational and social rehabilitation. The statute does not, however, require ex-residents to be furnished with any particular amount or level of services. A retarded client has a more substantial claim on departmental resources when he or she is placed in a community residence. These small hostels or group homes are defined by statute as a "long-term supervised residence to individuals whose mental disability is such that independent living is improbable."[166] At least in theory, the residents of these homes are eligible for rights and benefits substantially similar to those available to state developmental-center residents.

Site Selection Laws

The New York legislature, sensitive to neighborhood hostility to further deinstitutionalization, has, unfortunately, made it more difficult to open new homes. Enacted in 1978, the law on site selection is an illustration of how one arm of the state erects hurdles to community care while the other complains of these self-inflicted difficulties. Before an agency sponsoring a supervised residence for four to fourteen mentally disabled persons can obtain a license, it must now go through a time-consuming process of notifying the municipality, negotiating approval of a site, responding to alternative sites recommended by the municipality, and, if agreement cannot be reached, engaging in public planning hearings, administrative hearings, and judicial reviews. In reviewing any objections, the OMRDD commissioner considers the need for such facilities and the concentration of similar facilities. However, he must sustain the objection if establishing the new facility at the proposed site would substantially alter "the nature and character of the area."[167]

The stated purposes for this measure may seem benign, but the more affluent, politically sophisticated communities gain a potent legal weapon. It allows them to channel a backlash against deinstitutionalization into neutral, even paternalistic terms such as —the municipality is already oversaturated with facilities for "these people," or has traffic that will endanger their lives, or their presence will provoke hostility from other people. Despite legislative findings that announce the mentally disabled individual's right to the benefits of normal residential surroundings, the statute ironically leads to delay, heightened community opposition, and even the legalized veto of community residences by local communities. As the *Willowbrook* court noted, the net result of this law is a "self-imposed delay," and the loss of available sites and time in the already arduous fourteen-step process for obtaining a community residence.[168]

The Courts and Open Door Policies

Despite countermovements, New York courts have generally been supportive of *open door* policies and related efforts to relocate retarded persons released from institutions. For example, a long line of cases has sustained the propriety of group homes despite impediments based on local zoning ordinances. In *Little Neck Community Association* v. *Working Association for Retarded Children,* a unanimous Appellate Division held that a group home for mentally retarded children could be located in an area for single-family residences.[169] Classifying the group home as a family unit for the purposes of a zoning ordinance, the court noted that the home was not intended for transients, but would provide retarded children with "a stable environment" giving them "a real opportunity to develop to their full potential."[170] This judicial imprimatur has encouraged the state to fulfill its *parens patriae* responsibilities toward retarded people in community-residence programs rather than through institutionalization. Other decisions consistent with this trend have overturned local zoning interpretations restricting family-care programs for ex-mental patients, day and boarding schools for mentally disabled children, or the leasing of state-purchased buildings for a privately operated hostel for retarded adults.[171]

Negligence cases, in denying recovery to third parties harmed by released mental patients, have also expressed endorsement of more liberal discharge policies. The rule in New York cases is that the state will not be held liable in damages for the actions of a patient discharged or released from a state institution, even though the release was through an error of medical or professional judgment.[172] Recognizing the open door policy as a therapeutically valid approach to integrating mentally disabled persons into the community, courts have candidly acknowledged the policy rationale behind this rule: to impose a more stringent standard of liability against doctors, or the state would discourage releases and frustrate "the hope of recovery and rehabilitation of a vast number of patients."[173] Thus, in balancing the public interests in rehabilitating retarded persons and avoiding damage to adjacent property or injury to others, common-law judges have placed a high premium on the availability of open care.[174]

State Court Review

State judges, although sympathetic, have not played a significant role in helping retarded persons to leave institutions. In part, New York courts have simply not had that many cases to decide. Whenever they did order discharge or transfer, their opinions stressed the lack of any semblance of due process, for as one court wrote in 1967: "unbridled discretion, however benevolently motivated, is frequently a poor substitute for principle and procedure."[175] But apart from procedural defects, courts were reluctant to review retention decisions either for want of jurisdiction or expertise.[176]

The Court of Appeals, pointing to the risks of mentally disabled persons remaining in unduly restrictive surroundings, has required stricter reviews for mental patients facing prolonged hospitalization. In *Buttonow,* Chief Judge Fuld stressed that the "unknowing, meek or cooperative" patient, converted from involuntary to voluntary status, might not be able to invoke the "chimerical" right to release due to lack of outside aid or inability to understand written notices of rights. Judge Keating went further, sharply criticizing the state's due process failure to provide patients with representation and periodic review of the confinement's "propriety and suitability" before an "impartial forum."[177]

Subsequent cases have revealed the drastic inadequacies of the periodic review provided retarded residents. In *Renelli* v. *Department of Mental Hygiene,* the plaintiff, a Willowbrook resident, was misclassified during her twelve-year stay as "a hopeless case" to be relegated to "custodial care only.'' Out of dismay at the evidence uncovered and the state's unwillingness to provide a remedy without being ''forced by a Court of law to fulfill their obligations,'' Judge Titone urged stricter legislation. His recommendations included an ''independent case evaluation system'' to correct classification errors and provide a periodic accounting of the ''State's stewardship of these unfortunate human beings,'' and an ''objective panel or individual not connected with the institution'' to perform this oversight function.[178]

These judicial pleas to stop the warehousing of retarded people failed to evoke an affirmative state response. Family courts, notwithstanding their compassionate opinions, were also unable to cope with mistreatment on such a scale. *In re D,* an attempted class-action neglect proceeding for some three thousand Willowbrook children and youths, illustrates this frustration.[179] In denying jurisdiction, the family court described neglect proceedings as designed to determine if parental misbehavior warranted a child's removal from a home, holding that neither the state school nor the DMH were natural persons within the contemplation of the neglect statutes. Furthermore as ''a heavily overburdened court,'' the judge rationalized that he lacked the staff and facilities to undertake the necessary investigation and relief. Deploring the ''sub-human conditions'' at Willowbrook and the shocking public apathy which left its residents ''living 'on a thread of life, human vegetables rotting in inadequate warehouses,''' Judge Cory urged specific legislation strengthening judicial review. Calling upon the government to take voluntary action to remedy this ''blot on the conscience of New York State,'' the judge outlined some alternatives: provide sufficient funds for such institutions or ''phase them out altogether for smaller, more personal institutions or provide foster care in family units where possible, as is done in cases involving neglect.''[180] Ten years later, it is this replacement strategy that has prevailed.

Paradoxically, these larger solutions have been forged in federal rather than state forums. State courts, however, have been drawn into collateral controversies, particularly the question of treating equitably persons under the shield of federal class actions and those who are not. One notable example, *Sundheimer* v. *Blum,* rejected equal protection claims by the parents of noninstitutionalized retarded individuals who were ineligible for family-care payments granted a small group of natural parents of Willowbrook residents.[181] Although family-care providers are foster parents for retarded persons unable to function independently, the DMH extended this designation to some Willowbrook parents in an effort to comply with the deinstitutionalization decree. In reversing the trial court, the Appellate Division ruled that this temporary emergency measure, aimed at satisfying the consent judgment, was a reasonable classification.

If consent decrees cannot provide a basis for broader state obligations to similar groups, new litigation will follow. For example, a suit on behalf of six thousand homeless people released from state psychiatric hospitals, like a similar suit that led to a consent agreement, could turn state courts into fulcrums for wider reforms.[182] Even activist state courts, however, are no substitute for enlightened treatment professionals and a state bureaucracy committed to community-care goals. State class actions and habeas corpus writs are simply too rare and too circumscribed to fill the current deficiencies in the law on mental disability. Without larger visions and more potent remedies, New York, which invented the classic institution in the nineteenth century, could still be saddled with them in the twenty-first century.

Conclusion

At federal and state levels, the currents of legal change have swept away the old status quo. As this review demonstrates, it is no longer legally acceptable for state agencies to leave retarded persons stranded in prisonlike institutions. In principle, parents and guardians no longer possess an absolute veto to deny their wards the prospect of a beneficial community-based alternative. Neighborhoods, too, are losing legal battles to keep the retarded out of sight as exclusionary zoning gives way to new site-selection patterns for group homes. Statutes and case law have helped to legitimize these trends and neutralize political backlashes.

Continued progress, however, is far from inevitable. Until the advent of class-action litigation, state professionals just skimmed the surface in identifying candidates for community placement. Cases like *Willowbrook* and *Pennhurst* and others equally effective, although less publicized, will continue to change the professionals' notion of readiness for such placements. But their impact goes well beyond line-drawing. They successfully document new ways of preserving the lives, the rights, and the developmental capacities of highly vulnerable people. By focusing attention on how society cares for retarded people leaving institutions, the judges and litigants stimulated affirmative legislative and executive actions, as well as research and debate. Left alone, state bureaucracies might once again pursue the tempting paths of least resistance. To complete the humane revolution in mental care, legal advocates must now win durable support for a complex agenda: diligent monitoring of resettlement efforts, an array of living arrangements and services of intimate scale and high quality, and a more comprehensive legal reform. Without those elements, the counterfeit promise of deinstitutionalization will only provoke demands for new asylums. With them, states will one day replace rather than repair institutions like Partlow, Pennhurst, and Willowbrook.

Notes

1. *See, e.g.*, Parker v. Bernstein, 125 Misc. Rep. 92, 210 N.Y.S. 594, 597 (Sup. Ct., Oneida Co. 1925).

2. Halderman v. Pennhurst State School and Hospital, 526 F. Supp. 409, 410 (E.D. Pa. 1981).

3. W. Copeland & L. Iversen, Not Just the Aged, Not Just Health Care, and Not Just Nursing Homes: Some Proposals for Policy and Legislative Changes in Long-Term Care 28 (Jan. 14, 1981).

4. Ferleger & Boyd, "Anti-Institutionalization," 31 *Stan. L. Rev.* 717, 750 (1979). For mortality and release trends, see Lakin, et al., "One Hundred Years of Data on Populations of Public Residential Facilities for Mentally Retarded People," 87 *Amer. J. of Mental Deficiency* 1, 5 (1982).

5. New York Department of Mental Hygiene [hereinafter DMH], Table J-7: "Resident Clients and Admissions, All Facilities for the Mentally Retarded" (1977).

6. The [HEW] Secretary's Special Federal Team, The New York State Mental Retardation Program 21 (Oct. 1972).

7. For a study of postlitigation relocations of Willowbrook residents and the residents' improved self-esteem from "living free," see A. Birenbaum & S. Seiffer, *Resettling Retarded Adults in a Managed Community* (1976).

8. R. Crossley & A. McDonald, *Annie's Coming Out* (1980); "TV: After 46 Years in an Institution," *New York Times*, Dec. 22, 1981, at C15 (the story of Bill Sackter's stay in the Minnesota State School and successful community adjustment); Herr, "Civil Rights, Uncivil Asylums and the Retarded," 43 *U. Cin. L. Rev.* 679, 703 n.121, 716 n.164 (1974).

9. "Interview with Bernard Carabello," I *The Aide to Willowbrook* 2 (June 12, 1974).

10. Hearing on American Families: Trends and Pressures, 1973, Before the Senate Subcomm. on Children and Youth, 93d Congress, 1st Session 321, 326 (Sept. 24, 1973) (statement of Gunnar Dybwad).

11. *See* Solomons, "Counseling Parents of the Retarded," in *Psychiatric Approaches to Mental Retardation* 472 (F. Menolascino ed. 1970). For additional literature, see Teitelbaum & Ellis, "The Liberty Interest of Children: Due Process Rights and Their Application" 12 *Fam. L. Q.* 153, 194-97 (1978).

12. *E.g.*, Hammond, Sternlicht, & Deutsch, "Parental Interest in Institutionalized Children: A Survey," 20 *Hospital & Community Psychiatry* 338 (1969).

13. Guardianship of Becker, No. 101981 (Cal. Super. Ct., Santa Clara Co. Aug. 7, 1981), *aff'd*, No. A014309 (Cal. Ct. App., 1st App. Dist. Jan. 25, 1983).

14. *Id.* slip op. at 14.

15. *Id.* at n.69.

16. *In re* Vanessa R., No. M240496 (Cal. Super. Ct., Los Angeles Co. July 2, 1976) (habeas writ granted for minor's discharge over guardian's objection). *But see* Adamson v. Lackner, Civ. No. M243830 (Cal. Super. Ct., Los Angeles Co. 1978) (habeas denied for thirteen-year-old high-functioning institutionalized child). *See* Repp, "On the Ethical Responsibilities of Institutions Providing Services for Mentally Retarded People," 16 *Mental Retardation* 153, 154 (1978). *See generally* A. Stone, *Mental Health and Law* 123-24 (1975). On the unwritten Pennsylvania policy of not moving minors into the community when parents object and its rejection by a federal district court, see Halderman v. Pennhurst State School, 533 F. Supp. 660 (E.D. Pa. 1982) and Human Services Research Institute, Longitudinal Study of Court-Ordered Deinstitutionalization of Pennhurst: Historical Overview V (July 13, 1982).

17. *See* Guardianship of Becker, *supra* note 13, at 15; *In re* Hop, 171 Cal. Rptr. 721, 623 P.2d 282, 289 (Sup. Ct. 1981); *In re* Borgogna, 175 Cal. Rptr. 588 (App. Ct. 1981).

18. *See* S. Davies, *The Mentally Retarded in Society* 141 (1959); Sternlicht & Merritt, "Variables Related to Obtaining Natural Parents' Consent for Family Care Placement," 1 *Research to Practice* 275 (P. Mittler ed. 1977).

19. *In re* Wood, 355 N.Y.S.2d 885, 891 (Fam. Ct., St. Lawrence Co. 1974) (retarded child singled out from other neglected siblings as not "a candidate for adoption"); Matter of Anonymous, 76 Misc. 2d 1077, 352 N.Y.S.2d 743, 744 (Surr. Ct., N.Y. Co. 1968) (adoption decree abrogated on the possibility of the child's "mental retardation problem").

20. "More Couples Adopting Victims of Genetic Defect," *New York Times*, March 8, 1979, at 1; "Baby in Malpractice Was Put-Up for Adoption," *New York Times*, Feb. 17, 1973, at 23.

21. Braddock, "Deinstitutionalization of the Retarded: Trends in Public Policy," 32 *Hospital & Community Psychiatry* 607, 613 (1981); "Psychiatric Centers Cited in Levitt Audit," *New York Times*, May 1, 1978, at C39 (half of beds in new developmental centers remained empty).

22. Draft Memorandum from Peter Schuck, HEW Deputy Assistant Secretary to Benjamin W. Heineman, Jr., Executive Assistant to the Secretary, "Community Services Reform Initiative," 1-2 (April 21, 1978).

23. Decision Memorandum from Benjamin W. Heineman, Jr., Acting Assistant Secretary for Planning and Evaluation to the HEW Secretary, "Deinstitutionalization Task Force Recommendations" (March 12, 1979).

24. *See* Editorial: "Completing the Mental Care Revolution," *New York Times*, Nov. 1, 1977, at 36; "Suit on Homeless Mental Patients Asks New York State for Housing," *New York Times*, May 21, 1982, at A1.

25. 383 U.S. 107 (1966).

26. *Id.* at 111.

27. *See* R. Hunt & D. Wiley, "Operation Baxstrom After One Year," in Special Comm. of the Ass'n of the Bar of New York City, *Mental Illness, Due Process and the Criminal Defendant* 221, 225 (1968).

28. Steadman & Keveles, "Community Adjustment and Criminal Activity of the Baxstrom Patients: 1966-1970," 129 *Am. J. Psychiatry* 304 (1972).

29. Dixon v. Attorney General of Pennsylvania, 325 F. Supp. 966, 970 (M.D. Pa. 1971).

30. 422 U.S. 563, 575 (1975).

31. 102 S. Ct. 2452 (1982), discussed in chapter 8, *infra*.

32. 445 U.S. 480 (1980).

33. *Id.* at 495, quoting from Addington v. Texas, 441 U.S. 418, 430 (1979).

34. Southeastern Community College v. Davis, 442 U.S. 397 (1979). In University of Texas v. Camenisch, 451 U.S. 390, vacating 616 F.2d 127 (5th Cir. 1980), the Court found a preliminary injunction claim for a deaf graduate student's sign-language interpreter moot and remanded for a trial on the merits.

35. *Davis*, 442 U.S. at 413.

36. 429 U.S. 252 (1977). Under that test, the requirement of an annually renewable special-use permit did not violate group home residents' constitutional rights. Insight, Inc. v. City of Manassas, No. 79-1098 (4th Cir. June 2, 1981).

37. 416 U.S. 1, 9 (1974).

38. *E.g.*, Hopkins v. Zoning Hearing Board of Abington Township, 423 A.2d 1081, 1084 (Pa. Commonwealth Ct. 1980) (restrictive definition of family held unconstitutional, and denial of zoning permit reversed for community living arrangement placing mentally retarded persons into a family setting "as nearly normal as possible"). *See* text and notes at notes 169-171, *infra*.

39. Quoted in U.S. Dep't of Health and Human Services, "HHS News" (May 6, 1982).

40. 20 C.F.R. § 416.1161a (b), *printed in* 47 Fed. Reg. 24274-77 (June 4, 1982).

41. *Id.* at 24275. For discussion of the new Medicaid waiver, see chapter 4, text and notes at notes 84-86, *supra*.

42. 42 U.S.C. § 9501(1)(A)(i) (1981 Pamphlet). *See also* Adoption Assistance and Child Welfare Act of 1980, 42 U.S.C. § 5111 (Supp. Pamphlet 1982).

43. 29 U.S.C. § 794 (Supp. Pamphlet 1982).

44. 45 C.F.R. § 84.4(b)(1)(iv) (1981).

45. *Id.* § 84.4(b)(2).

46. Halderman v. Pennhurst State School, 446 F. Supp. 1295, 1323-24

(E.D. Pa. 1977), *aff'd on other grounds*, 612 F.2d 84 (3d Cir. 1979), *rev'd on other grounds and remanded*, 451 U.S. 1 (1981); New York State ARC v. Carey, 466 F. Supp. 479, 486 (E.D.N.Y. 1978), *aff'd*, 612 F.2d 644, 649 (2d Cir. 1979). *See also* Garrity v. Gallen, 522 F. Supp. 171, 205-18 (D.N.H. 1981).

47. Lynch v. Maher, 507 F. Supp. 1268 (D. Conn. 1981). On parental involvement in habilitation decisions, see Joyner v. Dumpson, 533 F. Supp. 233 (S.D.N.Y. 1982) (requirement transferring parents' custody to state as a condition for receiving out-of-home residential services violates § 504).

48. In baby Doe's few days of life, the Monroe County prosecutor and a guardian *ad litem* unsuccessfully sought a court order authorizing treatment from the trial court and the Indiana Supreme Court on April 14, 1982. The infant died before a *certiorari* petition to the United States Supreme Court could be prepared. On federal reactions, see President Reagan, Memorandum for the Attorney General [and] the Secretary of Health and Human Services, Subject: Enforcement of Federal Laws Prohibiting Discrimination against the Handicapped (April 30, 1982); The President's Comm. on Mental Retardation, "The Infant Doe Resolution" (June 14, 1982).

49. U.S. Dep't of Health and Human Services, Health Care Financing Administration, "Medicare Part A Intermediary Letter, Transmitted No. 82-11, Subject: Implementation of Section 504 (P.L. 93-112) to Assure Non-Discrimination Against Handicapped Persons" (May 18, 1982).

50. 42 U.S.C. § 1382e (Supp. 1982). This statute provides for annual certification of compliance by states, public reviews of the standards and their enforcement.

51. *See* C. Sherwood & M. Seltzer, *Board and Care: Review of the Literature* (Jan. 1981).

52. 42 U.S.C. § 1997a (1981).

53. United States v. Solomon, 563 F.2d 1121 (4th Cir. 1977); United States v. Mattson, 600 F.2d 1295 (9th Cir. 1979). Since passage of the act, the Justice Department has renewed its investigation of Maryland's Rosewood State School.

54. Santana v. Collazo, 89 F.R.D. 369 (D.P.R. 1981) (right to treatment for juveniles in least restrictive setting); Davis v. Henderson, No. 77-423 (D. La. May 28, 1982) (conditions and treatment in forensic mental facility).

55. *See, e.g.*, D.C. Welfare Rights Organization v. Thompson, No. 71-1150-J (D.C. Super. Ct. June 18, 1981), reported in 5 *Clearinghouse Rev.* 263, 419 (1971); Gary W. v. Louisiana, 437 F. Supp. 1209 (E.D. La. 1976); Dixon v. Weinberger, 405 F. Supp. 974 (D.D.C. 1975); United States v. Alsbrook, 336 F. Supp. 973 (D.D.C. 1971).

56. *E.g.*, Suzuki v. Quisenberry, 411 F. Supp. 1113 (D. Hawaii 1976).

57. Dixon v. Attorney General, 325 F. Supp. 966 (M.D. Pa. 1971).

58. *E.g.*, Wyatt v. Stickney, 344 F. Supp. 387, 395 (M.D. Ala. 1972).

59. L. Clark, The Martti Wuori Case: Report to the Court: How Maine Cares for its Retarded Citizens at 5 (July 20, 1981).

60. For a useful survey, see Special Project, "The Remedial Process in Institutional Reform Litigation," 78 *Col. L. Rev.* 784 (1978).

61. *Cf.* Halderman v. Pennhurst State School, 446 F. Supp. 1295, 1325, 1327 (E.D. Pa. 1977) *with* Brewster v. Dukakis, No. 81-1687 (1st Cir. June 28, 1982).

62. Poe v. Harris, No. 74-1800 (D.D.C. Feb. 25, 1980) (stipulation).

63. D.C. v. Surles, No. 78-91 (D. Vt. Aug. 1, 1979) (stipulation).

64. *E.g.*, Meisel v. Kremens, 405 F. Supp. 1253 (E.D. Pa. 1975) (summary revocation of patient's leave of absence "almost completely devoid" of due process of law). *See* Frederick v. Mulcahy, No. 76-257 (D. Vt. July 6, 1978) (suit challenging conditional discharge procedures from retardation institution ended by adoption of remedial regulations and legislation).

65. Johnson v. Brelje, 521 F. Supp. 723 (N.D. Ill. 1981) (transfer to more restrictive setting requires prior written notice to patient and attorney disclosing individualized basis for proposed transfer and an opportunity for a contested hearing); Herwald v. Schweiker, 658 F.2d 359 (5th Cir. 1981) (preliminary injunction denied where private nursing home involuntarily discharged retarded resident); Boarding Home Advocacy Team, Inc. v. O'Bannon, 525 F. Supp. 1181 (E.D. Pa. 1981) (procedures adequate for consensual transfers from state hospital to less restrictive nursing home).

66. Stanger v. Ambach, 501 F. Supp. 1237, 1243 (S.D.N.Y. 1980).

67. People of the State of New York v. Eleven Cornwell Company, No. 80 C 2139 (E.D.N.Y. Nov. 23, 1981).

68. N.Y. Exec. Law, § 296(5)(a)(1) (1982).

69. Stoner v. Miller, 377 F. Supp. 177 (E.D.N.Y. 1974).

70. *See* U.S. District Court Monitor, Report to the Court at 80-83, 128-32 (Feb. 1981) (equal treatment for all class clients recommended in the five Massachusetts mental retardation consent decrees).

71. Welsch v. Likins, No. 4-72 Civ. 451, Memorandum Findings of Fact, Conclusions of Law, and Order for Judgment at 30 (D. Minn. Oct. 1, 1975).

72. No. 75-80-SD (D. Maine July 14, 1978).

73. Report of the Special Master to the United States District Court, "Community Placement for Pineland Residents" at 6, 10 (Nov. 24, 1980).

74. Medley v. Ginsberg, No. 78-2099 CH, slip op. at 21 (S.D. W. Va. Oct. 8, 1981) (order and consent decree).

75. Welsch v. Noot, No. 4-72 Civ. 451 (D. Minn. Sept. 15, 1980) (consent decree).

76. On orders requiring legislative action to satisfy this decree, see

Welsch v. Noot, No. 4-72 Civ 451 (D. Minn. Mar. 23, 1982); *Id.* memorandum order of Jan. 13, 1982, discussed *infra* at note 147.

77. Interview with Neil Mickenberg, Deputy Director, Vermont Legal Aid Society (Mar. 17, 1979) (quoted with permission).

78. *D.C. Family Welfare Rights, supra* note 55, at 40: "Petitioners have been denied their rights to equal treatment and opportunity afforded other dependent children under the statute: some children receive an adequate home substitute through foster home care, while the children placed at Meriwether, for no reason other than administrative convenience and lack of responsibility, do not."

79. 446 F. Supp. 1295 (E.D. Pa. 1977), *rev'd and remanded on this point*, 612 F.2d 84, 113-15 (3d Cir. 1979).

80. No. 76-4432-F (D. Mass. Dec. 7, 1978).

81. Brewster v. Dukakis, 675 F.2d 1 (1st Cir. 1982); No. 81-1687 (1st Cir. June 28, 1982).

82. Michigan Ass'n for Retarded Citizens v. Smith, 475 F. Supp. 990 (E.D. Mich. 1979); 657 F.2d 102 (6th Cir. 1981) (intervention of labor union denied as untimely). *Cf.* Lapeer Oakdale Parents Ass'n for Retarded Citizens v. Ochberg, 492 F. Supp. 1035, 1037 (E.D. Mich. 1980) (reductions in resident population from 1,300 to 886, with further transfers contemplated; court warns that "budget cuts cannot under any circumstances justify depriving the residents of their rights").

83. *E.g.*, Lelsz v. Kavanagh, S-74-95-CA (E.D. Tex. July 9, 1981) (intervention by pro-institution parents' group denied); Florida Ass'n for Retarded Citizens v. Graham, No. 79-418 (M.D. Fla., filed Aug. 22, 1979); Washington Ass'n for Retarded Citizens v. Thomas, No. C-78-168 (E.D. Wash., filed June 16, 1978); Iasimone v. Garrahy, No. 77-0727 (D.R.I. April 29, 1982) (consent order).

84. 344 F. Supp. at 396 (standard 3.c.).

85. *Id.* at 397-98 (standards 9.d., 9.f., 14.h.). Modifications have since limited such plans to residents with prospects for release as well as permitted retention of multiply handicapped, but mildly retarded residents.

86. *Id.* at 396 (standards 2 and 3).

87. On the limitations of lay committees performing that role, see Drake, "Judicial Implementation and *Wyatt v. Stickney*" 32 *Ala. L. Rev.* 299, 307 (1981).

88. *Wyatt*, Order of April 12, 1978.

89. *E.g., Wyatt*, Memorandum of April 18, 1975: "Recognition of a resident's constitutional right to habilitation was the basis upon which the judgment and decree in this case were founded, and it remains this Court's primary concern and criterion in reviewing the adequacy of defendants' efforts at implementation."

90. Wyatt v. Ireland, Memorandum and Order of Oct. 25, 1979.

91. *Id.* at 7.

92. Wyatt v. Hardin, Petitioners' Motion for Modification at 7 (Oct. 20, 1978).

93. J. Rubin, *Economics, Mental Health, and the Law* 130 (1978).

94. Wyatt v. Ireland, No. 3195-J (M.D. Ala. Jan. 15, 1980), discussed in Johnson, "The Role of the Federal Courts in Institutional Litigation," 32 *Ala. L. Rev.* 271, 278 (1981).

95. Memorandum from R. Sanders to Professional Advisory Committee re Modifications in the Court Ordered Standards at 3, 5 (Feb. 18, 1981).

96. *See* Barbakow, "Partlow and the Wyatt Case: A Personal Experience," 20 *Mental Retardation* 141, 143 (July 1982).

97. Halderman v. Pennhurst State School and Hospital, 526 F. Supp. 409, 410 (E.D. Pa. 1981) [hereinafter cited as *Pennhurst*].

98. 446 F. Supp. 1295, 1312 (E.D. Pa. 1977), *aff'd in part*, 612 F.2d 84 (3d Cir. 1979), *rev'd on other grounds*, 451 U.S. 1 (1981).

99. Office of the Special Master, Plan for the Interim Operation of Pennhurst (Dec. 4, 1978).

100. *Pennhurst*, No. 74-1345, Order of April 26, 1979.

101. 612 F.2d 84, 115 (3d Cir. 1979).

102. *See id.* at 116: "[I]nstitutionalization is a disfavored approach to habilitation. Only where the court or the Master finds that an improved Pennhurst is the only appropriate place for individual patients should it be used."

103. Since the district court vacated its 1980 order requiring hearings as to the voluntariness of every placement, hearings are limited to questions of whether a placement is beneficial. *Pennhurst*, Order of Feb. 22, 1982.

104. 612 F.2d 84, 111-12 (3d Cir. 1979); 673 F.2d 628, 630-31 (3d Cir. 1982).

105. 102 S. Ct. 2956, *cert. granted* (June 21, 1982).

106. Human Services Research Institute, Longitudinal Study of Court-Ordered Deinstitutionalization of Pennhurst, Historical Overview IV at 63 (Dec. 21, 1981).

107. *Pennhurst*, Order of June 8, 1979.

108. *Pennhurst*, Order on Implementation of Mar. 2, 1981.

109. 526 F. Supp. 414 (E.D. Pa. 1981).

110. 533 F. Supp. 631 (E.D. Pa. 1981), *aff'd*, 673 F.2d 628 (3d Cir. 1982). On the disposition of those fines totaling $1.2 million, see 533 F. Supp. 641 (E.D. Pa. 1982).

111. 526 F. Supp. 428 (E.D. Pa. 1981).

112. For a detailed account of the pangs of this process, see Human Services Research Institute, Longitudinal Study of the Court-Ordered Deinstitutionalization of Pennhurst, Implementation Analysis (Mar. 5, 1982).

113. Conroy, Efthimiou, & Lemanowicz, "A Matched Comparison of

the Developmental Growth of Institutionalized and Deinstitutionalized Mentally Retarded Clients," 86 *Am. J. of Mental Deficiency* 581 (1982).

114. J. Conroy, Pennhurst Study Brief Report No. 10, Survey of Families of Clients Deinstitutionalized from the Date of the Court Order to April 30, 1980 (July 31, 1981). *Accord*, Schroeder & Henes, "Assessment of Progress of Institutionalized and Deinstitutionalized Retarded Adults: A Matched-Control Comparison," 16 *Mental Retardation* 147 (1978) (those placed in group homes showed greater gains in skills).

115. Preliminary Draft of Consent Judgment, jointly submitted by plaintiffs and the United States 64-69 (1975).

116. New York State Ass'n for Retarded Children v. Carey, No. 72 Civ. 356/357 (E.D.N.Y. April 30, 1975) (consent decree paras. V.1 & V.9), *approved* 393 F. Supp. 715 (E.D.N.Y. 1975) [hereinafter *Willowbrook*].

117. *Id.* at V.6.

118. *Id.* at V.4 and V.5.

119. *Id.* at V.4, discussed at text accompanying note 143, *infra*.

120. *Id.* at V.13.

121. 393 F. Supp. at 717.

122. Statement of Dr. Herbert J. Grossman, quoted at 357 F. Supp. 752, 755 (E.D.N.Y. 1973).

123. *Willowbrook*, consent decree, at V.2.

124. *Id.*, Proposed Community Placement Plan for the Members of the Willowbrook Class at 7 (1976).

125. *Id.*, Stipulation and Order on Consent at 1 (Mar. 10, 1977).

126. *See* 456 F. Supp. 85, 94 (E.D.N.Y. 1978).

127. *Willowbrook*, Order Modifying Order of March 10, 1977 (Sept. 30, 1978).

128. *Cf. id.* at para. J. *with* Willowbrook Review Panel, Report to the Court 43 (Dec. 1978).

129. 409 F. Supp. 606, 608 (E.D.N.Y. 1976).

130. *Willowbrook*, Order of Feb. 8, 1977.

131. *Id., supra* note 125, at para. 15.

132. Memorandum Decision and Order of June 10, 1977, at 4.

133. *Id.* at 11.

134. 456 F. Supp. 85 (E.D.N.Y. 1978).

135. 438 F. Supp. 440, 446 (E.D.N.Y. 1977).

136. Stipulation of Oct. 22, 1979. On the absence of program activity for clients and concern over the "massive and life-threatening problems" at the hospital, see Willowbrook Review Panel, Report to the Court 7, 16-23 (Dec. 1978).

137. Willowbrook Consent Decree, at paras. W.3, V.11.

138. *See* N.Y. DMH, Division of Mental Retardation Memorandum No. 76-5 (July 28, 1976).

139. *Id.* at para. B.10. Residents are also classified as correspondent or non-correspondent, on the basis of whether or not a parent, legal guardian, or interested relative has communicated with the facility or visited the resident at least once in the previous year. Non-correspondents are entitled to *in loco parentis* representation. On the mandatory nature of due process procedures in all transfers, see N.Y. OMRDD Operating Standards for Intermediate Care Facilities § 681.5(f) (Feb. 8, 1980).

140. *Id.* at para. B.6.

141. New York State ARC v. Carey, Memorandum on Motion for Declaration of Noncompliance and Appointment of a Special Master (E.D.N.Y. April 28, 1982). Rudy Magnone, the newly appointed master, must walk a delicate line: to plan, report and "assist in the accomplishment" of the consent decree's community placement provisions and to monitor its other provisions, but not to adjudicate disputes or control, manage or supervise state operations.

142. *Id.* at 21.

143. *Id.* at 49.

144. Evidence suggests that many of these children returned to their natural families with supportive services, while many adults were able to enjoy apartment living on an independent or semi-independent basis. *See* N.Y. State OMRDD, *Comprehensive Plan for Services to Mentally Retarded and Developmentally Disabled Persons in New York State, 1981-1984* (Oct. 1980). There is concern, however, on locating some "community status" clients who may not be receiving adequate services. *See* Willowbrook Review Panel, Report to the Court 13-14 (Dec. 1978).

145. Memorandum of April 28, 1982, *supra* note 141, at 55. Although the defendants' attributed their main difficulty to a real-estate scarcity, the court observed that these problems could be alleviated by new construction, relaxation of the "county of origin" rule for residents from Manhattan and Bronx (where the housing shortage is most acute), the hiring of additional site selection staff, and development of equivalent but less rigid building safety codes.

146. Johnson, *supra* note 94, at 279.

147. *See* Welsch v. Noot, No. 4-72 Civ. 451 (D. Minn. Jan. 13, 1982) (legislative action required to equalize costs to county of institutional and community care).

148. *E.g.*, Woe v. Arlington County General District Court, 620 F.2d 296 (4th Cir. 1980) (individual litigants must exhaust state remedies before claims of ineffective assistance of counsel can be heard). *See also* Petition of Ackerman, Ind. App., 409 N.E.2d 1211 (1980).

149. New York State, *Comprehensive Plan for Services, supra* note 144, at 134.

150. Ellis, "Model Statute," *Disabled Persons and the Law: State Legislative Issues* 426 (B. Sales, D. Powell & R. Van Duizend eds. 1982).

151. *E.g.*, Halderman v. Pennhurst State School, 673 F.2d 647 (3d Cir. 1982), *aff'g in substantial part*, 446 F. Supp. 1295 (E.D. Pa. 1977); Kentucky Ass'n for Retarded Citizens v. Conn, 510 F. Supp. 1241, 1247-50 (W.D. Ky. 1980); Dixon v. Weinberger, 405 F. Supp. 974 (D.D.C. 1975). *See* Davis v. Buckley, 526 F. Supp. 985 (E.D. Va. 1981) (least restrictive alternative statute, Va. Code § 37.1-84.1, may "require community placements where warranted").

152. *In re* Schmidt, 429 A.2d 631 (Pa. Sup. Ct. 1981); *In re* Angelo P., No. J-194157 (Pa. Ct. of Common Pleas, Philadelphia Co. Fam. Div. Dec. 6, 1976) (ordering foster care, public school enrollment, and discharge from a retardation institution).

153. *E.g.,* Vermont Stat. Ann., tit. 18 §§ 8824, 8834(e) (Cum. Supp. 1981); New Mexico Stat. Ann. § 43-1-8 (1979 Pamphlet); Ky. Rev. Stat. §§ 202B.040(c), .060(12)-(13)(1980); Tenn. Code Ann. § 33-1601, Art. IV (1977); Cal. Welf. & Inst. Code § 4502(a) (Supp. 1982). *See In re* Hop, 171 Cal. Rptr. 721, 623 P.2d 282 (Sup. Ct. 1981) (lack of due process hearing for nonprotesting developmentally disabled persons renders statute and transfer to more confining facility unconstitutional, notwithstanding "benevolent intent" or legislative mandate on least restrictive placements).

154. Dixon Ass'n for Retarded Citizens v. Thompson, No. 81 CO 2731 (Ill. Cir. Ct., Cook Co. June 3, 1982), *rev'd*, No. 56831 (Ill. Sup. Ct. June 29, 1982) (state has authority to close mental retardation facility).

155. For a clinician's perspective on parallel directions in mental health care, see James, "State Hospitals Should be Replaced," *State Mental Hospitals: Problems and Potentials* 117 (J. Talbott ed. 1980).

156. 1927 N.Y. Laws, ch. 426, § 125 (repealed 1972).

157. N.Y. Mental Hygiene Law [hereinafter M.H.L.] § 15.35 (1978).

158. New York State ARC v. Rockefeller, 357 F. Supp. 752, 756 (E.D.N.Y. 1973). Interviews with Willowbrook residents, New York City (Sept. 29, 1974).

159. The Mental Health Information Service must annually review the suitability and willingness of a resident to remain in voluntary status, and the retention of non-objecting residents. M.H.L. § 15.25(d).

160. 14 NYCRR §§ 36.1, 36.4(a) (1973).

161. "28% Are Held in Mental Hospitals Needlessly, New York Study Finds," *New York Times*, Jan. 15, 1978, at 1; S. Taylor et al., *Title XIX and Deinstitutionalization* 98-101 (Center on Human Policy, 1981).

162. M.H.L. § 29.11(a).

163. *See* M.H.L. § 1.03(30)-(31). *Cf.* Lewis v. Donnahue, 437 F. Supp. 112 (W.D. Okla. 1977) (status revocation statute unconstitutional).

164. *Id.* at § 29.17.

165. *Id.* § 29.15(g)(1). An interdisciplinary team, including the client and "client's correspondent," must develop this "Community Service Plan." N.Y. OMRDD, Policy and Procedures, Topic No. 2.5.1, "Process for Discharge or Conditional Release" (Nov. 1981).

166. *Id.* § 1.03(28).

167. M.H.L. § 41.34(b)(5) (Supp. 1981); Town of Pound Ridge v. Introne, 81 A.D. 2d 890, 439 N.Y.S.2d 54 (1981).

168. Memorandum of April 28, 1982, *supra* note 141, at 57.

169. 52 A.D.2d 90 (1976).

170. *Id.* at 95.

171. Ganim v. Village of New York Mills, 75 Misc. 2d 653, 347 N.Y.S.2d 373 (Sup. Ct., Oneida Co. 1973); Rogers v. Ass'n for Help of Retarded Children, 308 N.Y. 126, 123 N.E.2d 806 (1954); Connors v. N.Y. State Ass'n for Retarded Children, 82 Misc. 2d 861, 370 N.Y.S.2d 474 (Sup. Ct., Rensselaer Co., 1975).

172. *See* Cameron v. State, 37 A.D.2d 46, 322 N.Y.S.2d 562, 564 (1971), *aff'd*, 30 N.Y.2d 596, 331 N.Y.S.2d 30 (1972).

173. Taig v. State, 19 A.D.2d 182, 241 N.Y.S.2d 495, 496 (1963). In one case imposing liability, an award of damages against the state was based on the mental hospital's failure to conform to its own internal administrative procedures for discharge, the negligence arising from an administrative rather than a medical act. Homere v. State, 79 Misc. 2d 972, 361 N.Y.S.2d 820 (Ct. Cl. 1974).

174. *E.g.*, Seavy v. State, 21 A.D.2d 445, 451, 250 N.Y.S.2d 877, 882 (1964): "The use of the open door policy in psychiatric hospitals has been widely accepted. Most spectacular developments have occurred during the last two decades in the area of rehabilitation where attempts have been made to return the mentally deficient to full participation in community activity."

175. People *ex rel.* Goldfinger v. Johnston, 53 Misc. 2d 949, 280 N.Y.S.2d 304, 307 (Sup. Ct., Dutchess Co. 1967), quoting *In re* Gault, 387 U.S. 1, 18 (1967).

176. *E.g., In re* Perez, 65 Misc. 567, 120 N.Y.S.2d 870 (Dom. Rel. Ct., N.Y.C. 1953) (teenage girl committed to Willowbrook as "incorrigible" and "mentally defective" based on reports of sexual intercourse, but court had no jurisdiction to hear parent's petition for release).

177. *In re* Buttonow, 23 N.Y.2d 391, 297 N.Y.S.2d 97 (1968).

178. 73 Misc. 2d 261, 340 N.Y.S.2d 498, 501 (Sup. Ct., Richmond Co. 1973).

179. 70 Misc. 2d 953, 335 N.Y.S.2d 638 (Fam. Ct., Richmond Co. 1972).

180. *Id.* at 649-50.

181. (Sup. Ct., Bronx Co. May 28, 1979), *rev'd*, 79 A.D.2d 512, 433 N.Y.S.2d 456 (1980).

182. Callahan v. Carey, No. 42582-79 (Sup. Ct., N.Y. Co. Aug. 26, 1981) (consent decree); Klosterman v. Carey, No. 11270-82 (Sup. Ct., N.Y. Co., filed May 20, 1982). *But see* Sherrin & Abrams, "Equal Protection Challenges to Consent Judgments in Right-to-Treatment Litigation: Are the States Getting More Than They Bargain For?" 45 *Albany L. Rev.* 613 (1981).

Part III
New Directions

7 Advocates for Retarded People

The emergence of legal rights for retarded people has led to expectations that advocates will be available to defend those rights. During the past dozen years, as this book documents, there has been an explosive surge in defining those rights through the courts, legislatures, and regulatory bodies. This has transformed the concept of advocacy for mentally retarded as well as for mentally ill and other handicapped persons from an esoteric notion to an established fact. On international and national levels, an era of advocacy has arrived.

Despite this acceptance, the advocacy movement is threatened on two fronts: internal disagreement on what constitutes advocacy and external constraints on its more dynamic practitioners. These issues surface sharply in efforts to define the types of advocacy that the taxpayer should support or the foundation subsidize. No discussion of this topic can overlook the intertwined relationship between poverty and mental retardation. Though some retarded persons may have the financial resources to retain a private counsel, the overwhelming majority lack sufficient control of their resources or the sophistication to enter the fee-for-services market. In a period of shrinking legal-aid allotments, the retarded poor, who until recently had little or no access to the legal system, will be the first to suffer. Without the help of specialized offices prepared to assist those hampered by disability or institutionalization, they will be in no position to claim their rights or to compete for this scarcer generic service. If diligent and zealous advocacy is then reserved only for handicapped persons who can pay for it, this could set back human rights progress and aggravate social inequities. Politically, this would also erode the broad base of support that sustains the civil rights movement for *all* handicapped children and adults.

This chapter outlines some critical unmet advocacy needs and the spectrum of advocacy approaches. It then proposes a model for the realization of client rights and various strategies for its implementation. These developments suggest a greater emphasis on advocacy by as well as for retarded people.

Definitions and Needs

The many usages of the term *advocacy* raise the risk of a debased concept. At its loosest level, for example, some clinicians refer to advocacy as "raising a fuss'' or ''meeting clinical needs.''[1] This confused notion of equating advocacy with satisfying services needs has its origins in the writings of health professionals who promoted child advocacy as the ''added ingredient'' to ensure that the ''child's developmental needs are met.''[2] It was not long before state commissioners of education, institutional superintendents, protective-service workers, and other planners and providers of services had joined this bandwagon and labeled their work as advocacy.

The debate on who is entitled to be called an advocate has raged long and loud. It is more than a matter of semantics, ideology, or a petty jurisdictional dispute. At its core is a problem of truth in advertising: giving the public and potential clients clear notice that those who purport to be advocates will in fact discharge that role with credibility, competence, and freedom from distorting conflicts of interest. For instance, unless an advocate is trained and can be relied upon to preserve client confidences, the integrity of client-advocate communications is compromised.

Because of its historic roots, ethical codes, and professional mores, legal advocacy in this field has avoided some of the previously mentioned pitfalls. This role refers to formal and informal persuasive activities on behalf of a client or group of clients, efforts grounded in legal and human rights and subject to client control. In this context, legal advocacy is a shorthand for a broad range of client-oriented methods to secure the client's rights, aspirations, and dignity. Although guardianship implies advocacy aspects, a guardian assumes decision-making control over a ward whereas a legal advocate is subject to the decisions made by a client, and attempts to achieve the client's lawful goals.

Notwithstanding popular associations, this form of advocacy is neither the monopoly of lawyers nor synonymous with adversarial action. In addition to legal representation in a courtroom or an administrative setting, it may include counseling, legal planning, negotiation, investigation, and participation in developing individual service plans. On a systemic level, legal advocates act for individual or organizational clients through legislative, regulatory, administrative, and other processes. Beyond possessing legal skills and knowledge, to be effective, advocates for mentally disabled persons must be sensitive to interpersonal dynamics and the workings of public bureaucracies.

If defining unmet needs for traditional forms of legal assistance is a difficult task, doing so for mentally retarded persons is still harder. Surveys of the American public have analyzed the frequency of certain civil legal problems,[3] but there are no data to tell us whether retarded people have higher or lower rates of evictions, consumer credit, family law, and other common legal problems. Moreover, because of inexperience and incapacity, retarded persons are less likely than others to identify a problem as legal and to locate, retain, and guide a lawyer in seeking its resolution.

But apart from their ordinary legal problems, retarded persons (or those so labeled) have special needs related to or complicated by this status. Thus, laws on civil commitment, guardianship, special education, and antidiscrimination raise unique legal risks and opportunities. Given the geometric increases in asserting rights under those laws, any assessment of advocacy requirements based on historic patterns of consumer demands will be highly unreliable. A sounder approach focuses on the rights at stake, that is, the requirements of existing court decrees, statutes, regulations, and constitutional mandates, and the experience of special advocacy projects in seeking substantial compliance with those rights.

By any measure, the unmet needs of retarded persons for legal assistance are stark and overwhelming. Sometimes they involve life-and-death situations, such as the baby Doe case or the pervasive problem of unequal access to medical care on the basis of a diagnosis of retardation.[4] The right to a free, appropriate, and personalized education also generates an enormous demand for legal services, including parent training, counseling, representation in administrative hearings, litigation, and group advocacy with regard to regulatory policies and legislative actions. Furthermore, the legal rights of persons with mental disabilities to habilitation have burst forth in recent years as courts, legislatures, and regulatory agencies have set standards of quality, restrictiveness, and periodic review. Yet according to a Legal Services Corporation study, these and other special legal problems of 4.4 million retarded Americans go "largely unaddressed."[5]

For those in institutions, existing groups have only begun to outline the great needs for legal representation. Among the 1.8 million elderly and handicapped persons in this country's 27,203 institutions, retarded residents have little or no access to local legal-aid services.[6] As of 1980, one program in one hundred had an office in a retardation institution. With funding cutbacks in legal aid, now there is less case intake and outreach in such facilities than before. Yet the average resident is burdened with two to three serious legal problems, and studies document an ocean of unmet needs with respect to such issues as institutional conditions, individual service planning, aftercare, movement to and from institutions, and systemic advocacy.[7] Since retardation facilities—traditional and community-based—are within the rule of law, their populations should not be deprived of advocacy which can make legal safeguards meaningful. As presidential commissions have recognized, despite the best intentions mentally disabled pesons are exposed to exploitation and abuse, and need public legal advocacy services to protect their rights.[8]

The Advocacy Spectrum

Clearly not all advocacy needs can or should be referred to legal advocates. Even if sufficient numbers of lawyers, paralegals, and legally supervised lay advocates were available, it would be overkill to rely on technical, highly professional approaches where self-help methods would suffice. Indeed, a movement that aims to reduce dependencies should not foster new ones by encouraging overreliance on legal advocacy. That risk is more hypothetical than real, since there is now a profusion of advocacy approaches, each with its own *modus operandi* and mission.

Self-Advocacy

The self-advocacy movement challenges the stereotyped view that others always have to speak for retarded people because they cannot speak for themselves. Since the early 1970s, local self-help groups, composed and led by persons with handicaps, have come together to speak up for their rights and to protest stifling paternalism and prejudice. Under such names as People First, The Fifth Strand, and Project Two, these groups seek to bolster their members' self-esteem, to train them to advocate effectively on their own behalf, and to alter public attitudes and service provisions. This activity is based on the assumption that "disabled individuals can best speak about their needs, conditions, and concerns as they experience them throughout their own lives."[9] Self-advocacy, then, is part consciousness-raising, assertiveness-training program, and springboard to direct consumer involvement in a field that has seen relatively little of that in the past.

Although still in its early stages, the self-advocacy concept is spreading rapidly in this country and abroad. Following the early lead of retarded people in Sweden and Oregon, self-help groups have organized in thirty-five states, as well as in Canada, Australia, and the United Kingdom. In addition to consumer conferences, self-advocacy groups stress training in the rights and responsibilities of adulthood, voter registration, training in communication and assertiveness skills, and ways of working with other advocacy organizations. In observing these groups, Dr. Rosemary Dybwad has concluded that members gain self-confidence and "experiences which will prepare them to make choices, to assume responsibility, to participate in the life around them."[10] Furthermore, the very existence of such groups and their demands for respectful treatment can create more favorable public attitudes toward and perceptions of retarded people. As these groups intensify their efforts to affirm their rights through petitions, demonstrations, membership on boards, lobbying, lawsuits, and other expressive means, the general public and their fellow advocates must modify old notions of "the retarded" as a monolithic and silent minority.[11]

Family Advocacy

Advocacy by family members is critical for the child and the incapacitated adult. The point needs no belaboring, since retarded children, even more so than other children, need supportive adults who will prepare them for a life of growing independence as well as interdependence on others. Under the U.S. Constitution, it has long been understood that the parental role implies a vigorous assertion of the child's interests, since "those who nurture him and direct his destiny have the right, coupled with the high duty, to recognize and prepare him for additional obligations."[12] Current federal legislation on special education similarly places a high value on parental involvement in educational planning. Certainly, those parents who do participate in that process and understand their child's rights have a far better chance of securing appropriate education and related services than those who remain aloof.[13] Yet despite the obvious importance of legal rights at every stage of a retarded person's life, family members—parents, siblings, other relatives, and parental surrogates—have few opportunities to learn of those rights or to receive basic advocacy training.

Too many retarded persons, however, lack familial protection. Those in institutions are at special risk. Their contacts to the outside may shrink as a result of a relative's death, distance, or disinterest. As Congress has recognized, parents all too frequently are not effective advocates for their handicapped children's rights because they have been "erroneously led to believe that their children will not be able to lead meaningful lives."[14] For the parent of a retarded individual, there is the classic problem expressed in the question, "What will happen to my child when I am gone?" and the search it can provoke for someone or something to safeguard that individual's interests. The lack of reliable, long-term protective services surely accounts for some of the durability of discredited institutional solutions.

Friend Advocacy

Friend advocacy developed as a form of one-to-one volunteer assistance to meet a protégé's emotional and instrumental needs. Some theorists conceived of it as a less restrictive, noncoercive alternative to guardianship. In 1972, Wolfensberger defined the citizen advocate as "a mature, competent citizen volunteer representing, as if they were his own, the interests of another citizen" with unmet needs for practical or emotional support.[15] Under the auspices of associations for retarded citizens and similar organizations in thirty-two states, coordinators recruit and match citizen advocates and protégés.

Friend advocacy is a commendable and valuable source of altruistic assistance to people who lack other benefactors. Predictably, however, there is a shortage of competent volunteers willing to assume the burdens of a long-term fiduciary relationship with no thought of remuneration. Even if the citizen advocate's role is scaled down to providing companionship, at present the volunteer pool is insufficient to help more than a small fraction of those with identified needs. Though the numbers obviously fluctuate, in 1977, during this program's early stages, approximately five thousand developmentally disabled Americans received this one-to-one assistance. In any event, if the individual requires long-term continuity of representation, technical advocacy skills, or adversarial interventions, other forms of aid may prove more suitable.

Disability Rights Advocacy

Advocacy specialists deal on a regular basis with particular needs of recipients of human services at both the systemic and individual case levels. They occupy a useful but conceptually untidy middle ground between the one-to-one volunteers and the legal advocates. This is reflected in the varied terminology for essentially similar or overlapping tasks: *lay advocacy, systems advocacy, residents' representative, residents' rights advocacy, mental health advocacy, collective advocacy,* and *nonlegal advocacy* form only part of this list.[16] The labels tell little about the players, and even less about their auspices and allegiances. To make the literature and the reality even more confusing, new and uncoordinated roles have sprung up under particular processes: *surrogate parents* for children without familial protection in special-education planning, *in loco parentis* representatives for "noncorrespondent" (individually unrepresented) Willowbrook class members, and *patient advocates* to validate sterilization and other medical procedures for persons with borderline capacities for giving consent.[17] On a collective basis, organizations such as the national and local units of associations for retarded citizens or mental health associations have long been focal points for interest-group representation and defense of basic legal rights. Concentrating primarily on lobbying for new laws and appropriations as well as monitoring service-delivery systems, many of these units have not had the resources to pursue low-visibility individual cases on a systematic basis.

The common denominator in any activity deserving the good name of advocacy is its partisanship on behalf of the client's rights and interests. Despite the abundance of papers on advocacy, the actual availability of advocates is a far different matter. Especially in its purer forms, that species of advocacy is endangered by dwindling governmental support and stiffer competition for charitable contributions. And yet courageous groups like Advocating Change Together (ACT) of Minneapolis continue to function effectively, even as its staff struggles against budget cuts. At the same time, its consumer members must be helped to handle problems of financial assistance, residential services, employment, and housing on their own.[18] Grass-roots efforts of this kind must survive if persons with disabilities are to maintain their toehold grip on dignified community living.

Human Rights Advocacy Committees

Citizen review committees offer a method of monitoring the implementation of disabled people's legal and human rights at a local level. Under such designations as human rights committees, human rights advocacy committees, or human rights authorities, they perform review, fact-finding, educative, advocacy, and advisory roles. Composed of volunteers with lay and professional backgrounds, such committees can probe allegations of abuse, provide informal dispute resolution, and offer policy recommendations. Their mandates, duties, and scopes of authority will vary with their specific charge and mode of empowerment: legislative, executive, judicial or service agency.[19] A detailed evaluation of these oversight mechanisms is outside the scope of this study,[20] but some committees have had considerable success in casting sunlight on human rights abuses and in acting as quasi-independent critics and watchdogs of agency practices.

Unlike the impartial classical ombudsman, human rights committees may conceive of themselves as both arbiters and advocates. This can provoke tensions when the professional's claims to clinical or administrative autonomy clash with the committee's interest in wide-ranging inquiry to protect the rights of consumers. For instance, the institutional superintendent will prefer a docile committee that lobbies for his concerns and confines itself to advisory rather than confrontational activities. From the members' perspective, their posture is at best ambiguous and sometimes frustrating since they lack the power to compel compliance with their recommendations. If the appointing agency ignores their recommendation or appears to cover up a serious violation of clients' rights, they face the dilemma of whether to air their complaint in newspapers, courtrooms, or other external forums.[21] Whatever role they assume, given the constraints of limited staff, training, and time, these volunteers are clearly only a link to and not a substitute for independent full-time client advocates.[22] In general, such committees are forums for identifying and ventilating consumer complaints, not sources of representation for mounting formal complaints.

Internal Advocacy

The great divide in rights protection lies between those actors who are supervised and financed within an organization that provides treatment services and those who are not. That distinction lies at the root of the internal versus external advocacy debate. The internal advocates are known by such names as *human rights officers, rights advisors, ombudsmen* and the like.[23] They tend to perform investigative roles inside their agencies, counsel and educate other employees on rights-related matters, and otherwise try to minimize infringements upon residents' rights and dignity. Typically they rely on methods such as monitoring reports, operating an internal-complaint system, and informing residents how to exercise their rights. Yet in the field of developmental disabilities, there is little uniformity in job descriptions for this role, such services are spotty and sporadic, and there is doubt as to the reliability of efforts to notify residents (and/or their representatives) of their rights. In fact, most states are reluctant to commit substantial resources to fashioning a credible rights component within their service-delivery systems.

Indeed, some states have taken an entirely different and sounder tack: the creation of a public advocacy and monitoring capability in an agency separate from service providers. The foremost examples of this are the New York Commission on the Quality of Care for the Mentally Disabled and the Illinois Advocacy and Guardianship Commission.[24] Though they are still within state government, their independence from the direct-care sector and their explicit rights-protection mandate are formidable advantages.

Although there are valid rights-related functions to be performed by service agencies, it serves neither clarity nor client interests to brand them as advocacy. Otherwise, it is then a short and slippery step to categorize complaint processors, case managers, quality-assurance specialists, program brokers, and so on under the rubric of client advocacy.[25] Moreover, evidence suggests that the impetus for internal rights-protection mechanisms was in part to forestall or preempt more aggressive outside checks. It is desirable and understandable that treatment professionals should wish to assist the mentally disabled to exercise their rights "to the extent possible, rather than be ordered to do so by courts."[26] But even the sincerest and most dedicated insiders face inherent conflicts of interests. This results in temptations to underplay consumer complaints and to defend the values and frailties of the system one is intended to monitor. Thus, the internal advocates' dependence on the very institution or program that treats the client is bound to undermine independence and assertive vigor.

Legal Advocacy

Legal advocacy has high credibility, but it is often inaccessible to those who most urgently need legal protection. Until recently, the legal profession provided scant help to retarded people. This apathy and neglect extended even to those situations where the lives and liberties of persons so labeled were at grave risk. Despite efforts to involve the traditional private sector, those who now form the mental-disability law bar are drawn primarily from nonprofit organizations—public-interest law projects, protection and advocacy agencies, legal-aid offices, and academia—along with a scattering of private and government attorneys.[27]

Litigation, especially the class-action suit, is often regarded as the cutting edge of reform. It is not, however, as we shall see, the principle tool in resolving cases. Moreover, compared with prisoners (who filed over 10,000 federal civil rights suits in 1979), the residents of mental institutions—filing less than 50 similar cases in that year—could hardly be called litigious.[28] In fact, lawyers and paralegals were devoting significant energies to the drive for legislative, regulatory, and administrative reforms. Paradoxically, the very success and visibility of these efforts to consolidate and enforce their clients' rights has led to increased difficulties in financing their work. The remainder of this chapter explores the principles that characterize this potent advocacy and some ways of overcoming its access problems.

A Model for Legal Advocacy

The following model of independent, legally trained advocates offers an effective basis for representing clients in mental retardation or mental health systems. Indeed, one federal court has already recognized it as "an absolute necessity" for protecting the legal rights of people labeled as mentally disabled who are subject to institutionalization or deinstitutionalization.[29] Initially developed in the context of court mandates to explore the advocacy needs of some ten thousand individuals in six Massachusetts class actions, this model can be tailored to fit problems of different dimensions. Its features are derived from literature and practical experience, and from national as well as international perspectives.[30] Its principles flow from the widely shared conclusion and the historically documented record that without trained legal advocates, people with mental disabilities will suffer abuse, devaluation, and chronic disregard of their rights.

The advocate's strict independence and separation from service providers is the hallmark of this legal approach. Vigorous advocacy for the client requires that the advocate must be free of administrative or financial conflicts of interest that tend to dilute zeal or compromise effectiveness. Such conflicts or their appearance will corrosively affect staff morale, the advocacy office's credibility, and consumer trust or willingness to bring problems to advocates in the future. Any advocacy system must therefore be free of undue influence by agencies that provide treatment services.[31] This independence is not only required by the Code of Professional Responsibility,[32] but is essential to enhancing client control of the advocacy function.

To work effectively in this difficult field of legal assistance, an advocacy staff must have a high degree of knowledge, skill, and motivation. They will require substantial legal training in order to recognize and defend a complex, rapidly changing body of rights relating to disability or institutionalized status. Even if they are lawyers or paralegals experienced in other fields, they will need further skill training in interviewing, fact-finding, assessing expert opinion, counseling, and otherwise assisting clients whose cognitive limitations or impaired ability to communicate may hamper the assertion of their legal rights. Moreover, the very act of gaining entry to and acquiring "staying power" within an institution can be a heroic test of the advocate's stamina and diplomacy. In short, these legal advocates operate at an uncomfortable frontier where new rules of law are applied in the context of desperately needy clients, wary clinicians, and a state bureaucracy buffeted by change.

Even in advocacy offices that rely heavily on paraprofessionals, attorneys are indispensable to ensure clients of qualified legal representation and outreach assistance. In addition to guaranteeing the client's access to court, the lawyer has critical roles in giving legal advice, drafting complex documents, and undertaking both routine and sophisticated forms of legal planning. An attorney's supervisory function over lay advocates working under his or her direction is not only a quality-control and an ethical requirement, but a means of reinforcing that advocate's access to clients and their records. Given the vastly uneven power between retarded clients and the state provider system, the presence of attorneys also gives advocates the clout to bargain effectively and to gain satisfactory results through informal dispute settlements. Access to legal counsel thus means not only the availability of judicial redress if necessary, but the ability to resolve over 95 percent of the problems clients present without ever going to court.[33]

Explaining, defending, and asserting the legal rights of mentally disabled people is a tough, full-time job. It requires the services of talented professionals and paraprofessionals who should be compensated at levels commensurate with their experience. Donated assistance and self-help groups can offer valuable supplementary aids, but it would be an error to overlook the staff needed to support their efforts, provide consultation, and ensure competent, experienced attention across the range of the client's special legal problems. Furthermore, in comparing delivery systems that rely on hit-or-miss legal referral services with specialist advocacy offices, an office with full-time staff will provide more effective representation with greater efficiency, continuity, quality, and economy than a system of appointed counsel.[34] It is also in a better position to offer services responsive to wider client needs and to pursue time-consuming law-reform strategies.

The legal advocate's role is to be a zealous partisan of the client's interests and goals, not a paternalistic surrogate or a detached "counsel for the situation."[35] This role not only comports with prevailing expectations for attorney-client relationships, but affirms the very dignity of choice and risk-taking that care systems are supposed to encourage for their clients. Here again, advocacy offices are best equipped to train and guide lawyers and legal advocates on the hazards of slipping out of role, of usurping the role of guardian, judge, or ombudsman, or of simply signing up as another member of an interdisciplinary "helping team." Although the debate on the theory and practice of adversarial-advocacy versus best-interest roles waxes furiously,[36] participants often overlook a basic fact: the overwhelming majority of persons classified as mentally retarded can express an understandable preference and can provide counsel with substantial assistance in ascertaining their wishes and interests. That there are exceptions to the rule, principally mute or profoundly retarded persons, is neither a basis for abrogating the general rule nor for the attorney's failure to make some effort to discover an incompetent person's desires and interests.[37] In hard cases, the attorney may be compelled to rely on substitute decision makers: guardians, guardians *ad litem*, legally sanctioned next friends, or even to engage in substituted-judgment analysis.[38] These, however, are narrow exceptions to the general principle of client-guided and client-directed representation.

For a host of reasons, an advocacy office must have the capacity and authority to provide the full range of effective advocacy methods. First, as an ethical matter, an advocate must be free to pursue the remedies that will best serve the interests of clients, whether they be individual or class clients. Second, based on studies and experience, advocacy projects that achieve the most satisfactory results for their clients in fact use the entire continuum of advocacy methods.[39] Third, clients who receive full legal representation may reap indirect therapeutic benefits by gaining a sense that they are not helpless in the face of unfairness and by resolving socioeconomic problems that might otherwise impede habilitation. Lastly, while the vast majority of resident grievances can be handled informally, the advocate's ability to seek outside administrative or judicial redress gives officials an added incentive to maintain fair and timely internal grievance mechanisms. Not only can the advocate go to the next tier of remedies, but in the event of an emergency, a breakdown in the system, or a client's specific interest, the advocates can leapfrog over the bureaucratic chain of command and seek swift outside action.

The regular presence of advocates in major institutions is also vital to overcoming barriers to legal representation. The right to an independent advocate is a hollow right if its realization depends on institution staff to identify the clients' legal problems and obtain competent legal assistance. Moreover, though staff may wish to summon advocates who will channel their efforts to ordinary civil legal aid or to getting guardianships, advocates on-site are more likely to act on client-defined problems such as day-to-day routines or living conditions. To develop the necessary rapport, trust, and contacts with clients, their families, and staff, advocates need sheer physical presence. This will require offices or suboffices in facilities, careful listening to the clients themselves, participation in decision-making processes on individual services, and extensive outreach efforts for community-based clients.

Without reasonable access to institutionalized residents and their living areas, advocates cannot monitor conditions, provide residents with information, or otherwise protect their rights. Because of their disabilities and the dependency fostered by institutionalization, residents are unlikely to avail themselves of existing remedial procedures without such assistance. In recognition of these vulnerabilities, a growing body of legislation confers extensive monitoring functions on advocacy organizations, including investigating instances of neglect, abuse, or other violations of rights in mental facilities.[40] And in fulfilling statutory mandates to notify residents of their rights, an independent advocacy office is not only free of the role conflicts that distort such efforts by institutional staff, but also is a more reliable source of accurate information, explanation, and advice. Furthermore, the ability to visit wards and cottages is critical to legal representation. If that access is denied, the emphasis on fact-finding and negotiation will invariably shift to adversarial methods. Since unreasonable state restrictions on the flow of information can have crippling effects on legal representation, courts and legislatures should reaffirm the advocate's access to client records and opportunities to interview staff.[41]

Advocacy programs should strive for focus and a coherent identity. Too often advocacy agencies have faltered by undertaking inconsistent functions or by promising a supermarket of advocacy formats, social-work services, and publicity campaigns. Instead, a realistically drawn plan should aim at competent performance of a basic function, for example, meeting the need for legal representation of a population within a particular delivery system. This includes assisting clients in such matters as grievances, periodic reviews, conditions of care, mistreatment, guardianship, and client movement. In formulating its mission and engaging in individual and group representation, programs should weigh a community thrust—assuring clients of access to generic services, benefits, and systems, as well as relieving those persons exposed to discrimination, stigma, and segregation. For example, a legal-advocacy program could justifiably concentrate on deinstitutionalization and the concurrent creation of alternative services. Such decisions involve difficult trade-offs, but it is not unreasonable for a small, specialist project to concentrate its resources and to help clients with their ordinary civil or criminal legal problems primarily through referral to general legal-aid agencies or other suitable practitioners.

With the inevitable rationing of subsidized legal assistance, special programs should adopt a conscious priority-setting process. Based upon a periodic assessment of overall client needs, a project can devise realistic goals, priority objectives, and caseload policies. Clients, consumer groups, advocacy staff, and advisory boards can participate in identifying issues and functions that seem to demand the highest attention. Typically, priority-setting sessions are held on an annual basis, although changing conditions and unanticipated needs may require more frequent revisions. Although statutes and funding sources may constrain advocacy agencies from imposing strict caseload guidelines, those agencies have obligations to assure clients of competent services and fair intake policies. To avoid frustration and misunderstanding, all are better served when such policies are reached by design rather than by default.

Advocacy coalitions can offer practical help in coordinating resources and clarifying goals. Through agreements on reciprocal referrals, coalition members can assist disabled people to reach an advocate skilled and able to resolve their particular problem. As a means of pooling scarce resources and speaking with a more politically potent voice, a coalition can work together on major shared objectives such as reforms in statewide practices and policies, revised regulations, legislation, or impact litigation. In a few states, coalitions for disability rights are underway, with participation from consumer groups, legal services offices, protection and advocacy agencies, public-interest lawyers, and clinical law-school programs.[42]

Training and evaluation plans are also vital to the integrity of the advocacy mission. A workable model must ensure that clients, in fact, have the services of trained, experienced attorneys and paraprofessionals. As documented in litigation and studies, court-appointment systems have too often failed that test. In the more egregious situations, they have done little more than provide a "greased runway to the county mental health center."[43] In the developmental disabilities field, the risks of ineffective assistance of counsel are equally substantial when practitioners lack systematic training, continuing legal education, and peer review. In contrast, specialist offices can offer preservice orientation, inservice training, and supervision. Larger advocacy programs can establish central training units, though smaller programs must look to their own experienced supervisors or to outside resources such as law schools, bar associations, or new multidisciplinary training programs.[44] As another means of instilling a sense of direction, coalitions of advocates can collaborate in training sessions adapted to their shared needs.

Although advocacy programs for the developmentally disabled now operate on a national and state basis, programs of regional scope are sorely lacking. As the major service-delivery systems organize within states on a regional catchment basis, an advocacy counterpart should be available to clients. At present, statewide offices cannot provide local coverage or begin to handle the demand for individual representation, and the handful of institutional projects are often parochial and restricted to aiding current residents. The proposal for a solitary lawyer in each major public institution would create problems of isolation, unless that individual was linked to an outside legal-advocacy group.[45] Otherwise, it would not meet the range of needs addressed in this model nor assure the necessary training and peer support for advocacy in a sometimes hostile and always emotionally and professionally challenging environment. The architects of regional programs need not build from scratch. Ideally, such programs would form a link in a statewide advocacy network, either as components of an existing agency or as extensions of institutional advocacy projects.

The costs of implementing this model are miniscule compared with public expenditures on mental retardation or the costs of inhumane and overly restrictive care. According to the Massachusetts data, an adequate and effective program of advocacy could function on a regional basis for less than one-half of one percent of the annual operating budget of a DMH region.[46] The proposed advocacy model, with its extensive use of full-time, trained lay advocates, is cost efficient. Moreover, in assessing cost-benefits to the states, it should be noted that the life-time care costs for a single, inappropriately institutionalized resident can exceed $2 million. Similarly, without an advocate, the unlawful termination of Supplemental Security Income (SSI) benefits for a disabled client in the community can force reinstitutionalization and a huge shifting of costs from federal to state and local governments. Given the values and rights at stake and the budgets of thoughtfully planned public advocacy programs in leading states,[47] these implementation costs are indeed modest.

Implementing the Model

To varying degrees, the nation's legal advocates for retarded persons have begun to provide the types of services described here. Although class actions and other impact cases continue to capture the greatest attention, the vast majority of cases are settled with little fanfare through negotiation, mediation, counseling, administrative remedies, routine individual representation, and referral.[48] Such case advocacy is, however, neither glamorous nor well paid. Unfortunately, as the demand for quality individual representation increases, the supply of advocates trained for work in this field shrinks. Although it takes years to develop teams of knowledgeable, sophisticated legal advocates, it takes only months for budget cuts to disband them. But there are several alternative ways of funding elements of the proposed advocacy model.

The advocacy system can, in part, be mandated by judicial order. Of the various ways of implementing the model, none is more intriguing or as little tested as the argument based on the judicially enforceable right of access to the courts. When basic due process rights hang in the balance, the courts have repeatedly required the right to counsel in situations such as civil commitment, release from institutions, and transfer to a mental facility.[49]

There is a strong case to be made for a wider right of access to legal resources. As the Supreme Court emphasized in *Bounds* v. *Smith*, prisoners have a constitutional right of access to the courts, a right requiring states to make available to them legal materials through adequate law libraries or legal-aid programs.[50] In urging new legal-assistance programs, Justice Marshall, speaking for the Supreme Court, articulated rationales that could equally apply to advocacy programs for those detained for mental care: legal aid can provide more skillful handling of cases, assure fairness, and spur mediated solutions to complaints that might otherwise burden the courts or go without remedy.[51] The logic of *Bounds* ought surely apply to an involuntarily committed mental patient who seeks legal advice to perfect a claim to liberty or freedom from outrageous conditions of confinement. By analogy, retarded persons who cannot read, use a telephone, or communicate fluently, and who are confined to state institutions, should also have their day in court. But to ensure their meaningful access to the courts and other public officials, they will need affirmative assistance in lieu of the provision of pen, paper, and a law library.

In class-action litigation, federal courts have already begun to order such aids under a variety of theories. Thus, states have been required to supply mentally disabled class members with friend-advocates,[52] *in loco parentis* representatives,[53] and attorneys.[54] In *Brad G.* v. *Treen*, the federal court permanently enjoined Louisiana officials from failing to provide counsel to indigent persons at any significant stage of commitment (including periods "subsequent to their judicial hearings"), and the legislature responded by funding a mental health advocacy system.[55] The constitutional predicate for these affirmative duties has ranged from the due process clause, the right to nondiscriminatory habilitation, the right to protection from harm, and the right to adequate treatment. These cases have as their common denominator a legal obligation upon the state to fund some independent advocacy. Faced with the appropriate case, a state court could also act to ensure that retarded persons receive adequate representation.[56]

Where violations of law are found or admitted, courts have ordered advocacy plans as part of remedial packages. For instance, under a deinstitutionalization and right-to-habilitation decree, the defendants were required to fund a plan for the provision of advocates to assist in the protection of the rights of each plaintiff class member.[57] Under a similar consent decree in Maine, a system of full-time resident advocates was established to monitor compliance with judicially approved standards.[58] Armed with extensive powers of access, the advocates (two lawyers and a lay advocate) deal with allegations of abuse, deficiencies in client-service plans, and provide other forms of individual advocacy. And in a federal action establishing admission procedures for long-term retardation care, the state was required to appoint a lawyer automatically for each potential resident.[59]

Brewster v. *Dukakis* posed the question of a federal court's power to order state-funded legal advocacy to ensure consent-decree compliance.[60] Under that decree the court-appointed monitor was to investigate and report on the need for independent, trained advocates to protect the class plaintiffs' rights. On the basis of the monitor's and the expert consultant's reports and an evidentiary hearing, the district judge issued detailed findings on the absolute necessity of advocacy services. Citing its supervisory authority under the degree to settle unresolved issues and its inherent equitable powers to respond to changed circumstances, the district court ordered implementation of the recommended plan. Judge Freedman's order included a timetable and budget for a system of legal advocacy capable of representing class clients in connection with legal issues "arising from the clients' disability or status of prior or current institutionalization."[61]

On appeal, the defendants conceded that an independent legal-advocacy program is "highly desirable." Though they did not dispute the soundness of the monitor's and the court-appointed consultant's recommendations, they denied any legal responsibility and the court of appeals agreed that the district court lacked the legal power to compel the Commonwealth of Massachusetts to fund the proposed program. Based on a narrow interpretation of the consent decree's language, structure, and purpose, the First Circuit held that a general legal-services program for the mentally ill was not closely enough related to the decree's basic deinstitutionalization goal to have been intended as necessary to attain that objective. The court, however, left the door ajar to a more specifically focused order on advocacy. If the program (mischaracterized by the appellate court as general representation of the mentally ill and retarded persons in western Massachusetts) were to emphasize the deinstitutionalization rights grounded in the decree or if the district court should enter findings of legal violations, a different result could ensue. Alternatively, the plaintiffs' representatives could decide to fund the program, as originally recommended, through the $386,000 in court-awarded attorneys' fees.

Congress and state legislatures can and ought to respond to these well-documented findings of advocacy needs on a more systematic basis. Existing federal legislation provides the necessary authority, but not sufficient funds for addressing some of the problems identified in this chapter. The Mental Health Systems Act for a brief period also promised a federally financed "protection and advocacy" (P & A) system for the mentally ill in interested states, but that section has since been repealed.[62] In every state, P & A systems for developmentally disabled persons operate under a federal mandate to protect the legal rights of such persons receiving habilitation services.[63] With their mission to uphold these rights, to redress grievances, and to examine situations in which the disabled person's rights may be violated in the service-delivery system,[64] those agencies must be able to pursue legal, administrative, and other appropriate remedies. Since this requires both local and centralized capabilities, various P & A programs such as those in Massachusetts and New York have established regional offices through contracts with existing legal-services providers.

Although states bear the primary responsibility for securing the rights of dependent persons under their care or supervision, their record of supplying advocacy resources for that task is a mixed one. In a handful of states, statutory-based advocacy services provide substantial state-funded legal assistance to residents of public mental facilities. The oldest and best-known of these public agencies are the New Jersey Public Advocate, the Ohio Legal Rights Service, and the New York Mental Health Information Service (MHIS).[65] Although the American Bar Association has drafted model state advocacy legislation, only twelve states had any advocacy system law in 1978 and few states have added such statutory provisions since then.[66] Even in wealthy and industrialized states, legislative support for legal advocacy to mentally disabled people amounts to mere pennies in per-capita terms. For example, Massachusetts appropriates less than two cents per year per citizen for this purpose.[67]

Executive-branch officials also have a legitimate role in fostering advocacy. By grant or contract, they can fund independent advocates as spokespersons for otherwise unrepresented clients, a role frequently mentioned in regulations and policies.[68] Local prosecutors and state attorney generals have both legal and ethical duties to initiate actions to curb abuse of retarded persons and to take affirmative steps to assert their civil rights.[69] Because states and municipalities have often defaulted on those duties, the federal Department of Justice must play a larger part in safeguarding the federal rights of retarded citizens. At the same time, state agencies should make good-faith efforts to develop or reinforce speedy and locally relevant remedies such as human rights committees, grievance mechanisms, and credible investigative procedures for handling complaints of rights violations. At a minimum, retardation professionals can give more than lip service to advocacy principles; they can at least refrain from unreasonably interfering with the two-way access of residents and qualified legal advocates.[70]

The nonprofit corporation offers another means of organizing advocacy services, one with less risk of governmental or political obstruction. With its greater flexibility and freedom of action, this mode of governance has provided a popular way of conducting P & A programs, legal aid, and other potentially controversial advocacy services.[71] As a funding and regulatory device for statewide advocacy services, it could initiate regional programs, serve as a conduit for public and other funds, and act as a buffer between funding sources and local advocacy offices. This arrangement could thereby minimize friction and undue interference with the advocate's functioning, while upholding the advocate's accountability to meet reasonable standards of professional performance.

The concept of group legal services for disabled persons also deserves detailed exploration. At a time of waning public subsidies, advocacy agencies should, as a start, consider the ability of more affluent clients to pay for some or all of the services they receive. This can range from sliding fee structures based on income to assistance from clients with out-of-pocket costs. Although group legal services have not yet been developed in the disability field, what could be described as privately funded group advocacy services have been started in the United Kingdom, New Zealand, and various parts of this country. Under the auspices of or with seed monies from associations for retarded citizens, developmental disabilities councils or other consumer-oriented organizations, more elaborate plans, with a greater range of services, could be offered. For example, a legal-services plan could not only address certain class-representation needs, but could also arrange individual legal advice, advocacy participation in service-planning contexts, and contacts with disabled persons who for various reasons lack familial support. Serious problems of enrollment, coverage, and control would have to be resolved, but consumer groups recognize that the need for some type of group advocacy service is real and widespread.

A confederation of advocacy organizations poses another possible approach toward structuring a statewide network. Coalitions of legal advocates as well as the wider spectrum of avocacy groups have often come together for civil-rights objectives. Even though these coalitions are often short-lived and for limited purposes, there is a place for a standing organizational structure. Whether labeled a Council of Advocates, or a Coalition for Clients' Rights, its membership would have the immediate aim of increasing the effective use of resources to achieve consensus priorities. It could also work to expand vigorous, independent advocacy programs to uncovered geographic regions. Furthermore, by recruiting interested attorneys and stimulating bar associations and law schools to increase *pro bono* and fee-generating activities in the disabilities law field, such a council could help identify and fill gaps in advocacy services. Ultimately, a durable coalition could work to minimize needless duplication of efforts through joint training, publications, systems planning, fund-raising, legislative advocacy, and other collaborative activities. At present, this type of cooperation and cohesion is still an isolated phenomenon.

Specialized projects are essential for quality legal services for retarded persons. But their efforts will be little more than episodic unless linked with cooperating attorneys. In the 1980s, small law firms with public-interest orientations could become a major source of assistance. Courts have taken judicial notice of the shortage of lawyers skilled and committed to litigation for handicapped persons,[72] and the potential for court-awarded attorneys' fees may begin to change that. For example, federal courts are empowered to grant attorney's fees to prevailing parties in cases of civil rights violations[73] and discrimination based on handicap[74] (including limited special-education matters).[75] This is part of a broader trend toward fee-shifting in discrimination and consumer-protection areas of law. Thus, 125 federal and many state laws now provide an exception to the American Rule that each side in a lawsuit pay for its own counsel.[76]

For many lawyers, especially graduates of law schools in the 1960s and veterans of legal-services programs in the 1970s, the motivation to engage in advocacy in the disabilities field remains more idealistic than financial. Emulating the American Civil Liberties Union or the NAACP Legal Defense Fund, public-interest law firms in this field could formalize cooperating-attorney and other collaborative arrangements. Unless ways are found to tap the knowledge and commitment of experienced lawyers, this advocacy movement may lose some of its momentum and verve.

Conclusion

For the first time in history, advocacy *by* as well as *for* retarded people is now a reality. Despite hardships and obstacles, genuine advocacy in many forms is a spreading force in the United States and abroad. It is a force that will not fade away as long as the criterion of limited intelligence exposes a minority to exclusion and disregard of their legal rights and human dignity. This is one movement that clearly has a place for the crusader and the technician, linking professional skills to the aspirations of self-advocates, volunteers, family members, and other activists. By one means or another, they will animate advocacy models and develop the networks to implement hard-won rights.

Despite recent progress, persons with mental retardation, like other persons with disabilities, still face threats to their full citizenship and even survival. Against those stubborn menaces, the advocacy movement must act for those who are too young, too incapacitated, or too vulnerable to act for themselves. This chapter reveals that there are many ways to defend this minority within a minority from abuse or detriment. But even if every retarded person received only kindly care, many would still require aid in asserting their fundamental rights. When these rights are waived through unawareness, disability, or the lack of a representative, the retarded person can forfeit chances to learn and to live as fully as possible. A working model of legal advocacy is not only a check on such waivers; it is an essential component of an early-warning system to deter mistreatment and to remedy or mitigate its consequences.

Notes

1. *E.g.*, Lourie, "The Many Faces of Advocacy," *Advocacy for Child Mental Health* 69 (I. Berlin ed. 1975).

2. J. Westman, *Child Advocacy: New Professional Roles for Helping Families* (1979). *See* Joint Comm'n on the Mental Health of Children, *Crisis in Child Mental Health* (1969).

3. *E.g.*, B. Curran, *The Legal Needs of the Public* (1977).

4. On the unwillingness of some physicians to extend equal medical treatment to Down's Syndrome children or to seek a court order to preserve such a child's life, see D. Crane, *The Sanctity of Social Life* (1975); Affleck, "Physicians' Attitudes toward Discretionary Medical Treatment of Down's Syndrome Infants," 18 *Mental Retardation* 79 (1980).

5. Legal Services Corporation, *Summary of the Study on the Special Difficulties of Access and Special Unmet Legal Problems of the Elderly and Handicapped* 31, 48 (May 1980).

6. *See id.* at 53-58.

7. S. Herr, *Advocates for People With Mental Disabilities: Report to the United States District Court Monitors on Advocacy Needs and Models for Massachusetts Class Clients* 12-39 (Sept. 1980), admitted into evidence, Brewster v. Dukakis, 520 F. Supp. 882 (D. Mass. 1981); Boston Bar Association, I *Action Plan for Legal Services* 73 (1977).

8. U.S. President's Comm'n on Mental Health, I *Report to the President* 42 (1978); U.S. President's Comm. on Mental Retardation, *Century of Decision* 65 (1976).

9. M. Coile, N. Cohen, & B. Harter, *Self-Advocacy in Florida* (Florida Governor's Comm'n on Advocacy for Persons with Developmental Disabilities, 1981).

10. R. Dybwad, *The Retarded Child Today—The Adult of Tomorrow*, in ILSMH, Symposium Proceedings 13 (1979). *See generally* P. Williams & B. Shoultz, *We Can Speak for Ourselves: Self-Advocacy by Mentally Handicapped People* (1982).

11. *Cf.* U.S. President's Comm. on Mental Retardation, *Silent Minority* at iii (1973) ("Many mentally retarded citizens cannot organize themselves. They need others to speak with and for them.") *with* 8 *Washington People 1st Newsletter* 4 (Summer 1982) ("One of our most important goals is to reach out to people with severe and multiple handicaps because they are very important people.").

12. Pierce v. Society of the Sisters, 268 U.S. 510, 535 (1925).

13. *Cf.* Board of Ed. v. Rowley, 102 S. Ct. 3034 (1982) *with* Guardianship of Becker, No. 101981 (Cal. Super. Ct., Santa Clara Co. Aug. 7, 1981).

14. S. Rep. No. 94-168, 94 Cong., 1st Sess. at 9 (1975). Institutionalization can lead to the resident's complete loss of family contact. *See* Halderman v. Pennhurst State School, 446 F. Supp. 1295, 1303 (E.D. Pa. 1977).

15. W. Wolfensberger, *Citizen Advocacy for the Handicapped, Impaired, and Disadvantaged: An Overview* 12 (1972).

16. See National Institute of Mental Health, *Mental Health Advocacy: An Emerging Force in Consumers' Rights* (L. Kopolow & H. Bloom eds. 1977).

17. See 20 U.S.C. § 1415(b)(1)(B) (1978); New York State ARC v. Carey, 596 F.2d 27 (2d Cir. 1979); Ass'n for Voluntary Sterilization, "Model Voluntary Sterilization Act" § 6 (1981).

18. Advocating Change Together, Inc., [ACT] "Annual Report: Status of Instrumental Advocacy Cases from 10/1/80 to 10/8/81." The vast majority of consumers reported their satisfaction with ACT's case work, and their perception of advocate partisanship and interest in resolving their problems. Through active consumer involvement, ACT also won significant legislation requiring a rule on aversive and deprivation procedures. 1982 Minn. Sess. Law Serv. Ch. 637.

19. *E.g.,* Fla. Sta. Ann. § 20.19(6)-(7) (Supp. 1982) (statewide and district Human Rights Advocacy Committees to protect the constitutional and human rights of clients in facilities and programs of Department of Health and Rehabilitative Services); 104 CMR §§ 15.03(13), 20.14 (1980) (Human Rights Committees in institutions and community-based programs of Massachusetts Dep't of Mental Health); Wyatt v. Stickney, 344 F. Supp. 387, 392 (M.D. Ala. 1972) (Partlow Human Rights Committee created to guarantee that residents are afforded constitutional and humane habilitation); Accreditation Council for Services for Mentally Retarded and Other Developmentally Disabled Persons, *Standards for Services for Developmentally Disabled Individuals* 62 (1980) (establishment of a human rights committee as a prerequisite for accreditation).

20. For a working paper on this subject, see S. Herr, "Guarding the Guardians: Roles of Advocates, Ombudsmen and Human Rights Committees" (Columbia U. Center for the Study of Human Rights Symposium, April 3, 1981). *See generally* Florida Statewide Human Rights Advocacy Comm., *Annual Report* (1979); Davis v. Buckley, 526 F. Supp. 985, 989 (E.D. Va. 1981) (plaintiffs not required to exhaust remedies before human rights committee at institution).

21. *See, e.g.*, "Fernald School Rights Probe Asked," *The Boston Globe*, Feb. 4, 1982, at 20; Area VI Developmental Disabilities Board v. Riles, No. 284172 (Cal. Super. Ct., Sacramento Co. Aug. 12, 1980) (pursuant to statutory mandate, watchdog board for developmentally disabled persons sought least restrictive educational settings for 160 state hospital residents).

22. For a rule that human rights committees make "special efforts" to monitor and secure rights compliance for clients incapable of making informed decisions, see Massachusetts Dep't of Mental Health, Regulations for Department Investigation, 104 CMR § 24.11 (Jan. 13, 1983).

23. The use of the term *ombudsman* to describe an in-house advocate or a superintendent's troubleshooting assistant is misleading hyperbole. *Cf.* W. Gellhorn, *Ombudsmen and Others: Citizen's Protectors in Nine Countries* (1966) *with* Mallory, "The Ombudsman in a Residential Institution: A Description of the Role and Suggested Training Areas," 15 *Mental Retardation* 14 (1977).

24. N.Y. Mental Hygiene Law §§ 45.01-45.19 (1978). On its oversight functions and efforts to develop a statewide advocacy network, see N.Y. State Comm'n on Quality of Care for the Mentally Disabled, *Annual Report 1980-81* (Feb. 1982). Ill. Rev. Stat. ch. 91 1/2 §§ 701-735 (Supp. 1982). *See generally* Paull, "The Creation of an Ombudsman: The Guardianship and Advocacy Commission," 29 *De Paul L. Rev.* 475 (1980).

25. *E.g.,* Record at 108-18, Brewster v. Dukakis, 520 F. Supp. 882 (D. Mass. 1981) (examination of F. Wilson, Director of Quality Assurance, July 16, 1981).

26. American Public Health Ass'n, Resolution 8019: Rights Protection Within the Public Mental Health System (adopted at the 1981 annual meeting).

27. Herr, "Legal Advocacy for the Mentally Handicapped," 3 *Int'l. J. of L. & Psychiatry* 61, 70-78 (1980).

28. *See* Bonner v. City of Pritchard, 661 F.2d 1206, 1213 n.11 (11th Cir. 1981). *Cf. In re* Green, 669 F.2d 779 (D.C. Cir. 1981) (a prisoner litigant filed 600 to 700 lawsuits in a decade) *with* Jackson v. Indiana, 406 U.S. 715, 737 (1972) (infrequency of litigation by institutionalized mentally disabled persons).

29. 520 F. Supp. 882, 892 (D. Mass. 1981), *vacated and remanded on other grounds*, (1st Cir. June 28, 1982), discussed *infra* at text and notes 60-61.

30. *See, e.g.*, note 7 *supra*; U.N. Declaration on the Rights of Disabled Persons, G.A. Res. 3447, 30 U.N. GAOR Supp. (No. 34) 92, U.N. Doc. A/10034 (1975), art 11; International League of Societies for the Mentally Handicapped, *Step by Step: Some Analytical Guidelines for National Societies* (1978); S. Herr, *The New Clients: Legal Services for Mentally Retarded Persons* (1979).

31. U.S. HEW, Developmental Disabilities Office, Draft Guidelines for the Planning Stage 10 (May 1976); Ohio Rev. Code § 5123.94(E) (Supp. 1978).

32. American Bar Ass'n, *Code of Professional Responsibility* EC 5-1, 5-24 (1976).

33. Government Studies & Systems, 3 *Evaluation of Models of Advocacy Programs for the Mentally Ill and Developmentally Disabled: Final Report* 82 (NIMH Dec. 17, 1980).

34. *See* Elkins, "Legal Representation of the Mentally Ill," 82 *W. Va. L. Rev.* 157 (1979); Governor's Comm'n for Revision of the Mental Health Code of Illinois, *Report* (1976) (Court-assigned public defender or private

counsel "generally provided inadequate representation"), *reprinted in* 1 *M.D.L.R.* 279 (1977); Andalman and Chambers, "Effective Counsel for Persons Facing Civil Commitment: A Survey, a Polemic and Proposal," 45 *Miss. L.J.* 43, 80-82 (1974).

35. For the argument that the lawyer in a mental institution should primarily act as a fact-finder, mediator, counselor, and ombudsman, see Brakel, "Legal Aid in Mental Hospitals," 1981 *Am. Bar Foundation Research J.* 21, 89-92.

36. *Cf.* Schwartz & Fleischner, "Legal Advocacy for Persons Confined in Mental Hospitals," 5 *M.D.L.R.* 274 (1981) with *Brakel, id.* On the obligation to act as a zealous, adversary counsel rather than in a paternalistic role for the mentally disabled client, see State *ex rel.* Memmel v. Mundy, 249 N.W.2d 573, 577 (Wis. Sup. Ct. 1977); *In re* Hutchinson, 421, A.2d 261, 265 (Pa. Super. Ct. 1980).

37. *See, e.g.*, Minn. Stat. Ann. § 252A.09 (1982) (counsel's duty to visit with and, to the extent possible, consult with the proposed ward).

38. *E.g.,* Superintendent of Belchertown State School v. Saikewicz, 373 Mass. 728, 370 N.E.2d 417 (1977). *See generally* Mickenberg, "The Silent Clients: Legal and Ethical Considerations in Representing Severely and Profoundly Retarded Persons," 31 *Stan. L. Rev.* 625 (1979).

39. Although the individual client's satisfaction may hinge on the swiftness and the concreteness of the results obtained, "impact litigation," despite its delays, is sometimes the preferred method for making new resources, powers and life changes available to disabled persons. *See generally* Georgetown Univ. Health Policy Center, *Protection and Advocacy Systems for the Developmentally Disabled* (G. Clarke & J. Stearns eds. 1977).

40. *E.g.,* N.Y. Mental Hygiene Law § 29.09 (1978); 42 U.S.C. § 1997 (1981).

41. *See, e.g.*, Mass. Gen. Laws Ch. 221 § 34E (1974); 42 U.S.C. § 9501(1)(I), (M) (1982 pamphlet); Lynch v. King, No. 78-2152, Order and Memorandum (D. Mass. Mar. 8, 1982); Barbara C. v. Moritz, No. C-2-77-887, Consent Decree para. 24 (S.D. Ohio Oct. 19, 1981) (access to records and staff).

42. *E.g.*, Coalition for the Legal Rights of the Disabled, *Newsletter* No. 14 (May 10, 1982) (members include twenty-one Massachusetts organizations and Rhode Island Legal Services).

43. State *ex rel.* Memmel v. Mundy, No. 441-417 (Wis. Cir. Ct., Milwaukee Co. Aug. 18, 1976), *appeal dismissed and declaratory judgment entered*, 75 Wis. 2d 276, 249 N.W.2d 573 (1977).

44. *See* National Legal Services Corporation, *Legal Advocacy for the Handicapped: A Legal Services Practice Manual* (1981); S. Schwartz, R. Fleischner & D. Ferleger, Establishing and Maintaining an Institutional Advocacy Program: Representing People With Handicaps (Sept. 1981).

45. *See* Brakel, *supra* note 35, at 91.

46. Monitor's Report Regarding Necessity for Trained Advocates, Brewster v. Dukakis, 520 F. Supp. 882, 898. On staffing and costs, see S. Herr, *supra* note 7, at 174-82.

47. For example in fiscal year 1981, the Illinois Guardianship and Advocacy Comm'n had state appropriations of $3,086,300, the New York Mental Health Information Service had $3,550,100, and the New Jersey Div. of Mental Health Advocacy had $858,000.

48. *See* Government Studies & Systems, *supra* note 33; Herr, "The New Clients," 31 *Stan. L. Rev.* 553 (1979).

49. *E.g.*, Heryford v. Parker, 396 F.2d 393 (10th Cir. 1968); Lessard v. Schmidt, 349 F. Supp. 1078, 1098 (E.D. Wis. 1972), *vacated on other grounds*, 414 U.S. 473 (1973), *on remand*, 379 F. Supp. 1376 (1974), *vacated on other grounds*, 421 U.S. 957 (1975), *on remand*, 413 F. Supp. 1318 (1976); Vitek v. Jones, 445 U.S. 480 (1980); Johnson v. Solomon, 484 F. Supp. 278, 290-94, 305, 316 (D. Md. 1979) (ordering plan to implement the right to mandatory appointed counsel).

50. 430 U.S. 817 (1977).

51. *Id.* at 831.

52. Halderman v. Pennhurst State School and Hospital, 446 F. Supp. 1295, 1327 (E.D. Pa. 1977), *aff'd*, 612 F.2d 84, 113 (3d Cir. 1979), *rev'd*, 451 U.S. 1 (1981), *on remand*, 673 F.2d 647 (3d Cir. 1982).

53. New York State ARC v. Carey, 596 F.2d 17 (2d Cir. 1979), *cert. denied*, 444 U.S. 836 (1979). As parent substitutes, Citizen Advisory Board members and their paid staff participate in the preparation and review of development plans and transfer plans for otherwise unrepresented individual members of the plaintiff class. Garrity v. Gallen, 522 F. Supp. 171, 241-42 (D.N.H. 1981) (ordering surrogate parents and guardians).

54. Davis v. Balson, No. C73-205, Second Interim Order (N.D. Ohio Sept. 1, 1976) (mandating independent patient advocacy program at Lima State Hospital and the hiring of a full-time attorney and lay advocates).

55. No. 81-1094 (E.D. La. April 15, 1981); La. Rev. Stat. Ann § 28.64 (Supp. 1982). Although statutory authority for a program of direct legal representation for mentally disabled persons had been on the books since 1977, it took five years before the legislature passed its first annual appropriation. With $250,000, this will permit five staff attorneys, a director, and paralegals to be hired.

56. *See, e.g.*, *In re* Weberlist, 79 Misc. 2d 753, 360 N.Y.S.2d 783 (Sup. Ct., N.Y. Co. 1974); Guardianship of Becker, *supra* note 13, (lawyer appointed as guardian ad litem); Michigan Ass'n for Retarded Citizens v. Wayne County Probate Judge, 79 Mich. App. 487 (1977); *In re* Residents of Los Lunas Hospital and Training School, No. 111-Misc., Stipulation and Appointment of Counsel (N.M. Dist. Ct., Valencia Co., filed Feb. 1, 1978); *see In re* Hutchinson, 421 A.2d 261 (Pa. Super. Ct. 1980); *Mem-*

mel, supra note 43, (court authorized Milwaukee Legal Aid Society to hire the necessary attorneys and staff; order approved as a temporary, emergency measure).

57. *See* note 52, *supra.*

58. Wuori v. Zitnay, No. 75-80-SD, Appendix A, § U.7 & Appendix B, § J.5 (D. Maine July 14, 1978). That system is not only "in place," *id.*, The Marti Wuori Case: Report to the Court 11 (July 20, 1981), but has a permanent status under the decree and state statute. Me. Rev. Stat. tit. 34, § 1-A (1978).

59. Saville v. Treadway, 404 F. Supp. 430 (M.D. Tenn. 1974). While the original decree called for a plan of lay advocacy, this was changed to a system of appointed counsel.

60. 520 F. Supp. 882 (D. Mass. 1981), *vacated and remanded*, No. 81-1687 (1st Cir. June 28, 1982).

61. *Id.* at 892.

62. 42 U.S.C. § 9502 (repealed 1981).

63. 42 U.S.C. § 6012 (1981 Pamphlet). *See generally* S. Herr, *Advocacy under the Developmental Disabilities Act* (1976); U.S. Comptroller General, *How Federal Developmental Disabilities Programs are Working* 61-72 (Report to the U.S. Subcomm. on the Handicapped, Senate Comm. on Labor and Human Resources, Feb. 10, 1980).

64. S. Rep. No. 160, 94th Cong., 1st Sess. 38 (1975).

65. N.J. Stat. Ann. § 52:27 E-21 (Supp. 1982); N.Y. Mental Hygiene Law § 29.09 (1978); Ohio Rev. Code Ann. § 5123.94 (Supp. 1978). For example, the nine attorneys and four social services personnel of the Ohio Service have filed broad class actions and represented mentally disabled individuals in commitment, nursing homes, juvenile, education, employment, guardianship and housing matters. Ohio Legal Rights Service, *Annual Report, Fiscal Year 1980.*

66. American Bar Ass'n Comm'n on the Mentally Disabled, *Advocacy for Developmentally Disabled Persons* 5-7 (1978); Ill. Rev. Stat. ch. 91 1/2 § 710 (Supp. 1982); Ark. Stat. Ann. § 59-1417 (Cum. Supp. 1981) (patient's advocate at mental health facilities). On statutory status for a P & A agency, the Division of Advocacy for the Developmentally Disabled, in the Department of the Public Advocate, see N.J. Stat. Ann. § 52:27E-41 (Supp. 1982). On the provision of counsel in proceedings relating to institutionalization, with court appointments giving preference to nonprofit organizations or specialist public advocacy agencies, see Ill. Ann. Stat. ch. 91 1/2 § 3-805 (Supp. 1982); New Mexico Stat. Ann. § 43-1-4 (1978).

67. S. Herr, *supra* note 7, at 126.

68. Contracts for such legal advocacy exist or have existed in Maine, Massachusetts, Pennsylvania, Vermont, and Washington. *See* 104 CMR §§ 21.87(f), 21.46(1)(b), 21.49(2)(g).

69. *E.g.*, People of the State of New York v. 11 Cornwell Co., No. 80 C 2139, Memorandum of Decision and Order (E.D.N.Y. Nov. 23, 1981).

70. *Cf.* Developmental Disabilities Advocacy Center v. Melton, 521 F. Supp. 365 (D.N.H. 1981), *rev'd and remanded*, No. 81-1727 (1st Cir. Sept. 22, 1982), *with* Becker v. Hobby Horse Ranch School, No. 79-303 (D. Ariz. Dec. 17, 1979) (consent decree on access to privately owned residential facility). *See* 42 U.S.C. § 9501(1)(M) (1981 Pamphlet).

71. For example, the Mental Health Law Project and some 60 percent of the nation's P & A's are organized as private nonprofit entities.

72. *E.g.*, Society for Goodwill to Retarded Children, Inc. v. Carey, 466 F. Supp. 722, 730 (E.D.N.Y. 1979).

73. 42 U.S.C. § 1988 (1981). *E.g.*, Donaldson v. O'Connor, 454 F. Supp. 311 (N.D. Fla. 1978); Halderman v. Pennhurst State School and Hospital, 533 F. Supp. 649 (E.D. Pa. 1982); Brewster v. Dukakis, No. 76-4423-F (D. Mass. July 16, 1982) ($386,000 awarded for deinstitutionalization case). *See generally* E. Larson, *Federal Court Awards of Attorney Fees* (1981); Comment, "Civil Rights Attorneys' Fees Cases Resolved on State Pendent and Federal Statutory Grounds," 130 *U. of Pa. L. Rev.* 488 (1981).

74. 29 U.S.C. § 794a(b) (Supp. Pamph. 1982). *E.g.,* Fells v. Brooks, 522 F. Supp. 30 (D.D.C. 1981).

75. As a general matter, there is no right to free counsel in special-education proceedings, or to court-awarded attorneys' fees under P.L. 94-142. *But see* Jose P. v. Ambach, 669 F.2d 865 (2d Cir. 1982); Tatro v. Texas, 516 F. Supp. 968, 985 (N.D. Tex. 1981) (attorneys' fees of $24,000 awarded under the Rehabilitation Act, where catheterization upheld as a "related service" under 94-142); Campbell v. Talladega County Bd. of Ed., 518 F. Supp. 47 (N.D. Ala. 1981) (fees of $36,700 awarded under Rehabilitation Act where severely retarded child denied appropriate education and contact with nonhandicapped children); Hymes v. Hernett County Bd. of Ed., 664 F.2d 410 (4th Cir. 1981) (attorney fees can be recovered for relief obtained under § 1983, such as return of child to classroom placement but not for administrative procedures under 94-142).

76. *See* Lloyd, "Presenting Claims for Attorneys' Fees in the District," 6 *District Lawyer* 36 (No. 4 1982).

8 Beyond Benevolence

This book has traced the beginnings of an extraordinary legal and human struggle—the attempt to end the enforced isolation of retarded children and adults from the rest of society. Seldom in American legal history has a group as powerless and forgotten as the mentally retarded managed to transform an area of law with such speed, drama, and success. That they had the help of skillful advocates and ardent friends is clear. Less than twenty years ago, President Kennedy could only plead for the day when the retarded child would emerge "from the attic of society to take his place on the school playground," and when the retarded adult would move from an "institutional ward to the day center and workshop."[1] American law now commands that persons with mental as well as physical handicaps be given such opportunities suited to their needs.

This study has focused on an unfinished battle in a far larger campaign: the desegregation of retarded people and their legal challenge to a conspicuous legacy of their ostracism, the institution. Part I documented the historical and policy background and part II analyzed the profound changes in decisional and statutory law. This concluding chapter considers the impact of those changes and suggests some directions for the advocacy movement that mounted this rights campaign.

The Failure of Good Intentions

Benevolent rhetoric has often cloaked unsavory interventions into the lives of retarded people. "Experience should teach us," Justice Brandeis cautioned, "to be most on our guard to protect liberty when the Government's purposes are beneficient."[2] That warning aptly characterizes the tragic history detailed in this book: the abuse and neglect of dependent people in the name of care, treatment, and compassion. In theory, institutions were schools or at least centers for therapeutic care. Sworn testimony, however, in such court cases as *Wyatt*, *Willowbrook*, and *Pennhurst* exposed that pretense. In theory, *parens patriae* laws authorizing confinement guaranteed these so-called objects of charity the solicitude of a kindly substitute parent. But institutions with hundreds or thousands of beds and shifting staffs could never approach the environment of a nurturing home.

During long decades of silence, the public and the courts acted as if legal rights had no relevance for children and adults placed within an institution's gates. Over a century ago, Dr. Samuel Gridley Howe, a pioneering figure in the field of mental retardation, boldly suggested that "even idiots have rights which should be carefully considered."[3] Sadly, his call was ignored. Those who pleaded the cause of the retarded had appealed to the public's pity, its patriotism, and its sense of religious charity, but the only rights receiving sustained discussion were the presumed rights of society to protect itself from the retarded, rather than the rights of the retarded to some affirmative protections from society. While legislatures enacted procedural safeguards to benefit mentally ill persons, the weak-minded were treated casually, without even the illusion of legal protection.

Under this laissez faire approach to retardation care, the recipients of charity rapidly became the targets of scorn and exclusion. Until the last decade, the legal rights and human amenities afforded retarded persons in most U.S. institutions compared unfavorably to those of incarcerated felons. In an increasingly competitive industrial society, those banished from their communities to settings known as idiot asylums or state schools came to be regarded as a surplus and devalued population. The very buildings and the laws regulating their keeping proclaimed the stigma, inferiority, and perceived dangerousness—and even subhumanity—of those clustered within.

In surveying this scene and urging checks on commitments, a presidential panel would state: "the law cannot deal in good intentions."[4] Yet for the most part, the actions of institutional caretakers, whether measured against their intentions, their results, or their legal authority, received no judicial review. Although the law on the books prescribed safeguards, the law in action was largely ritualistic.

Undoing the Segregationist Legacy

New laws and civil rights processes have had to pierce myths and undo the harms generated by the older custodial approaches. Civil rights lawyers set the tone and framed the tactics for the legal enforcement of the rights to freedom from confinement and to live in the community. Consumer organizations welcomed this advocacy as a powerful tool for accomplishing basic reforms that had eluded other forms of redress. The leadership of professional associations, though often wary of these newcomers, knew that outside intervention was required to revitalize their field. Following the lead of the courts, Congress recognized that as a matter of both human rights and the national interest, services for disabled persons should reduce or eliminate the need for institutional care. Progress at the state level, however, has remained highly uneven. In the absence of a concerted national policy of deinstitutionalization and in the face of resistance to change from state legislatures, court action has remained necessary to maintain progress.

Litigation offered a relatively inexpensive legal response to a serious moral wrong. Stated simply, the wrong was to treat persons with mental handicaps as if they were nonentities, relegated to institutions that had spent less for their care and maintenance than would be spent on animals in the public zoo. Because the children and adults in congregate care generally lack almost all forms of political power, a lawsuit was one of the few channels of persuasion and influence open to them. Unlike the journalistic probes of the past, the courts and plaintiffs' attorneys had the tenacity and the techniques for disciplined investigation. More importantly, they had the duty to insist that remedial promises be kept, even if this required indefinite monitoring. Systemic litigation of this kind thus provided a compelling source of documentation on the breakdown of existing laws, policies, and care regimes. Beyond their courtroom impact, those suits had publicity value in prodding the public conscience and embarrassing public officials.

Unquestionably, this sustained sense of crisis gave administrators the leverage to obtain more funds or to resist budget cuts. Court cases also offered a focus for mobilizing reform-minded professionals and consumer groups, for changing the public outlook on mental retardation, and for demonstrating that community care could work. Measured against the prelitigation status quo, the results have been overwhelmingly positive. Institutional admissions were avoided. Care was improved. Residents were resettled. New homes and learning opportunities were created.

This is not to claim that all the positive changes were attributable to the legal process. It is clear, however, that the courts and federal laws were major factors in the drive for more stringent admission criteria and procedures. Certainly many professionals were in sympathy with those aims, and many administrators used the laws to resist pressures for improper admissions. Legislative, planning, and other reform packages were needed to establish a coherent system for caring for people. Procedural reforms alone would not cure this field's deeper ills.

The courtroom had obvious limitations as an arena for thoroughgoing reform. With problems as complex as harmful institutions and the lack of home substitutes, no court had the resources, the time, or the authority to forge truly comprehensive remedies. Even if all the relevant expertise could be marshalled, the interests of nonlitigants could not be adequately represented. Hence, class actions always carried the risks of unintended consequences such as the diversion of resources from other retarded persons or dependent persons. Moreover, detailed remedial orders were difficult to monitor, enforce, and modify. The line between minimum and optimum standards was subject to constant debate. Making assessments of the efficacy and the ethics of behavioral interventions for mentally retarded persons raised especially thorny regulatory issues. No one imagined that model laws could substitute for models of competent and compassionate habilitation.

Lawyers and judges were keenly aware of these problems and of the need for multidimensional change. Time after time they invited enlightened legislative action and conscientious administration to remedy the faults uncovered by litigation. "Appropriate and workable standards," Judge Bazelon wrote, "are developed through a process that traces a spiral from legislature to agency to court and back to legislature."[5] But in the field of mental retardation, the legislatures left institutions to fester, without such standards, without resources to fulfill habilitation promises, and without impartial agents to review controversial treatment modalities. The spiral process is still being created.

Meanwhile, retarded people suffer needlessly. Retarded infants and children cannot wait indefinitely for an appropriate education without suffering developmental loss. Retarded young adults cannot remain in institutional limbo without becoming habituated to those surroundings. At any age, retarded persons, like other persons, can become overwhelmed by a lack of intimate emotional relationships. Although courts have imposed standards to relieve this suffering, there remain glaring distances between the relevant legal standards and the realities of institutional care. For example, despite a fall in institutional censuses from 200,000 to 130,000 persons, there are still some articulate, only mildly handicapped individuals in public institutions. Their presence there in 1982 is made the more stunning by the knowledge that they are exceptions, that even the most severely disabled persons with major medical, behavioral, and physical limitations can be, and have been, successfully placed in desirable community settings.

The legal process must be more conscious of the urgency of these needs. However, the courts did not create the delays in the community-placement process. Their interventions may sometimes help residents around that gauntlet line, but the underlying barriers remain largely unchanged.

Part of the solution involves a massive job of recruiting, training, and socializing a professional and paraprofessional workforce to translate the new norms on human rights and normalization into practice. In addressing an audience of those professionals, Judge Frank Johnson was especially sensitive to the limits of judicially spawned reform: "No court order can permanently accomplish the ultimate and real purpose of litigation over the provision of social services: fair, adequate and humanitarian treatment."[6] Along with other jurists, he understood that law reform is but a step in that direction.

New Directions

Law reform through the courts will continue to send powerful messages of what this society expects of its human-services professionals. Although they break little new ground, recent Supreme Court decisions provide a precedential and psychological boost for certain long-disputed claims.

The Supreme Court Trilogy

In June 1982, the Court handed down opinions representing its first rulings on three vital issues. In *Romeo* a unanimous Court considered the substantive constitutional rights to habilitation of involuntarily committed mentally retarded persons. In *Rowley* it defined the statutory right to a free appropriate education for handicapped children. Only in *Rogers* did the justices sidestep the issue presented: the involuntarily committed mental patient's constitutional right to refuse antipsychotic drug treatment. Yet taken together, the Supreme Court's address of these three controversies—cases on restraints, related services, and refusals of drugs—marks the end of the first era of the campaign for the legal rights of mentally retarded people.

Youngberg v. *Romeo* finally puts the Supreme Court's seal of approval on a constitutional right to "minimally adequate treatment."[7] It confirms that people committed to state institutions for the mentally retarded have rights to essential care, including adequate food, shelter, clothing, and medical treatment. Adopting the basic premise that such persons have constitutional rights no less than those of convicted criminals, the Court holds that their rights to safe custody and freedom from unreasonable restraints are entitled to substantive protection under the Due Process Clause.

Framing their holding to the narrow claims posed by Nicholas Romeo, the Court endorsed a limited constitutional right to habilitation. Given the facts and focus presented, the justices had only to require minimally adequate training to ensure safety and freedom from undue restraint. Speaking through Justice Powell, the Court deliberately left open a wide array of questions on the existence of broader rights to habilitation for retarded residents.

Romeo has, however, settled the threshold question. After ten years of lower court decisions on treatment rights, the Supreme Court has firmly acknowledged the justiciability of those claims, instructing courts to "start with the generalization that there is a right to minimally adequate training."[8]

For the reformer, the cautionary flags in this opinion should be carefully noted. Once again, the Supreme Court sounds the theme of judicial deference to qualified clinicians acting within reasonable professional limits. Consequently, *Romeo* will not likely lead to a proliferation of damage awards. Under the Court's opinion, the decisions of professionals are presumptively valid, and liability is reserved for the supposedly rare case of "a substantial departure from accepted professional judgment, practice or standards."[9] Thus, this rule for finding a constitutional tort is considerably stricter than the standards of liability in conventional malpractice actions. Moreover, the opinion gives facility staff explicit immunity when the breach is due to budgetary constraints. This decision does not, however, fix the boundaries for judicial review in declaratory or injunctive relief cases. Because *Romeo* was an initial step in announcing damage liability under the Constitution, the Court concentrated on claims of outrageous inattention to or abuse of committed residents.

The Court has also issued a call for judicial restraint in matters of special education. In *Board of Education of the Hendrick Hudson Central School District* v. *Rowley,*[10] the Court held that the Education for All Handicapped Children Act requires personalized instruction conferring some benefit on a handicapped child. The decision overturned lower court orders for a sign-language interpreter for a deaf child, but the Court stressed that it did so because this particular child was receiving a variety of adequate services. The opinion emphasizes her academic progress and the school's efforts to provide her with a substantial package of special services. The Court declined to adopt a standard that would have obligated states to maximize the full potential of handicapped children commensurate with the opportunities provided other children. The proper scope for judicial inquiry, according to the Court, is twofold. Lower courts must ensure compliance with the Education for All Handicapped Children Act's procedural requirements, including the development of an individualized education program tailored to meet each child's special needs. Furthermore, they must determine whether the individual program developed under this process is "reasonably calculated to enable the child to receive educational benefits."[11] In sum, courts were urged not to substitute their notions of preferable educational methods, theories, or policies for those of the agencies under review.

Although denying a costly supplemental service for an already favored student, *Rowley* reaffirms the power of trial courts to ensure appropriate educational programs for handicapped children. This decision holds, as a matter of statutory interpretation, that each child covered under the act is entitled to "personalized instruction with sufficient support services" to permit educational benefit from that instruction.[12] Recognizing that the act covers a spectrum of students from those labeled profoundly retarded to those with mild handicaps, the Court rejects any single test for determining the adequacy of educational benefits. Although the majority opinion described meaningful access to public education as the primary substantive aim under the act, this narrow reading slights the congressional emphasis on equal protection. Congress intended the handicapped child not only to enter the schoolhouse, but to have his or her unique needs addressed. Indeed, the Court approvingly refers to the formidable statutory checklist for determining whether the required free appropriate public education has been achieved. This list includes both procedural and substantive criteria. Although not all educational needs must be satisfied in full, advocates and courts can still hold school districts accountable. The legislative promise of a full educational opportunity for the handicapped child continues to be measured not by any particular academic outcomes, but by the delivery of reasonably designed services.

Without reaching the merits of the right to refuse treatment, the justices in *Mills* v. *Rogers* strongly implied that this claim will fare better under state than under federal law. The plaintiffs, a class of present and former state-hospital patients, obtained injunctive relief to refuse forcible medication, and the Supreme Court granted review. Based on an intervening decision by the highest Massachusetts state court, which upheld the right of a noninstitutionalized but incompetent mental patient to refuse antipsychotic drugs, a unanimous Court vacated and remanded *Mills.*[13] It thereby avoided a premature constitutional adjudication by the federal courts. The Court reasoned that the procedural and substantive liberty interests under Massachusetts law could well exceed the minimum guarantees of the Constitution. For example, although state law required an overwhelming state interest to defeat the patient's interest to be free from potentially harmful antipsychotic drugs, federal courts may be unwilling to impose so strict a balancing test. Similarly, the judicial review and the substituted judgment test mandated by the Massachusetts Supreme Judicial Court appear to set higher hurdles than this Supreme Court bench would interpose between mental patient and clinician.

In states that give generous legal protection to the interests of the mentally disabled, the ideal complement could involve federal court relief based on independent state law grounds. The viability of that strategy and the utility of the doctrine of pendent jurisdiction will be better understood after the *Pennhurst* case is decided in 1983.[14] Thus, for the third year in a row, a case involving the institutionalized retarded in general and this facility in particular has claimed the attention of the High Court.

Though advocates for retarded people cannot wholly avoid this forum, they should exert as much discipline as possible in case and issue selection. Taking the long view, it is an immense distance from the jurisprudence of *Buck* v. *Bell* to *Romeo* v. *Youngberg.* Yet the Court's uncertain grasp of modern concepts of habilitation, its reluctance to regulate treatment professionals, and its cool attitude toward disability rights underscores the need for conscious strategies of incremental law reform.

Federalism and Forum Shopping

Advocates for disabled persons have always engaged in some type of forum shopping. If the executive branch was unresponsive to their pleas, they turned to the legislatures. When neither proved satisfactory, they turned to the courts. The judicial process, even though at times cumbersome, enabled litigants to stir other branches of government to action.

Despite the allure of the judicial arena, the field of mental retardation is likely to remain far more sensitive to regulatory fluctuations than to Supreme Court pronouncements. Dollars not doctrines are the administrator's primary concern.

Despite recent shifts in executive funding priorities, the historic role of federal law will not be permanently altered. It will remain as a source of innovation; a means of raising standards for dependent persons, enforcing civil rights, and reducing disparities in services among states and within states. From Dorothea Dix to the ARC (association for retarded citizens) movement, a long line of reformers have petitioned Congress for legislative programs to improve care, education, and research in this field.

Unlike earlier legislation, the current programs have broad enough constituencies to weather political squalls. If the Education for All Handicapped Children Act is the classic example of such a program, then equally classic is its defenders' resistance to attempts to dilute that act through reduced appropriations, legislative amendments, and regulatory revisions. The antidiscrimination provisions of the Rehabilitation Act have equally dedicated supporters, but stand in greater peril because most of its substance is embodied in regulation rather than in statute. The possibility of congressional veto, however, should place restraints on radical revision.

Like earlier cycles of reform and retrenchment, the current swings in regulatory climates and civil rights appear to be more a pause than a turning point. During the Nixon administration, the country witnessed something similar. What seems qualitatively different is the current administration's sophisticated and steady attack on the roots of the disability rights movement such as the efforts to dismantle the Legal Services Corporation and to weaken other means by which disabled persons can assert their rights and have their views heard in governmental forums.

At this point, state governments are likely to resist trends toward further defederalization. Not only are they in no position to take up the slack, but many are still saddled with outdated facilities and legislative frameworks. They can be expected to lobby for federal support for the transition from containment and commitment of retarded persons to systems of community-based care.

The private sector offers no real alternative funding. It has often provided superior and less restrictive community services, but its capacity to do so has been weakened by federal funding cuts. Thus, it may be added to the constituency that will hold the federal government to its core statutory and public-policy commitments.

Although their exact details may be altered, the major legislative enactments for disabled persons will survive this period. Among those who will make common cause to ensure that this is so are advocates of the elderly, the physically disabled, the young, the ethnic minorities, and the mentally disabled. This book has documented another rationale for the federal government's continued role: the national problems that led to remedial legislation in such fields as special education and residential care are far from resolved. For many compelling reasons, Congress will continue to champion disabled persons and their interests: practical politics, compassion, equal rights, and a more humanistic cost-benefits accounting.

The Unfinished Agenda: Choices of Conscience

This analysis points to a need for greater diversification of strategies. After a decade of unprecedented activism, advocates can count some impressive achievements. International declarations, landmark cases, and legislative milestones marked the 1970s as a period for discovering the human and legal rights of retarded people. The future poses an equally arduous challenge: replacing laws and practices that rely on coercion and segregation with those maximizing choice and community affiliation. Even if sound laws are enacted and humane services provided, not all persons with disabilities will be treated justly. As is also the case with other formerly disenfranchised groups, the advocates' agenda is always unfinished.

The broad outlines of that agenda are found not only in state and national laws, but in international human rights standards. Applied nationally, the declarations of the United Nations and of the International League of Societies for Persons with Mental Handicap can represent a measure of achievement, a set of minimum guidelines transcending the socio-legal culture of any particular nation. In a world in which some children and adults are still denied essential medical treatment on the basis of a diagnosis of mental retardation, activists must frame legal responses to this cruel discrimination. In doing so, their arguments can link international with national guarantees of equal rights and minimum habilitation.[15] This illustration is only suggestive of the many uses of international standards in developed as well as developing nations.

In the courts, lawyers confront increasingly subtle claims and tactical choices. In the United States, with its tradition of litigation as a tool of social reform, judges are deciding questions that go to the quality as well as the locus of care and habilitation. If the courts had done no more than freeze new admissions or scatter retarded residents to uncaring communities, legal victories would have proved social disasters. Because lawyers and judges have looked beyond institutions to the systems that would sustain more compassionate care, this has not happened.

Federal courts and constitutional claims will not, however, vindicate *all* the rights of these residents. State courts and administrative tribunals will become increasingly important in resolving problems related to mental retardation. Whether the issue is resident abuse or SSI benefits, educational exclusion or related services, those forums have critical but often overlooked roles in protecting the legal rights of retarded persons. State courts, for example, have primary jurisdiction over guardianship, commitment, negligence, family, and criminal laws. It is therefore remarkable that so little scholarly and activist attention has focused on how those courts actually deal with persons of significantly subaverage intelligence.

For their part, the lobbyists are engaged in struggles on two fronts: to retain federal rights already conferred and to overhaul antiquated state laws to incorporate the insights of developmental and civil rights models. Earlier legislation viewed retarded persons as hopeless, unchanging, and essentially useless burdens to be put away "among their own kind." Newer legislation acknowledges a different set of assumptions: the individual's potential for growth and change; for movement to less restrictive settings; and for exercising rights and choices. One expression of this trend is the growing number of countries and jurisdictions that have either abolished involuntary commitment of retarded persons outright or simply declined to use such laws.[16] It can also be seen in model laws and progressive states that raise the legal requirements for institutional care for any person regardless of legal status, and which offer civil rights pledges to any client within the care system. Those changes in the legal rules are an important step in eliminating archaic stereotypes and planning more appropriate services.

At federal and state levels, funding laws should be reexamined to create financial incentives that foster rather than hinder community reintegration of retarded people. As more states apply for Medicaid waivers, Congress should expand the funds tied to plans that subsidize community and home-based habilitation services.

Activists can also fashion grievance mechanisms to secure the rights of retarded persons on a continuing basis. As supplements to the adversarial process, oversight agents can serve to reduce the costs, delays, and frictions in resolving disputes. Various agents can identify and prevent potential violations of rights through monitoring, investigative, and problem-solving techniques. As one example, human rights committees will become more commonplace. Operating on a local level, they can constitute an easily accessible grievance procedure for isolated clients as well as a means of reviewing ethically sensitive practices and policies. On a statewide level, professionally staffed commissions can organize, train, and support such committees. They can also be empowered to perform other functions, such as investigating the quality of publicly supported habilitation services, monitoring the implementation of liberty-related laws, and publicizing conditions threatening the safety, well-being, or rights of mentally disabled persons. Properly designed, such entities should be able to foster neutral review and informed public debate before rather than after individuals are seriously harmed.

The long-term challenge can be stated simply: to increase the probability that all disabled people can exercise their human and legal rights. In our highly developed society, with its wealth and inventive capacities, this is not an idle goal. In theory, the United States has committed itself to realizing equality and full participation for persons with mental and physical disabilities. By tradition and outlook, its legal culture is uniquely equipped to help honor that pledge. New services or freedoms won in our courts and legislatures can inspire disabled persons, their families, and friends to educate themselves to identify and to claim their specific rights. Habilitation professionals should also be sensitized to the rights of their clients and be informed of methods to aid them in their quest for self-determination. For those persons who have difficulties in asserting their own rights, a just society has an obligation to back up rights with remedies. Nonprofit legal-advocacy groups should therefore have the standing and authority to reach those prospective clients and to engage in this collective advocacy.[17]

To translate abstract rights into practice and to safeguard vulnerable human beings from callous harms, a system of durable and diversified advocacy is essential. Historic patterns of abuse, exploitation, and disregard of the rights of retarded persons has clearly proved that. Without the strategic interplay of litigation, legislation, and administrative reform, retardation institutions would still be overcrowded and forgotten places. The advocacy movement led to an unprecedented infusion of public funds for the field of mental retardation, and helped its professionals to resist budget cuts and to reclaim their role as educators rather than custodians. But while progress has been dramatic at test-case and federal legislative levels, the resources to secure the rights of specific individuals have lagged far behind. The work of assisting clients to retain public benefits, to claim statutory entitlements, or to gain basic freedoms occurs on a largely episodic and haphazard basis. Despite often-heroic efforts by advocacy and legal-aid offices, retarded people have regular access to trained advocates in only scattered sections of this country.

For retarded persons as for others, the advocate's classic role is to be a partisan for the client's objectives. That role cannot lightly be forsaken. The presumption of client competency and capacity to give directions should remain a starting point for advocate-client interactions. In this context, the lawyer's task is to clarify and amplify the client's voice. At times, this effort may require giving the lawyer special training or aid in eliciting instructions from a retarded client. When a client is incompetent or non-communicative, this may involve the appointment of a substitute decision maker or a corporate nonprofit advocacy entity. Group representation may overcome some practical and ethical difficulties, but it still places unusual burdens on the lawyer to ascertain and accommodate the objectives of classes of hundreds and even thousands of disabled individuals. With all its difficulties, this mode of representation is still one of the best ways of shielding clients from the extremes of therapeutic bombardment or a not-so-benign societal neglect.

On both individual and group levels, there is also an affirmative agenda: the private enforcements of laws and regulations for disabled persons government agencies might otherwise choose to disregard. Public and private care providers may sympathize with this agenda, but only independent advocates can press forward without risk to job security or other compromising conflicts of interest.

If eternal vigilance is the price of liberty, disabled persons and their friends have special reasons for watchfulness. For people with mental handicaps, whose liberty interests have long been devalued, the right to make choices must be nurtured and defended. Consequently, their advocacy movement has remained deeply involved in guarding the various guardians. It is not because the courts, caretakers, legislators, and leaders are lacking goodwill or good intentions toward dependent people. After all, everyone proclaims their commitment to doing what is best for the retarded. As we have seen, professional and consumers' groups alike endorse the broad concepts of habilitation and normalization, of human rights and equal protection. But consensus on generalized principles frequently dissolves in practice, and pledges of decent and humane services are lost in the crush of competing interests. Inevitably, the social distance between scientist and subject, clinician and client, guardian and ward, renders people diagnosed as retarded subject to an additional risk, the hazard of being smothered, however kindly, for one's own good.

Like the rest of us, individuals with mental retardation need both services and liberty to grow and prosper. The errors of the past led to overprotection, to paternalistic philosophies that completely swamped civil rights principles. Even today, debate often drifts into a false dichotomy between rights and needs, as if there were no rights to education, habilitation, or shelter. The old concept of segregating retarded people is bankrupt. The future demands a flowering of the least restrictive principles and the service arrangements that will permit each disabled person to live as independently, happily, and productively as possible.

The social costs of preserving the rights of sometimes inarticulate, inconvenient, or unpopular people are high. The costs of abandoning that effort are even higher. They are counted in the diminished lives and wasted productivity of people consigned to enforced idleness. They are manifest in the soaring expenses of life-time institutional care that brings neither credit nor satisfaction to resident, staff, relative, or taxpayer. Legislatures should recognize that continuation of this status quo detracts from human dignity and coarsens attitudes toward a whole range of dependent persons.

In a nation in which human solidarity is too often a frail bond, the appeal for legal protection can be a search for refuge. Faith in the old asylums is gone. Massive institutions set retarded people apart from the rest of society without guaranteeing their physical security or psychological integrity. Resort to the judicial process occurred not because judges, let alone lawyers, are more nurturing or benevolent than their fellow citizens. It happened because the vindication of legal rights hinges on principles and precedents, not on market forces or political arenas. Legal protection is not a panacea. It has, however, helped thousands of retarded people in the United States to avoid or to leave institutions for fuller and more dignified lives.

Out of that process, states will come to realize that outdated facilities can be closed, and homelike, normalized environments provided. If that advocacy pressure continues, the classic institution will not outlast the twentieth century. If that pressure recedes, the bureaucracies will again gravitate toward the paths of least resistance: grudging respect for rights, dual systems of institutional and community care, and the sacrifice of the interests of unrepresented clients. Thoughtful professionals already recognize that the institutions are anachronisms, too costly to run and too large to police. It is not easy, however, to persuade politicians and labor unions to act on that knowledge. Yet their interests and the interests of retarded persons can be safeguarded without a large, central edifice. Within a few years, the first developmental centers will close their doors. Before long, other states will set timetables to replace residential institutions with community care. When that happens, an important psychological barrier will be broken.

A postinstitutional society will not be the end of the road. Advocacy and legal checks will simply have to be refocused to prevent abuses and custodial practices from taking hold in newer forms of long-term care. Certainly the legal challenges will change as clients increasingly look to generic services for the satisfaction of their medical, educational, and vocational needs. Equal housing opportunities, job opportunities, availability of public entitlements, and the freedom to participate in habilitation decisions will only be a portion of that agenda.

In this country and in this context, the law has worked as an instrument for social integration. The lessons of this experience deserve close study. For those whose attention centers on other fields of human services (especially mental health, physical rehabilitation, and children's services), there are profitable analogies and common problems to be explored. For scholars and activists in the United States and in other countries, it is hoped that this book will stimulate further research and debate.

In a deep sense, the real heroes of this account are the disabled persons and their families who made claims on society for rights, not pity. When they first turned to the law, they risked retaliation by breaking the conspiracy of silence with their testimony and their example. Together with enlightened professionals and advocates, they will continue to press for the realization of rights long declared but so tardily enforced. And in gaining the experience to shape their own fates and be their own advocates, the people we call retarded will take us beyond benevolence.

Notes

1. Letter from President John F. Kennedy to Dr. Stafford L. Warren, Sept. 18, 1963, *printed in* The White House Conference on Mental Retardation, *Proceedings* 9 (Sept. 18-20, 1963).

2. Olmstead v. United States, 227 U.S. 438, 479 (1928) (Brandeis, J., dissenting).

3. S. Howe, *Twenty-Seventh Report of the Superintendent of the Massachusetts School For Idiotic and Feeble-Minded Youth* 24 (1874).

4. President's Panel on Mental Retardation, *Report of the Task Force on Law* 20 (1963).

5. Bazelon, "Implementing the Right to Treatment," 36 *U. Chi. L. Rev.* 742, 747 (1969).

6. Johnson, "Court Decisions and the Social Services," 20 *Social Work* 343, 347 (1975).

7. 102 S. Ct. 2452 (1982). The facts and lower court holdings in the *Romeo, Rowley* and *Rogers* cases are discussed in chapter 5, *supra.*

8. *Id.* at 2460 n.25.

9. *Id.* at 2462.

10. 102 S. Ct. 3034 (1982).

11. *Id.* at 3051.

12. *Id.* at 3049.

13. 102 S. Ct. 2442 (1982). The case is now before the Massachusetts Supreme Judicial Court, a tribunal generally sympathetic to the claims of disabled persons. See Guardianship of Roe, 421 N.E.2d 40 (1981).

14. Pennhurst State School and Hospital v. Halderman, *cert. granted,* 102 S. Ct. 2956 (1982).

15. Brief of Amici Curiae Ass'n for Retarded Citizens of the United States, American Ass'n on Mental Deficiency, The Ass'n for Retarded Citizens—California, and Protection and Advocacy, Inc., Guardianship of Becker, Civil No. 53419 (Cal. Ct. App., First Div. Aug. 20, 1982).

16. Denmark has recently joined the abolitionist jurisdictions. Danish Dep't of Social Welfare, Decree of Dec. 21, 1979, *applying* Act No. 333 of June 19, 1974, *as amended by* Act No. 258 of June 8, 1978.

17. *See* Developmental Disabilities Advocacy Center v. Melton, No. 81-1727 (1st Cir. Sept. 22, 1982).

Index

About the Author

Stanley S. Herr is an associate of the Columbia University Center for the Study of Human Rights and senior adjunct associate of the Institute of Society, Ethics, and the Life Sciences. A graduate of Yale College and the Yale Law School, he also holds a doctorate in law from Oxford University. Since 1970, he has been involved in the field of law and mental disability as a public-interest lawyer, researcher, clinical teacher, lecturer, and consultant. He has also served in various positions in the American Association on Mental Deficiency, the International League of Societies for Persons with Mental Handicap, and the National Legal Aid and Defender Association. Dr. Herr is the author of *The New Clients: Legal Services for Mentally Retarded Persons* (1979) and a coauthor of *Legal Rights and Mental-Health Care* (Lexington Books, 1983).